I0127878

Decolonisation in Aotearoa: Education, research and practice

Edited by Jessica Hutchings and Jenny Lee-Morgan

NZCER PRESS

NZCER PRESS
New Zealand Council for Educational Research
PO Box 3237
Wellington
New Zealand

© The authors 2016

ISBN 978-0-947509-17-0

No part of the publication may be copied, stored or communicated
in any form by any means (paper or digital), including recording
or storing in an electronic retrieval system, without the written
permission of the publisher.
Education institutions that hold a current licence with Copyright
Licensing New Zealand may copy from this book in strict accordance
with the terms of the CLNZ Licence.

A catalogue record for this book is available from the National Library
of New Zealand

Designed by Smartwork Creative Ltd, www.smartworkcreative.co.nz

Decolonisation in Aotearoa:
Education, research and practice

Contents

Acknowledgements

*Tuia te rangi e tū iho nei. Tuia te papa e takoto ake nei. Tuia te hunga
tangata. Ka rongo te pō, ka rongo te ao. Tuia te muka tangata i takea
mai i Hawaiki nui, i Hawaiki roa, i Hawaiki pāmamao, i te hono-i-
wairua ki Te Whai Ao, ki Te Ao Mārama. Tihei Mauriora! Ki o tātou
aituā tuatinitini, rātou kua wheturangitia ko rātou ērā e tiaho mai ana i
a rātou māramatanga ki a tātou ngā purapura whetu kua mahue iho ki
muri nei. Ko te hunga matai pō ki te hunga matai pō, ko te hunga matai
ao ki te hunga matai ao, tēnā hoki tātou katoa.*

This book has been inspired by the many kaupapa Māori thinkers,
writers, teachers, activists and theorists who have forged a strong pathway for kaupapa Māori in education, research and in our communities
of practice. These Māori leaders have encouraged us to not only adhere
to the teachings of our ancestors, but also give meaning to our traditions in our contemporary settings. They have encouraged us to have
faith that our own knowledge systems continue to provide guidance,
wisdom and the solution to many of the challenges we face today.

One of these leaders is Ranginui Walker. We mourn his recent death,
as one of the most significant Māori academics of our time intent on
our decolonisation. His work, in particular *Ka Whawhai Tonu Matou:
Struggle Without End* (Walker, 1990) continues to be a critical reader
for Māori. We acknowledge Ranginui's powerful body of work, and
here his support of, and contribution to, our book. He kura i tangihia,
he maimai aroha ki a koe Ranginui o Te Whakatōhea. Moe mai rā koe
e te rangatira i tō moenga kahurangi.

Many thanks go to the authors, for contributing to this anthology.
The ideas presented in the chapters are critical, fresh and inspiring and
provide a new way for us in Aotearoa to think about what is relevant
and important for decolonisation and Māori education in Aotearoa,
as defined by Māori. We thank the authors for their commitment to
working with the genre of pūrākau as the form of writing for the book.
For many authors we know it was your first time telling and narrating

your work and ideas in this way. What has resulted is a diverse and connected collection of critical ideas that reframe our thinking on how to decolonise education in Aotearoa.

Our deepest thanks go to Robyn Kahukiwa, who so generously provided the art work for the cover of this book. We are also grateful to NZCER Press for publishing this book and lending support with the editing and design work. We acknowledge our respective work-places, NZCER and The University of Auckland, for supporting us to undertake this project, and our colleagues who provided administrative support and a sounding board when needed. Our final thanks go to our whānau, our tamariki and our partners, whose dedication and commitment to understanding the importance of this project was unconditional.

Nā pango, nā whero i oti ai ngā rau whakaaweawe o tēnei pukapuka hei raumei mō ngā whakatipuranga e tū mai nei.

Ngā mihi
Jessica Hutchings and Jenny Lee-Morgan

Foreword Keeping a decolonising agenda to the forefront

Linda Tuhiwai Smith

Education and schooling have played a crucial role in the colonisation of Māori people in Aotearoa since the Native Schools Act 1867. There were schools before 1867 but the legislation identified schooling as having a role to play in the government's agenda for assimilating Māori people. Generally speaking, Māori leaders at the local community level accepted schooling as a means of survival and as a serious attempt to engage with Pākehā settler society. Since that time Māori have had a complicated relationship with education and schooling. While our communities have understood the significance of education, they have not fully experienced the social wellbeing that educational success should deliver. It is partly that tension that the chapters in this book address.

Decolonising Aotearoa: Education, research and practice provides ways to analyse, understand and address the unequal relations of power that structure Māori educational experiences in contemporary Aotearoa New Zealand. Despite improvements in educational success of Māori over time, there remain both unacceptable disparities in achievement between Māori and non-Māori students and unanswered deeper questions about the purposes the New Zealand education system should serve and how it should influence curriculum, teacher education and the organisation of institutions.

Why use a decolonising approach? Decolonising approaches focus on the history, colonial processes, ideologies and institutional practices that structure the relations of power between indigenous people and settler society. These approaches attempt to get under the skin of policy discourses, knowledge paradigms and practices that have sustained the myth of New Zealand as a good place for indigenous development. They seek to reveal the possibilities for social transformation as much as they seek to expose further colonising practices.

This book brings together a group of authors with different perspectives who offer thought-provoking ideas and examples that challenge our current educational practices and encourage further discussion and debate. The book covers topics that are not always included in standard books on educational matters. In the process it broadens the scope of a decolonising framework of analysis and demonstrates the deep influence of colonisation on knowledge systems and ways of living and being, the taken-for-granted way that society has been structured.

The book will provide an excellent text for those interested in the critical analysis of society and the reasons for resistance that many Māori people have taken to protect Māori values, language and mātauranga within Aotearoa. The different essays show how specific aspects of education can be unpacked and can reveal both reasons for discomfort and strategies for change.

**Kaupapa Māori in action:
Education, research and practice**

Jenny Lee-Morgan and Jessica Hutchings

Introduction

This book is timely as we recently marked the anniversary of 200 years
of schooling in Aotearoa. The first mission school house was opened by
Thomas Kendall in Rangihoua on 12 August 1816. At that time, te reo
Māori was the predominant language spoken in Aotearoa, and Māori
knowledge systems recorded, transmitted and developed inter-generational knowledge. Over these past 200 years the assimilation policies
of colonial schools and the imperialist nature of Western knowledge
systems have had a terrorising impact on Māori wellbeing. The Crown
continues to define and manage what it sees as important and relevant
in Māori education. This book seeks to counter that narrow world view.

Decolonisation in Aotearoa: Education, research and practice privileges
kaupapa Māori spaces to radically rethink what constitutes a kaupapa Māori and decolonised agenda for Māori education. This book
responds to the critical need for indigenous liberation strategies that
make space for ways of knowing and indigenous learning practices in
education. Concerned with the nexus of action and theory, we aim to
collectively extend the theoretical fields of kaupapa Māori by providing

a space for Māori educationalists, activists and scholars to engage in practice-led thinking for decolonisation in Aotearoa.

The notion of kaupapa Māori theory was first developed by Graham Smith and other Māori academics in Te Aratiatia (Māori Education), The University of Auckland, in the early 1990s (Pihama, 2001). It is now widely accepted in the academy as a legitimate form of academic inquiry (Smith, 2012). Kaupapa Māori brings a critical analysis of the power dynamics within relationships. Kaupapa Māori aims to alter the balance within power relationships so that all partners can operate from autonomous standpoints rather than from a position of subordination or dominance. Kaupapa Māori is grounded within diverse Māori knowledges and knowings, and is drawn from and connects with ancestral knowledges.

The chapters within this book aim to trigger and develop critical thinking that re-centres diverse indigenous realities in education in Aotearoa. The chapters are centred on three key areas imperative to both kaupapa Māori and decolonisation: education, research and practice. The Māori writers and intellectuals cover a wide range of topics, such as tribal education models, schooling, citizenship, maternities, the media, Christianity, wellbeing, food sovereignty, tikanga and identity. The book also aims to support Māori and other indigenous communities in the ongoing decolonisation process by reframing and contributing ideas in Māori education. By arguing for a wider remit for what is considered relevant in Māori education, this book contributes to the radical project of kaupapa Māori (Smith, 2012) and builds on and extends kaupapa Māori thinking and ideas to decolonise education in Aotearoa.

Kaupapa Māori

Although kaupapa Māori is not new (Nepe, 1991), it was actively developed as a term in the context of education in the 1980s, in particular in the context of te kōhanga reo and kura kaupapa Māori. The term 'kaupapa Māori' has subsequently become widely used across a range of sectors, including education, health, justice, agriculture, housing, economics and the media.

While kaupapa Māori has opened up new spaces for Māori in education and across the different sectors, Linda Smith draws attention to the potential of kaupapa Māori in practice. In her keynote address at the first Kei Tua o Te Pae Hui, "The Challenges of Kaupapa Māori Research in the 21st Century", Linda talks about the sort of spaces that kaupapa Māori continues to create:

> The other thing about kaupapa Māori is that it's not my creation, or Graham Smith's creation, or any single individual's creation. It is ours. It is our language, our terminology, and we will make it what it will be. When I think about kaupapa Māori research, I see it really simply: it's a plan; it's a programme; it's an approach; it's a way of seeing; it's a way of making meaning; it's a thought process; it's a practice; it's a set of things you want to do. It is a kaupapa and that's why I think it is bigger than a methodology. (Smith, 2011, p. 10)

Her comments affirm kaupapa Māori as a space *for* Māori *by* Māori and, in this case, encourage us to think about decolonisation in Aotearoa. In this regard, the book provides the reader with diverse ways of seeing, thinking and making meaning of decolonising education, research and practice in Aotearoa.

Decolonisation

While a kaupapa Māori approach has driven much of the work in this book, the decision to feature the decolonising dimension here is intentional. The term 'decolonisation' has been popularised as indigenous peoples around the world share their strategies of survival and commitment to leading positive, self-determining lives in their own homelands. Decolonisation reminds us that as Māori we are not alone in our struggle. It denotes the widespread and destructive impact of imperialism and, more specifically, the devastation of colonialism. If we understand the act of colonisation as the invasion of and control over indigenous peoples, whereby the colonisers secure and sustain the means to profit from the resources of the land—and as part of this process supplant indigenous social, cultural, political and economic ways of being with their own (Waziyatawin & Yellow Bird, 2012)—the task of decolonisation is no easy feat. The challenge is made more difficult by the insidious normalisation of the coloniser's power and control, until the indigenous people become alienated in their own land. Worse still, they start believing in their own inferiority, adopting what Kenyan intellectual Ngugi wa Thiong'o (1986) describes as a "collective death-wish".

In order to interrupt the colonisation process, Dakota activist Waziyatawin, and Sahnish and Hidatsa academic Michael Yellow Bird (2012) urge us to analyse the legitimacy of colonisation in each context. In Aotearoa, Māori have spent much time reasserting the covenants of the 1835 He Whakaputanga o te Rangatiratanga o Niu Tireni, which recognised the authority of iwi and signalled a move towards nationhood, and the 1840 Te Tiriti o Waitangi, signed between Māori and the Crown, which acknowledges Māori sovereignty. Since that time Māori have talked, worked, protested, fought and died challenging the betrayals of the Crown and its broken promises. The overarching call by Māori, based on our Treaty rights and common to the decolonising agenda, is tino rangatiratanga (sovereignty). Activating tino rangatiratanga as whānau, marae, hapū and iwi is not only the subject of our discussions, writing and research, but what we do.

In this sense we engage in what Graham Smith (2012) calls indigenous transforming praxis, participating in various ways in theory, action and reflection, to experience and ultimately achieve transformative outcomes. This book seeks to contribute to the praxis required for decolonisation by provoking critical thinking about the ways colonisation continues to be ever present and all-encompassing in Aotearoa today. It follows that this kaupapa Māori project is a challenge to everyday norms of 'whiteness' and Pākehā culture inherent in institutions and organisations in Aotearoa, including education (Milne, 2013). The work in this book actively attempts to dislodge, dislocate and detach from white, European-centred frameworks for thinking about education in Aotearoa. It does this by presenting our own narratives of experience about ourselves, our whānau and our communities with regard to decolonisation.

As is the case for other indigenous peoples, decolonisation here is premised on a belief in our own social, spiritual, economic, political and cultural knowledge systems, traditions, beliefs and practices. These traditions are not seen as a romanticised past, but continue to be a valid source for our sustainability and regeneration as a people, and at the heart of what decolonisation aspires to achieve. This brings us back to kaupapa Māori as a decolonising agenda. It validates our diverse ways of knowing as Māori and encourages us to hold a critical lens across discourses, ideas and practices. Bringing the ideas of kaupapa Māori and decolonisation together in this book strengthens the call for critical and insightful scholarship that addresses and connects political, social, environmental, spiritual and gendered critiques in relation to decolonisation in Aotearoa.

A pūrākau approach

Enacting kaupapa Māori in the framing of this book, we decided to invoke a pūrākau approach: a Māori pedagogical tool for teaching and learning. Inspired by the book *For Indigenous Minds Only: A Decolonization Handbook* (Waziyatawin & Yellow Bird, 2012), which provides activities alongside the narrative to systematically stimulate a deeper thinking about the issues discussed, pūrākau emerged as a way to think about our pedagogical approach to the book. How might we engage readers in a culturally relevant teaching and learning process that stimulates deeper reflection for action? Rather than prescribing activities within each of the chapters, we looked to the traditions of our pūrākau narratives.

Traditionally, pūrākau is a type of Māori narrative used to create, support and disseminate knowledge about ourselves and the world around us within whānau, hapū and iwi. The term is commonly used to describe ancient and historical stories of our atua, heroes and heroines, well-known people and places. Developed as a methodological approach in Jenny Lee-Morgan's (2008) doctoral work, the pedagogical element of pūrākau echoes the indigenous story-work movement of other peoples, influenced in particular by Stolo academic Jo-Ann Archibald (2008). An inherent part of pūrākau is its pedagogical potential. Pūrākau as a cultural imperative guides us to share our 'stories' in ways that engage with the audience, provoke a self-directed process of meaning making, raise questions and provide answers, or quench the thirst to learn more.

A pūrākau approach does not mean that one can carelessly write whatever comes to mind; nor is writing pūrākau easy. On the contrary, pūrākau are well-crafted, thoughtful narratives to effect engagement. This approach in a written document (book) about education primarily targeted at a wide Māori audience, including academics, professionals, community and whānau, is, therefore, not straightforward. Inevitably there are tensions about the who, how, what and why. While Lee (2008) suggests there are some key principles that can guide pūrākau as a form of narrative inquiry, there is no set format for telling or writing pūrākau. Rather, pūrākau are highly contextual and depend on the story-teller, topic, purpose and audience. In this regard, some authors in this book have not only chosen to position themselves as writers, but to reposition the writing in their worlds. Others have foregrounded their voice, and some have remained within the confines of a conventional format to 'write back'. Each has formulated their narrative in their own style to engage the reader in critical thinking and deep reflection, with the aim of inspiring action.

In this way, this work does more than just describe kaupapa Māori: it puts kaupapa Māori to work in diverse settings and in diverse ways that remind us of the importance of troubling the given, including: What counts as pūrākau? What counts as education? What counts as kaupapa Māori? The book presents a diverse collection of writings and ideas that intersect in some places and not in others. This has been central in our discussion with authors when thinking about how to compile these diverse narratives into an edited collection. During the development process of the book two writing retreats were held with authors. Much time was spent discussing pūrākau and the decolonising work that authors wanted their chapters to do. We considered it an important part of the kaupapa Māori process for developing this book and building a connected community of contributors to this collection.

Hence, a pūrākau approach to decolonisation in Aotearoa involves a range of styles and topic areas that appear across the chapters in this book. We have organised the chapters into three parts: Māori in education, Māori in research and Māori in practice. An emphasis on 'Māori in' highlights our agency as Māori, and our engagement in praxis. The part headings are intentionally broad, but each serves to guide the reader through the array of chapters.

Māori in education

The first part of this book directly examines education, both as a colonising tool and as a site for decolonisation, including tribal education initiatives, youth-led movements and flax-roots experiences of transformation. It begins with "Reclaiming Māori Education" by the late Ranginui Walker (Whakatōhea), which provides an overview of some of the key historical moments in the colonisation of Māori education in Aotearoa. Ranginui's narrative traverses the impact of the mission schools, Native Schools, Māori boarding schools, district high schools, and the government policy to exclude Māori language, culture and knowledge in the education system in order to assimilate and subordinate Māori to an underclass.

The re-presentation of this historical account, with a focus on power and control, connects with a critique of the 'gaps' rhetoric often heard in and for Māori education, and which is still evident in the contemporary 'capacity building' ideology posited as the solution to Māori disparity. Simultaneously, Ranginui weaves some key Māori responses to colonisation through the reclamation of education on multiple fronts, including leadership, teacher education, university, kōhanga reo, kura kaupapa Māori and wānanga, with the aim of developing a liberating pedagogy for the reclamation of Māori education.

Chapter Two presents a conversation with Moana Jackson (Ngāti Kahungunu, Ngāti Porou) on decolonising education. Drawing on his vast experience of fighting for Māori rights across all sectors, Moana reminds us that education is not culturally or politically neutral, but continues to be powerful in the colonisation process. This is evidenced in Moana's definition of colonisation as

> a deliberate process of re-education ... [by] which our minds were colonised to accept a particular political and social order where all power (and therefore all valid modes of thinking) is vested in the colonisers. (p. 40)

However, although he identifies the dilemma of 'educating' to colonise, and colonising to 'educate', he presents two key ways to think about what education does: educational or pedagogically specific impacts, and culturally deliberate impacts. While Moana acknowledges the important and significant work of teachers, whānau, academics and

researchers to improve educational outcomes, he encourages an exploration of what he refers to as "culturally deliberate impacts" to educate
for rangatiratanga, not just 'success'. Within the paradigm of education
Moana pushes us to think more deeply about constitutional change,
neo-liberalism and the advent of charter schools. Despite the amount
of decolonising work still required to achieve "colonisation-free rangatiratanga-embracing education", forever the optimist Moana urges us
to engage in a rigorous critique that leads to transformative change.

Chapter Three, by Ani Mikaere (Ngāti Raukawa), "Te Harinui:
Civilising the Māori with School and Church", examines the phenomenon of Christianity in colonisation through schooling, beginning
with the early missionaries. As we know, colonisation has not gone
away. To this end, Ani draws attention to the way Christian practices
have seeped into our Māori education environments and everyday
events. Christian prayers and hymns that often form an expected and
'natural' part of Māori protocols and rituals are described by Ani as
"Christianity masquerading as tikanga". Ani provides an important
critique that exposes the fundamental problem with incorporating
Christian beliefs within a Māori social system. Furthermore, she iden-
tifes the way Māori religious codes, such as Io, have been contaminated
by Christianity. In this pūrākau, Ani also grapples with her own personal experiences of Christian practices in education to portray the
courage required to confront the normalisation of Christianity implicit
in much of our tikanga. Ani reminds us that decolonisation is not easy,
but a process that requires courage if we are to create kaupapa Māori
spaces that are our own.

The next chapter, by Sarah-Jane Tiakiwai, "Ko te Mana Motuhake—
Ake! Ake! Ake!: Reclaiming Education for Waikato-Tainui", tells the
story of Waikato-Tainui College for Research and Development. This
version, however, is focused on the reclamation of tribal knowledge
through the construction and establishment of the tribe's Endowed
College. As the current Director and a tribal member, Sarah-Jane tells
a personal pūrākau, one that she has witnessed, experienced and continues to contribute to.

Chapter Five, by Jenny Lee-Morgan (Waikato, Ngāti Mahuta),
is titled "Marae-ā-kura: A culturally specific decolonising strategy in
schools". While marae-ā-kura (school marae) are an accepted part of

the secondary school landscape today, Jenny argues that they were always part of a kaupapa Māori education agenda to create both a peda-gogical and political space for Māori within monocultural mainstream schools. It draws on a recent research project of three marae-ā-kura in Auckland secondary schools, which allowed Māori students to voice their qualitatively different experiences of the sanctity of marae-ā-kura. Their experiences serve to highlight the continued struggle over ideol-ogy in schools, and in particular, the importance and validity of the marae-ā-kura to their teaching, learning and living as Māori at school. Jenny reminds us that marae-ā-kura have the potential to be a powerful decolonising strategy for teachers, learners and their whānau, a place that draws a boundary for space that falls within our own control.

Takawai Murphy (Ngāti Manawa, Ngāti Ruapani ki Waikaremoana, Tūhoe, Ngāti Kahungunu) shares his journey in "Reflections from the trenches: Decolonising hearts and minds in Aotearoa". As one of the most prominent community teachers of decolonisation in the country, Takawai developed and has delivered his programme "He Pūmaomao: A Nation-building Workshop" at more than 1,000 seminars over the course of 20 years. Such work, described as in the "trenches", must be fuelled by a personal commitment and passion. In this chapter Takawai reflects on his own story of becoming. He begins with his own experiences as a student, and then as a teacher, which saw him disillusioned, frustrated and stressed—a state that eventually became the motivation and source to reclaim and re-develop a new, inclusive educational experience. He writes: "My overall intent was to create a safe, empowering and engaging space for Māori and Pākehā to unpack tough issues around colonisation, power and identity" (p. 85). As his title suggests, Takawai's aim is to affect not only minds but also hearts in order to create positive active change. His pūrākau of decolonisation also acknowledges the many people who have shared their knowledge and provided support to his development and work, in recognition that none of us can do this work by ourselves.

The final chapter in this part, by Veronica Tawhai (Ngāti Porou, Ngāti Uepohatu), is titled "Matike Mai Aotearoa!: The Power of Youth-led Decolonisation in Education". Veronica tracks the prog-ress of Matike Mai Aotearoa Rangatahi, the youth project of the Independent Working Group on Constitutional Transformation. As well as documenting the innovative and effective programme designed and implemented by rangatahi, her chapter tells of the ways rangatahi engaged rangatahi with the complexities of constitutional change. An example of this is the dialogue for the "Dude, Where's My Mana?" exercise that begins the chapter.

More than just the way in which the rangatahi worked to decolonise themselves, understand and contribute to the discussion on constitutional change, Veronica reflects on decolonising the views of rangatahi. The positive outlook and power of rangatahi in this project are linked to the legacy of Māori leaders as rangatahi, and the essential role of rangatahi within decolonisation. Veronica pushes us to be agents of transformation, and reconsider educational spaces that are adult governed, that constrain and limit rangatahi.

Māori in research

The second part in the book explores kaupapa Māori in action, with a focus on research.

It opens with writing by Leonie Pihama, whose chapter examines the positioning of ourselves as Māori within kaupapa Māori research. Her chapter highlights the important place of kaupapa Māori in research, theory and practice and reminds us that this remains an ongoing, everyday struggle for many Māori. The chapter consciously brings a kaupapa Māori analysis of education to the forefront by examining the role of the colonial education system in constructing and facilitating the maintenance and reproduction of selected knowledges, thereby resulting in the suppression of Māori world views and ways of living. Her chapter is a clear reminder of the false neutrality and objectivity often claimed by Western research methods and approaches. Rather, she argues that research is culturally, socially, economically and politically bound.

The second chapter in this part, by Mera Lee-Penehira (Ngāti Raukawa, Rangitāne, Ngaiterangi), describes and discusses Māori research excellence through the eyes of Māori researchers. Māori and indigenous research is undeniably political and occupies a tenuous space that has been hard fought for and won. Her chapter looks at the relationship between colonisation and research, and how we set about designing research in such a way that we become active agents in the struggle for indigenous self-determination. The question she explores is how we organise ourselves as indigenous researchers in international collaborations while still developing independent indigenous research frameworks in our own lands. There is a particular emphasis on kaupapa Māori theory and how it might be applied in an international context, and some suggestions are given for how kaupapa Māori research can contribute to international indigenous collaborations.

In the final chapter in this part, Āneta Rāwiri (Ngāti Rangi, Ngāti Hine, Ngā Puhi) shares a pūrākau about her experience of decolonising research with Whanganui iwi. Her chapter describes a Whanganui iwi-led project that was firmly grounded within a fundamental aspiration of indigenous peoples: to live their ancestral heritage and pass it on to future generations in its full richness and vitality. It was in this space that Āneta was supported to think critically about decolonisation, and to embrace it as research practice. We learn that for Whanganui iwi, decolonising research is about participating on their own terms in today's world. This is based on a desire to continue to manage their own affairs—according to ancestral ways of life and values—as they have done for many centuries. It is about community continuity and dynamism, and self-determination. It challenges the neo-colonial and neo-liberal values of a dominant Western society, which are not life-affirming and place individual wellbeing over collective wellbeing, and the wellbeing of people over that of the natural world.

Māori in practice

The final part in the book centres on kaupapa Māori in action, with a focus on practice. This part contains a diverse collection of pūrākau from Māori writers, which range from decolonisation and Māori maternities, Māori Television, food knowledges, and our understandings of menstruation.

The part begins with a pūrākau by Naomi Simmonds (Ngāti Raukawa, Ngāti Huri) and Kirsten Gabel (Ngāti Kahu, Te Paatu) titled "Ūkaipō: Decolonisation and Māori maternities". The chapter encourages Māori readers to look to the narratives about maternities within our whakapapa. These tell of the unique place of women, the tapu of women's bodies, the power of female sexuality, the complementary roles of men and women in maternities, and the central role of tamariki within communities. In this chapter, Naomi and Kirsten make a strong case for seeing traditional pūrākau as not simply historical accounts but also as statements about our current realities. They unpack the impact of colonisation and patriarchy on our notions of ūkaipō and Māori maternities. In doing so, they retell and decolonise notions about maternities. This is a powerful chapter that encourages Māori women, Māori men and whānau to reclaim our most basic practices of birthing the next generation.

The second chapter in this part, by Jo Smith (Waitaha, Kāti Māmoe, Kai Tahu), looks at the aspirations or moemoeā for Māori Television. This chapter reminds us that since the 1960s, television audiences in Aotearoa have been fed a diet of monolingual narratives of nationhood premised on non-Māori perspectives. These stories, images and framings have generated some entrenched views, processes and institutional practices about Māori that still inform the present day. This unrelenting structure has influenced New Zealand media industries for many decades. It was not until 2004, when Māori Television emerged as a vehicle for revitalising te reo me ngā tikanga Māori in the wake of such devastating monolingualism that the media landscape began to shift. This chapter engages with the early aspirations, dreams and hopes for Māori Television from across a range of diverse and interested Māori communities, and gives thought to the decolonising potential of Māori Television in relation to these aspirations.

Next, Jessica Hutchings (Ngāi Tahu) explores decolonising food knowledges in her chapter on the impact of the global food regime. She argues that our indigenous ways of thinking about food have become so colonised in our everyday practices that what's required is a complete reorientation of how we think about, and are connected to, our food system. As a counter-practice to the global capitalist food regime, she presents a kaupapa Māori food initiative called Hua Parakore. Hua Parakore creates a pathway for Māori educationalists across all learning environments to bring kaupapa Māori to the everydayness of the plate. The Hua Parakore system, developed by Te Waka Kai Ora (National Māori Organics Authority of Aotearoa), is a kaupapa Māori food sovereignty and food security initiative that holds potential for decolonising knowledge around kai in Aotearoa.

Ngahuia Murphy (Ngāti Manawa, Ngāti Ruapani ki Waikaremoana, Tūhoe, Ngāti Kahungunu) describes decolonisation as healing, releasing, remembering, reviving, reclaiming, reasserting and confronting the continuing colonial agenda. Her pūrākau is about 're-storying'. By returning to our sacred stories—the ones that connect us to one another and our elders across the web of life, the ones that remind us who we are—we can reclaim and, where necessary, reconstruct them within a kaupapa Māori agenda of transformation. Ngahuia argues that this is necessary work because our sacred stories are labyrinths that house our cultural identities, and they have been purged and modified by the coloniser in a way that threatens our connections. In this chapter she uses the subject of menstruation to illustrate this history of redefinition. The river of ancestors and descendants—menstruation—provides a potent example of the retelling of our sacred stories in ways that desecrate and seek to sever our connections. In the quest to decolonise our stories, our tikanga and ourselves, she makes an insightful case that menstruation is a pivotal site for a decolonising educational agenda because it speaks to our very origins as Māori.

The final chapter in the book is by Debbie Broughton (Te Aitanga a Hauiti, Ngā Puhi, Taranaki, Ngāti Porou). Her pūrākau explores our relationships with tūpuna, whānau and the expansion of the mātauranga continuum to help ensure whakapapa continuity and the survival of Māori as a people. Her stories ask us to think about how we are connected to tūpuna who have passed and those who are yet to be born. She reminds us that since time immemorial, successive generations have deepened their understandings of these questions, not as siloed questions of science or religion, but as part of our understandings of whakapapa. Her chapter reminds us that Pākehā education systems and religions have interrupted this exploration, colonising and marginalising our understandings, branding them as religious superstitions of sub-humans with limited intellectual capacity. This chapter suggests that whānau can contribute to the mātauranga continuum and ensure whakapapa continuity by exploring and enacting our understandings of where we come from and where we go once this human experience has ended.

Conclusion

This book is premised on two key ideas: colonisation has not gone away, and the re-education required to combat the impact of colonisation must be broad and comprehensive. The nature of colonisation that affects all aspects of our lives demands a response that reaches to the breadth and depth of our experiences. In this way we have attempted to provide a diversity of topics from a range of Māori educators, researchers, intellectuals and activists. However, we are conscious that we have only touched the tip of the iceberg; we are aware, too, that key issues such as te reo me ōna tikanga and Te Tiriti have not been addressed directly. This is only a beginning, and in many ways an introduction to decolonising thinking in some of the domains in which we dwell.

Our approach in this book has been to assert kaupapa Māori as a decolonising methodology that not only engages in a critique, but also inspires action for transformation. In this regard, Waziyatawin and Yellow Bird's (2012) definition of decolonisation is useful here:

> Decolonization is the meaningful and active resistance to the forces
> of colonialism that perpetuate the subjugation and/or exploitation
> of our minds, bodies and lands. Decolonization is engaged for the
> ultimate purpose of overturning the colonial structure and realizing
> indigenous liberation. (p. 3)

Despite the size of the task before us, tino rangatiratanga will only be achieved by our collective contributions. We must have the courage to remember the taonga of tūpuna and the legacy of those who have gone before to reclaim and create spaces for self-belief as a people. It is in the spirit of a collective commitment to tino rangatiratanga that we hope this book will assist in the praxis needed if we are to improve our conditions, retain our knowledge and belief systems, our values and practices, our relationships with the natural and spiritual worlds, and most of all, our faith in each other.

Author wānanga held at Te Puna Wānanga, The University of Auckland. Left to right: Maryann Lee, Jo Smith, Jessica Hutchings, Veronica Tawhai, Whiutaikaha Tawhai-Porter, Jenny Lee-Morgan and Mera Penehira.

References

Archibald, J.-A. (2008). *Indigenous storywork: Educating the heart, mind, body, and spirit*. Vancouver, BC: UBC Press.

Lee, J. B. J. (2008). *Ako: Pūrākau of Māori secondary school teachers' work in secondary schools*. Unpublished doctoral thesis, The University of Auckland.

Milne, A. (2013). *Colouring in the white spaces: Reclaiming cultural identity in whitestream schools*. Unpublished doctoral thesis, Waikato University.

Nepe, T. M. (1991). *Te toi huarewa tipuna: Kaupapa Māori: An educational intervention system*. Unpublished master's thesis, The University of Auckland.

Pihama, L. (2001). *Tīhei mauri ora: Honouring our voices: Mana wahine as a kaupapa Māori: Theoretical framework*. Unpublished doctoral thesis, The University of Auckland.

Smith, G. (2012). Kaupapa Māori: The dangers of domestication. *New Zealand Journal of Educational Studies Te Hautaki Mātai Mātauranga o Aotearoa, 47*(2), 10–20.

Smith, L. (2011). Story-ing the development of kaupapa Māori: A review of sorts. In J. Hutchings, H. Potter, & T. Taupo (Eds.), *Kei Tua o Te Pae Hui proceedings: The challenges of kaupapa Māori research in the 21st century*. Wellington: NZCER Press.

Thiong'o, N. w. (1986). *Decolonising the mind: The politics of language in African literature*. London, UK: J. Currey; Portsmouth, NH: Heinemann.

Waziyatawin, A. W. & Yellow Bird, M. (2012). *For indigenous eyes only: A decolonisation handbook*. Santa Fe, NM: School of American Research.

PART 1: MĀORI IN EDUCATION

Māori in Education draws attention to education as both a powerful colonising tool and, more recently, a site to develop liberating pedagogies for the reclamation of Māori education. Education is discussed on multiple fronts, including educational institutions, tribal and community developments and rangatahi initiatives, as it relates to Māori in the past, present and future.

Chapter 1 Reclaiming Māori education

Ranginui Walker

Introduction

At the height of its power in the 19th century, the British Empire encompassed 11.5 million square miles and ruled over a quarter of the world's population (Waitangi Tribunal, 2012). The Empire's expansion at the expense of indigenous people in the New World was driven by trade, capitalism and consumerism. When Great Britain annexed New Zealand under the Treaty of Waitangi in 1840, it had considerable experience in the techniques of domination, subjugation and domestication of indigenous populations in North America, Canada and Australia.

Like its Greek and Roman predecessors, the British Empire portrayed itself as civilised and painted the people it encountered in the New World as savage, uncivilised and inferior. The British racial hierarchy placed Europeans at the top and 'natives' at the bottom. Although the culture of New Zealand's tangata whenua, with its hunting, fishing, gathering and gardening economy, was a sustainable design for living, it was almost destroyed by the colonial enterprise of converting the natives from barbarism to Christianity and civilisation. British colonisers saw Māori tribalism and communal ownership of land as the mark of primitive and barbaric people.

The techniques of the coloniser included: trade at the frontier; opening up new lands and resources for exploitation; cultural invasion by missionaries imposing their world view on the natives; treaty-making to gain a foothold on the land; taking advantage of tribalism to divide and rule; military invasion; political domination; confiscation and expropriation of land and resources by legal artifice; and state terrorism and intimidation of non-conformist pacifist populations. For Māori, the most adverse effects of the colonial encounter included population decline, domination of chiefly mana by a foreign power, political marginalisation, impoverishment, and the erosion of language, culture and self-respect.

The consequence of this historical process, enacted in New Zealand from 1840 to 1900, is a structural relationship of Pākehā domination and Māori subordination. Subsequent institutional arrangements, including Parliament and the apparatus of the state, functioned to maintain that structural relationship. This chapter examines how one facet of institutional arrangements, the education system, was manipulated by the power brokers to maintain an unjust social order between Māori and Pākehā.

Mission schools

The Anglican missionaries who arrived in New Zealand in 1814 were the advance party of cultural invasion. Their mission of converting Māori from 'barbarism to civilisation' was predicated on notions of racial and cultural superiority. They believed in a divine right to impose their world view on those whose culture they were displacing (Freire, 1972). Rev. Henry Williams thought Māori people were governed by the Prince of Darkness. Rev. Robert Maunsell abhorred Māori practices and thought their waiata (songs) were filthy and debasing. The Catholic Bishop Pompallier, who was admired by Māori converts to his faith, looked down on them as "infidel New Zealanders" (Elsmore, 1985).

Despite their prejudices towards natives, missionaries believed Māori could be raised from their primitive state to civilisation through schooling. The first mission school was opened by a teacher, Thomas Kendall, on 12 August 1816 at Rangihoua in the Bay of Islands (Jones & Jenkins, 2011). Others were established at Kerikeri, Waimate North and Paihia.

Although Māori had whare wānanga (schools for teaching their own genealogy of knowledge), they wanted to send their children to the mission schools to access the Pākehā knowledge that produced large ships, powerful weapons and an amazing array of goods. Perhaps schooling would unlock the secret to this material wealth. However, the Māori desire to access Western knowledge was thwarted by missionary control of the curriculum. Instruction in the mission schools was strictly confined to the scriptures, and reading and writing in the Māori language only. Secular and non-Christian knowledge was excluded from the curriculum (Elsmore, 1985). English was not taught because the missionaries did not want Māori contaminated by non-Christian influences (Jones & Jenkins, 2011).

In 1837, when Colenso printed the scriptures in Māori, the Bible became hot property among tribes. Māori believed that knowledge of European culture and material goods was contained in the Gospels. Within a decade a number of Māori in most villages throughout New Zealand had learned to read and write in Māori (Barrington & Beaglehole, 1974). Adults and children arrived at mission stations for lessons. Māori teachers spread literacy to remote tribes well in advance of the missionaries. Rev. William Williams went to Poverty Bay in 1840 to establish a mission station and found that people there could already read and write (Elsmore, 1985).

Although interest in missionary teaching waned when prosperity remained elusive, Māori made use of their ability to read and write to communicate by letter with other Māori. From the 1830s letters were delivered on horseback to all parts of the country. Community leaders also put up whenua rāhui, tapu and trespass notices on posts and houses (Jones & Jenkins, 2011). The spread of literacy in Māori communities enabled learned men in the traditions of their hapū and iwi to write their genealogy of knowledge in family manuscript books. But the transition from oral to written transmission of knowledge was an enterprise fraught with ambivalence and potential danger. In Māori epistemology, humans are born into the world with no knowledge. All knowledge emanates from the gods, who embedded it in the natural world to be discovered by humans. For this reason, the pursuit and transmission of knowledge was a sacred enterprise confined to whare wānanga.

Aperehama Taonui, who taught in the mission school at Mangungu in 1848/49, wrote *He Pukapuka Whakapapa mō ngā Tūpuna Māori,* which recounted the history of Hokianga ancestors from Kupe and Nukutawhiti to their modern descendants. Taonui learned the genealogies as a young man and was instructed not to write down the names of deified ancestors because they were tapu. There was also the danger that such a manuscript might end up in a box among profane things. When Taonui wrote the book, he understood it was for the edification of Pākehā scholars and feared that if other Māori saw the book it could arouse animosity and resentment.

Authors of family manuscript books resolved the problem by treating them as tapu and secreting them away from the public gaze, as the whare wānanga had been in the past. Some authors did put their knowledge out in the public domain. They were the modernisers, educated first in whare wānanga by their elders, then taught to read and write in the mission schools. Their writings paved the way for the writing of tribal histories in the 20th century. Perhaps the most influential of these modern-day tohunga was Wiremu Maihi Te Rangikāheke of Ngāti Rangiwewehi hapū of the Arawa confederation of tribes. Born in 1815, he was instructed in the genealogy of tribal knowledge by his elders. At 20 he also learned to read and write at Te Koutu mission.

Te Rangikāheke was a prolific writer. He set out his genealogy of knowledge in 21 manuscripts, and contributed to 17 others, authoring a total of 800 pages. His writing was based on the technique of genealogical recital, complemented by a narrative recounting of events at various levels of the whakapapa (genealogy), from the creation of the universe to the descent of man from the gods and the migration of his ancestors to Aotearoa New Zealand.

Te Rangikāheke was also a political realist who embraced modernity. He attached himself as an adviser to Governor Grey to teach him Māori language, traditions and customs so that he would be a good governor for both Māori and Pākehā. Unfortunately, Grey did not live up to Te Rangikāheke's expectations. Instead, he exploited Te Rangikāheke's manuscripts, which became primary sources for his publications *Kō ngā Mōteatea me ngā Hakirara ō ngā Māori* and *Kō ngā Mahinga ā ngā Tūpuna.* The latter was translated and published as *Polynesian Mythology* without citing Te Rangikāheke as a source.

Besides being a plagiarist, Grey was an unredeemed assimilationist. There was no room in his notion of governance for a dual administration of two cultures in one nation.

Schools for assimilation

The existence of the tangata whenua (people of the land) as the dispossessed owners of the soil was problematic for the coloniser. Assimilation was Governor Grey's solution to the Māori problem. His Education Ordinance of 1847 subsidised church boarding schools with a view to isolating Māori children from the "demoralising influence" of their villages. The aim was to assimilate Māori as quickly as possible into European ways (Barrington, 1970). Grey subsidised the church schools with the proviso that instruction was conducted in English. Māori was excluded from the curriculum. The system was reinforced by the Native Schools Act 1858, which gave an annual grant of £7,000 to boarding schools teaching in English.

The Government's motives for funding mission schools included civilising the natives and pacifying the country. It was thought that the schools would enhance the moral influence of government. They were also expected to develop ideas of individual ownership of property and displace communal ownership, thereby making Māori land more accessible (Simon, 1998). The Government also wanted the mission schools to provide industrial training and labouring on the land and gardens. The underlying objective was to prepare Māori for a future as a labouring underclass. The school inspector Henry Taylor declared:

> I do not advocate for the natives under present circumstances a refined education or high mental culture … they are better calculated to get their living by manual than by mental labour. (Simon, 1998, p. 11)

The mission schools became a tool of government to assign Māori to an underclass—the British brown proletariat, below the meanest of white men.

In 1867 William Rolleston reported to the Government on the progress of 13 Native Schools founded by the Anglican, Catholic and Wesleyan missionaries. Rolleston criticised the schools for failing to eliminate "Māori communism" and for emphasising religious instruction ahead of other subjects. He was also critical of the churches for not establishing a general system of primary schools (Walker, 1990). Rolleston's report encouraged the Government to introduce the Native Schools Act 1867 to establish primary schools in Māori communities. The Native Schools were controlled by the Department of Native Affairs. Māori leaders had to ask the Government to establish a school in their district and provide sufficient land for the school, but had no say in the curriculum. The genealogy of Māori knowledge was excluded and disqualified as inadequate, low down in the "hierarchy of knowledge" (Foucault, 1980).

Despite elimination of their own culture from the curriculum, Māori leaders supported the Native School system in the hope that their children would gain access to the benefits of the New World. By 1907 there were 97 Native Schools in rural Māori communities. Social life in tribal hinterlands was now centred on the new triad of school, church and marae.

The Inspector of Native Schools drew up a Native School Code in 1880. The Māori language was confined to the junior classes to induct infants into school routines. Thereafter it was progressively displaced by English as the medium of instruction in reading, writing and arithmetic. Although children became proficient in the three Rs, the authorities underestimated the strong resistance of Māori culture to assimilation. In 1897 the Inspector of Native Schools attributed poor progress to Māori difficulty with the English language. He instructed teachers to encourage children to only speak English in the playground. Teachers translated this into a general prohibition of the Māori language in school precincts. Subsequent generations of Māori, right up to the mid-20th century, claimed the prohibition was enforced by corporal punishment.

National system of education

The Education Act 1877 established a national system of secular and compulsory primary schools administered by 10 regional boards controlled by the Department of Education. The Native Schools were transferred from Native Affairs to the Department of Education. The objective was to phase out the Native Schools in communities that had become 'Europeanised', a euphemism for assimilation. However, the Māori desire to have their own schools increased the number of Native

Schools to a high of 166 well into the 20th century (Simon, 1998).

Despite the increase in Native Schools, by 1909 there were more Māori pupils attending Board schools than Native Schools. Over the next 50 years Māori attendance at Board schools increased as people migrated to towns and cities in search of work. There, the pressure to assimilate was irresistible. School demanded cultural surrender, the denial of Māori language and culture. For the majority of children, school became a site of resistance, an arena of cultural conflict exacerbated by teachers steering pupils towards manual labour and domestic service. Few went on to high school; most dropped out to join the workforce as manual workers. This dismal outlook was ameliorated by church boarding schools determining their own curriculum.

Hukarere

Napier's Hukarere Native School for Girls, established in 1875, was a joint venture between the Anglican Church and the Department of Native Affairs to Christianise, civilise and assimilate Māori. It aimed to domesticate girls for their future role as mothers and housewives. In addition to their lessons, they were expected to help prepare meals and do laundry, gardening and general housekeeping (Jenkins & Morris Matthews, 1995).

The school curriculum emphasised reading and writing in English, and rudimentary arithmetic, geography and sewing. Māori culture and tikanga (customs) were replaced by Pākehā beliefs and social practices. On leaving school, some girls went into domestic service and some went home. A small number trained as nurses, going against the prevailing educational objective of confining Māori to underclass status as labourers and manual workers (Jenkins & Morris Matthews, 1995).

Te Aute College

In 1854 Samuel Williams founded Te Aute College for Māori boys, near Pukehou, for the Anglican Mission. Initially the school struggled, but it changed for the better when John Thornton was appointed principal in 1878. Thornton prepared senior students for the matriculation exam to enable them to go on to university. The curriculum at Te Aute included English, arithmetic, algebra, Euclid, physiology, Latin, science, chemistry, Greek, French, geography and New Zealand law.

In the late 1800s three to four students a year were passing the matriculation examination. In the vanguard of Māori graduates was Apirana Ngata BA, LLB (1894). He was followed by Māui Pōmare MD (1899) and Te Rangihīroa (Peter) Buck MD. The appearance of Māori graduates so early in the colonial encounter constituted a challenge to the nexus of power and knowledge monopolised by Pākehā. All three of these modern pillars of Māori society became members of Parliament, determined to improve the lot of their people. The power-brokers in education moved to quench the flame lit by Thornton.

George Hogben, Director of Education, focused the curriculum of Native Schools on hand work, and manual and technical instruction. He wanted Te Aute to replace Latin, Euclid and algebra with agricultural and manual training (Calman, 2015). Official attempts to restrict the curriculum of Māori boarding schools were made even more explicit in the 1906 report of the Royal Commission of Inquiry into the Te Aute and Wanganui Collegiate School Trusts. William Bird, Inspector of Native Schools, argued that the objective of Māori education was to fit pupils for life among Māori and "not to mingle with Europeans and compete with Europeans in trade and commerce".[1] Bird also approved changes to the curriculum at Hukarere, replacing academic subjects with needlework, cooking and domestic work. When the school trustees resisted the instruction to tailor the curriculum towards instruction in agriculture, Bird suspended scholarships for the matriculation programme.

Hogben and Bird's control of the curriculum in Māori schools created a two-tier system of education that affirmed Pākehā dominance and Māori subordination. In 1931 T. B. Strong, Director of Education, reinforced policies laid down by Hogben and Bird. Teachers were not to encourage Māori pupils to take arithmetic beyond their present or even possible future needs (Simon, 1990). Māori education should train boys to be good farmers and girls to be good farmers' wives. The policy of tracking Māori away from high-level academic training created the 50-year hiatus between the first and second wave of Māori graduates.

Native district high schools

When the first Labour Government came to power in 1935, its education policy aimed to provide secondary education for every child "of the kind for which he is best fitted and to the fullest extent of his powers" (King, 2003, p. 335). High schools would be free of charge. The Education Department responded to the policy by establishing Native District High Schools located in rural Māori communities and controlled by the Department. The curriculum included metalwork, home management, cookery, decorating and infant welfare for girls.

In 1945, when Māori parents realised their children were being short changed, they requested that School Certificate courses be provided. Government policy meant the Department had to comply. Before leaving office in 1949, the Labour Government abolished the pejorative term 'native': Native Affairs became Māori Affairs and the Native Schools became Māori District High Schools.

Although Māori were able to influence the curriculum for the first time, the dynamic of Pākehā control at the chalk face hardly changed. With Māori urbanisation in the 1950s, more Māori were enrolled in Board schools than in Māori schools. For Māori children, schools became sites of resistance and culture conflict, exacerbated by teacher attitudes and low expectations.

Māori teacher training

Meanwhile, a breakthrough was made in reversing the policy of shutting Māori out of the professions. There was little chance the 166 Native Schools in isolated tribal areas, where Māori was still the first language, would become 'Europeanised'. Māori junior assistants from the community were employed in the infant school to help monolingual Pākehā teachers induct pupils into school routines. Teacher trainees were reluctant to be posted to Native Schools as probationary assistants. Headmasters recommended able junior assistants for teacher training to fill the shortfall in PAs. The Department of Education was obliged to institute the Māori quota system for teacher training, with trainees bonded to teach for 3 years in Native Schools.

The first intake of students under the Māori quota was admitted to Auckland Teachers' Training College in 1939, but their training was disrupted by the outbreak of war. Those who returned from the war completed their training and started teaching in the Native Schools.

The shortage of teachers in the post-war years led to an expansion of the Māori quota to upwards of 60 students a year at Auckland and

Ardmore Teachers Colleges. Others were trained at Wellington and Palmerston North. These teachers constituted the second wave of graduates and intellectuals who engaged in the praxis of liberating Māori from educational subjection. Their objective was to carefully incorporate elements of Māori culture (including art and songs) into their classrooms while avoiding a Pākehā backlash.

Whakapapa of the gaps

Apirana Ngata, the most influential Māori leader of the 20th century, was the first to recognise the economic and educational gap between Māori and Pākehā. His solution was to promote a Māori farming and land development scheme. However, many of the farms were too small to be economically viable. By 1939 most landless Māori had to look for labouring work outside their tribal areas.

In education, Ngata understood the relationship between power and knowledge and the role of the state in generating knowledge. To ensure Māori knowledge would have a place in education, Ngata had established the Māori Ethnological Research Board in 1923 to promote the study of Māori language, culture and traditions, and to publish the works of Elsdon Best, Peter Buck and Henry Skinner (Māori Ethnological Research Board, 1929). The Board also published *Te Wānanga,* a Māori counterpart to the *Journal of the Polynesian Society. Te Wānanga* ran for three issues in 1929/30.

In 1926 Ngata had proposed to the University of New Zealand that Māori language be included as a subject for the Bachelor of Arts degree. Ngata's strategy to overcome opposition was to designate Māori a foreign language. When the proposal went before the University Senate, opponents argued that Māori was not a written language. Ngata responded by citing a considerable body of literature. The University's Board of Studies capitulated and approved Māori as a foreign language for the BA degree, but did not implement the proposal. Ngata campaigned for the next 20 years to establish a lectureship in Māori, but his attempts to secure funding failed.

Māori studies

Ngata never gave up the fight to have Māori language and culture taught in universities. The breakthrough came at the Young Māori

Leaders Conference he sponsored at Auckland University College in 1939. A resolution was passed for the establishment of a Māori social and cultural centre to promote Māori adult education through Auckland University College, Teachers College and the Auckland Museum (Young Māori Leaders Conference, 1939). The outbreak of World War Two delayed action on the solution for a further 10 years.

In 1949 Maharaia Winiata was appointed Māori tutor in adult education at Auckland University. This first foot in the door of the academy was augmented by the 1951 appointment of Bruce Biggs as a junior lecturer in Māori in the Anthropology Department and Matt Te Hau in adult education. The trio pioneered the establishment of Māori studies at Auckland University. Winiata and Te Hau focused their pedagogy on cultural reconstruction and the validation and incorporation of Māori knowledge in the academy. Their courses in Māori language, culture, history and the arts of carving and weaving were held off campus on marae in Māori communities.

In 1951 Professor Ralph Piddington, head of anthropology at Auckland University, sought approval from faculty to teach Māori language. In doing so, he had to deal with the colonial mind-set rooted in the view of European superiority over natives. Piddington produced a pile of Māori text books to refute the claim that Māori was an oral, not a written, language. He argued that teaching the native tongue was essential to the discipline of anthropology, and his motion for the Māori language to be taught was passed.

At the outset the core business of Māori studies was teaching te reo Māori (the Māori language). The admission of Māori into the academy paved the way for the introduction of cultural studies as increments to the language programme. Māori studies expanded to include kawa o te marae (marae protocol), whaikōrero (oratory), waiata (songs and chants), pakiwaitara (legends), tribal traditions, and the arts of whakairo (carving), tukutuku (decorative fibre work) and raranga (weaving). Māori studies has since been extended to include topics such as Māori politics, the Māori response to colonisation, Māori resource management, indigenous studies, the Treaty of Waitangi and the settlement of Māori land claims against the Crown.

The Hunn Report

The 1960 Hunn Report on Māori Affairs made explicit for the first time in an official document the gaps identified by Ngata between Māori and Pākehā:

- Māori life expectancy was 15 years lower than that of Pākehā
- there was a 'statistical blackout' of Māori in higher education
- Māori unemployment was three times that of Pākehā (Hunn Report, 1961).

Although Hunn's findings were useful, he did not question the moral integrity of an education system that tracked Māori away from the professions and into manual work. Nor did he see structural inequality in the distribution of power as the root cause.

The Ministry of Education responded by establishing the Māori Education Foundation and the National Advisory Committee on Māori Education (NACME). To make education more congenial to Māori, NACME recommended the inclusion of "taha Māori" (Māori dimension) in the curriculum and the establishment of bilingual schooling. These initiatives had limited success because their application in so-called mainstream schools was managed mainly by Pākehā teachers and officials labouring under the influence of Hogben, Bird and Strong's earlier policies.

Māori responses to the gaps

In response to the findings of the Hunn Report, the growing body of Māori in the teaching profession adopted a co-operative and reformist strategy to education. No one questioned the moral integrity of education provision for Māori and its underlying agenda of subordinating Māori as an underclass of manual workers. They assumed there was a level playing field for Māori and devised their own strategies to close the education gap, including:

- the establishment of homework centres
- the formation of Māori education-advancement committees
- raising funds for the Māori Education Foundation
- establishing play centres for early childhood education.

Māori enthusiasm for the play centre movement was based on its kaupapa of parental participation. In 1963 Alex Grey, education lecturer at Auckland Training College, visited Māori communities throughout the North Island, promoting the play centre movement. Over 500 Māori play centres were established nationwide and affiliated to the New Zealand Play Centre Federation In theory, play centres were expected to make up the so-called deficits in Māori children, who were thought to be culturally deprived and spoke a restricted language code. It was thought they would give children a head start for primary school. In 1966 it was evident nothing had changed. The report of the Māori Education Foundation noted that over 85 percent of Māori pupils left secondary school with no qualifications. In 1969 the figure was still 79 percent, despite a decade of effort and financial input.

By this time there were several hundred Māori teaching in both primary and secondary schools. They initiated action from within by stepping up the teaching content on taha Māori in social studies, promoting school visits to marae (meeting houses), and, in the 1970s, establishing marae on school campuses. Teacher efforts to create a more congenial cultural environment for Māori students in mainstream schools were complemented by the efforts of Tūroa Royal, Advisor to the Officer for Māori Education in the Ministry of Education.

In 1971 the National Advisory Committee on Māori Education produced a seminal report written by Tūroa, recommending that:

1. cultural differences be understood, accepted and respected by children and teachers

2. the school curriculum must find a place for the understanding of Māoritanga (the Māori way of life)

3. special measures must be taken to achieve the goal of equal opportunity (Codd, Harker, & Nash, 1985, p. 75).

These resolutions enabled the Minister of Education to reverse the policy of excluding the teaching of Māori language in primary schools.

In the 1970s, to circumvent opposition to the insertion of Māori language and culture into the school curriculum, Māori intellectuals redefined assimilation and integration as taha Māori. Marae were established on school campuses to make schooling more culturally welcoming to Māori students. Māori language and cultural competitions expanded the footprint of Māori culture in previously monocultural Pākehā schools. The more embracing concept of biculturalism replaced the ideology of integration advocated by the Hunn Report.

Biculturalism is predicated on the fact that the new nation created by the Treaty of Waitangi is founded on two cultures. The base culture is that of the tangata whenua, the people of the land, whose mythology and tribal traditions connect them to their signifying symbols on the landscape. The overlying culture is that of the coloniser, who attempted to obliterate Māori culture by assimilation. The recovery and efflorescence of Māori culture in the second half of the 20th century negated the policy of assimilation by demonstrating that two cultures can co-exist and interact creatively to the benefit of both.

Generation 2000

Māori academics had their own agenda for cultural recovery through education. Leading the movement was Whatarangi Winiata, Professor of Accounting at Victoria University of Wellington. In 1975 a survey of his iwi, Ngāti Raukawa, found that most young people around Ōtaki on the Kāpiti Coast were unable to speak te reo Māori. Whatarangi devised a programme called Whakatupuranga Ruamano, Generation 2000, setting targets for language learning and entry into the professions. The pedagogy of Māori-language immersion at marae venues leaned heavily on the traditional values of whanaungatanga (kinship) and manaaki (support) from kaumātua (elders) fluent in Māori. Kaumātua taught for free, supported by kaiāwhina, (voluntary teachers). The reo rumaki (language immersion) programme began attracting adult learners from other iwi, and entry had to be limited to members of the Ātiawa, Raukawa and Ngāti Toa Rangatira (ART) confederation of iwi.

Kōhanga reo

As objects of cultural subversion through schooling, Māori had a radical potential to reform education, the portent of which surfaced in the Māori play centre movement. Māori mothers attending play centres in urban areas realised their children were being socialised to become brown Pākehā. Some withdrew their children from play centres to establish informal play groups in their own homes, where children would be socialised as Māori. This early breakaway movement provided a ready-made constituency for an authentically Māori preschool system of early childhood education.

In 1979 the most obvious effect of schooling on Māori culture was Richard Benton's gloomy prediction of Māori-language death (Benton, 1979). Māori leaders responded in 1981 by establishing kōhanga reo, preschool Māori-language nests. The Māori-speaking kuia (nannies and aunties) did the teaching, helping young mothers learn the language as well. Within 5 years, 550 kōhanga were established in rural and urban Māori communities, overseen by the Department of Māori Affairs. The Kōhanga Reo Trust and its constituents determined the curriculum and cultural procedures of kōhanga. In 1990 kōhanga reo numbers peaked at around 800. By 1993, 50 percent of Māori infants in early childhood education were in kōhanga reo.

In 1990 the Ministry of Education wanted an integrated system of early childhood education. It took control of kōhanga from Te Puni Kōkiri, the successor to Māori Affairs. Kōhanga were required to be staffed by teachers trained and qualified in early childhood education. The requirement triggered a decline, with over 400 kōhanga closing their doors. By 2006 the Kōhanga Reo Trust was desperate to arrest the decline and promote a recovery, and eventually lodged a claim against the Ministry of Education with the Waitangi Tribunal.

The Tribunal called for a moratorium on policy decisions from the Ministry on kōhanga reo pending discussions between the Trust, the Minister of Education and the Minister of Māori Affairs. An independent adviser was appointed to oversee the implementation of the recommendations in the Tribunal's report, released in October 2012.

Māori Educational Development Conference

The Māori Educational Development Conference at Tūrangawaewae marae in 1984 was a turning point in Māori understanding of the role of education in maintaining Pākehā domination and Māori subordination. The trigger was David Hughes's seminal paper on the School Certificate examination as a cause of unnecessary failure, and his challenge of the 50 percent pass/failure rate. School principals argued with the School Certificate Examination Board that the bright pupils who took academic courses in mathematics, science or French were unfairly penalised by the 50 percent pass/failure rate convention. This led to progressive lifting to 80 percent of the pass rate for academic courses.

Hughes's analysis of School Certificate examination results over a 10-year period revealed that the raw marks had been manipulated through a complicated formula of scaling to give pass rates of up to 80 percent for academic subjects. However, to maintain the convention of an overall 50 percent pass/fail ratio, the scaling formula lowered the pass rates for non-academic subjects such as art, woodwork and technical drawing. Māori language was classified among the non-academic subjects.

Confirmation of Hughes's thesis concerning the "subject hierarchy" pass rate came from Māori-language teachers, whose students did well in on-course assessment but more than 50 percent failed the School Certificate examination. In one year the pass rate in Māori language fell to 39.1 percent (Walker, 1990), a stark exposure of how the elites controlling the education system continued to determine negative outcomes for Māori.

Kura kaupapa Māori

The 300 delegates at the Māori Educational Development Conference concluded that the strategy of trying to reform a morally flawed education system to accommodate Māori culture over 25 years was a waste of energy. The conference resolved to establish alternative primary schools modelled on the precedent set by kōhanga reo. Three independent kura kaupapa Māori schools were established: Hoani Waititi Marae in 1985, Te Kura Kaupapa Māori ō Waipareira in 1987, and Te Kura Kaupapa Māori ō Maungawhau in 1988. The special character of kura kaupapa was their objectives of language and cultural maintenance. The kura trialled the teaching of the primary curriculum in the Māori language.

Te Aho Matua were the six principles underlying kura kaupapa:

- te ira tangata—the human essence of a child with physical, spiritual and emotional needs
- te reo—how kura can promote the advance of the Māori language
- ngā iwi—the tribes through which children make sense of their world and their place in it
- te ao—the world of light, where children come to understand fundamental truths about reality

- āhuatanga ako—learning that is congenial to the child and its whānau and is conducive to the requirements of the national curriculum

- ngā tino uaratanga—the values defining the character of kura kaupapa for transmission to children (Te Rūnanganui o ngā Kura Kaupapa Māori o Aotearoa, 1998).

In 1990 the proponents of kura kaupapa persuaded the Ministry of Education to fund a pilot scheme for six kura kaupapa Māori. Fortuitously, this coincided with policy changes in education under *Tomorrow's Schools*, which provided funding for a new category of schools with a "special character". Over the next 17 years the number of kura kaupapa nationwide increased to 71. At their inception kura were essentially primary schools, known as kura tuatahi, catering for children from Years 1 to 8. But there were also composite area schools in largely rural Māori communities catering for children aged 5–18. When these were converted to kura kaupapa they were designated kura arongatahi. In 2008 there were 15 schools in this category.

The gaps continue

In 1991 the *Ka Awatea* report (Henare et al., 1991) found that the gaps the Hunn Report identified 30 years earlier remained. The report proposed establishing commissions in education, health, employment and economic development to address the gaps, but this was criticised as creating a "super ministry" for the benefit of Māori. *Ka Awatea* was stillborn when the Government denied the programme funding and sacked the Minister of Māori Affairs, Winston Peters.

Undeterred, Te Puni Kōkiri (the Ministry of Māori Affairs) revisited the gaps issue in 1998. Its report, *Progress Towards Closing Social and Economic Gaps Between Māori and Non-Māori,* found that the gaps were as entrenched as ever. For example, although life expectancy had improved, Māori health overall had deteriorated. Furthermore, despite increased Māori participation in education, disparities between Māori and non-Māori persisted for most indicators of social status (Te Puni Kōkiri, 1998).

In 1999 incoming Prime Minister Helen Clark announced Labour's objective to close the gaps between Māori and non-Māori. Clark signalled her commitment to Māori by establishing and chairing the Gaps Committee, which was criticised for favouring Māori ahead of other deprived sectors of the population. 'Closing the gaps' was subsequently dropped from the political lexicon and replaced by the nebulous 'capacity building in Māori communities'.

Conclusion

The 2003 report *Decades of Disparity*, published by the Otago Medical School and the Ministry of Health, found that the mortality rate gap between Māori and non-Māori had increased between 1980 and 1999. Besides epidemiological risk factors, the report blamed social and structural factors for this growing disparity. The widening gap was seen as a downstream effect of the restructuring of the economy: "Inequalities between Māori and non-Māori had widened in employment status, education, income and housing, the key social determinants in health and social well being" (Ajwani, Blakely, Robson, Tobias, & Bonne, 2003, pp. 46–50).

This whakapapa of the gaps from the 1930s through to 2003 confirms the disparity as a structurally entrenched artefact of New Zealand's colonial history. Māori responded to the Hunn Report with co-operative strategies to make schooling more congenial to Māori culture. This included supporting the play centre movement, inserting Māori language and culture into the curriculum and establishing marae on school campuses. These transformations set the stage for the emergence and development of a truly liberating pedagogy in the form of kōhanga reo, kura kaupapa and wānanga.[2]

Since neither the Government nor its officials in the Ministry of Education had the stomach to deal with the gaps, it was up to the victim to do so. Māori, of necessity, must struggle to close the gaps and liberate themselves from Pākehā hegemony, as they have done in education for most of the 20th century. The downstream effect of wānanga has turned Māori on to education so that more people now aspire to gaining a tohu (qualification). The "blackout" identified by Hunn is being dispelled by a new dawn.

The noble purpose of education—to nourish the minds and hearts of children to realise their human potential in the world bequeathed to them by their ancestors—was perverted by the coloniser to subordinate

Māori as an underclass below the meanest of white men. With the exclusion of Māori language and culture from the curriculum, schooling became an arena of conflict and resistance, with the majority of students dropping out of school with no qualifications to join the workforce as domestics and manual workers. Schooling was doing exactly what it was designed to do when the Hunn Report in 1960 noted there was a "blackout" of Māori in higher education, a Freudian slip perhaps baring the truth that triggered Māori reaction.

References

Ajwani, S., Blakely, T., Robson, B., Tobias, M., & Bonne, M. (2003). *Decades of disparity: Ethnic mortality trends in New Zealand 1980-1999*. Wellington: Ministry of Health and University of Otago.

Barrington, J. (1970). A historical review of policies and provisions. In J. Ewing & J. Shallcrass (Eds.), *Introduction to Māori education*. Wellington: New Zealand University Press.

Barrington, J., & Beaglehole, T. (1974). *Māori schools in a changing society*. Wellington: New Zealand Council for Educational Research.

Benton, R. (1979). *Who speaks Māori in New Zealand?* Wellington: New Zealand Council for Educational Research.

Calman, R. 'Māori Education – mātauranga church boarding schools', *Te Ara – the Encyclopedia of New Zealand*. Retrieved from http://www.TeAra.govt.nz/en/maori-education-matauranga/page-4

Codd, J., Harker, R., & Nash R. (Eds.). (1985). *Political issues in New Zealand education*. Palmerston North: Dunmore Press.

Elsmore, B. (1985). *Like them that dream: The Māori and the Old Testament*. Tauranga: Tauranga Moana Press.

Foucault, M. (1980). *Knowledge/Power*. New York, NY: Pantheon Books.

Freire, P. (1972). *Pedagogy of the oppressed*. New York, NY: Bloomsbury.

Henare, D., et al. (1991). *Ka Awatea*. Wellington: Manatu Maori.

Hunn, J. K. (1961). *Report on Department of Māori Affairs: With statistical supplement, 24 August 1960*. Wellington: Government Printer.

Jenkins, K., & Morris Matthews, K. (1995). *Hukarere and the politics of Māori girls' schooling*. Palmerston North: Dunmore Press.

Jones, A., & Jenkins, K. (2011). *He kōrero: Words between us: First Māori Pākehā conversations on paper*. Wellington: Huia Publishers.

King, M. (2003). *The Penguin history of New Zealand*. Auckland: Penguin.

Māori Ethnological Research Board. (1929). *Te Wananga, 1*(1).

Simon, J. (1990). *The place of schooling in Māori-Pākehā relations*. Unpublished doctoral thesis, The University of Auckland.

Simon, J. (1998). *Ngā kura Māori: The Native Schools system 1867–1969*. Auckland: Auckland University Press.

Te Puni Kōkiri. (1998). *Progress towards closing the social and economic gap between Māori and non-Māori*. Wellington: Te Puni Kōkiri.

Te Rūnanganui o ngā Kura Kaupapa Māori o Aotearoa. (1998). *Including Te Aho Matua*. A submission to the Associate Minister of Education.

Waitangi Tribunal. (2012). *Te Raki stage one report*. Wellington: Ministry of Justice.

Walker, R. (1990). *Ka whawhai tonu matou: Struggle without end*. Auckland: Penguin.

Young Māori Conference. (1939). *Young Māori conference*. Auckland: Auckland University College.

Endnotes

1 *Appendix to the House of Representatives*, 1906, pp. 95–96. Retrieved from http://atojs.natlib.govt.nz/cgi-bin/atojs?a=p&p=browseall&e=-------10--1------0--

2 The three wānanga providing post-secondary education have distinctive objectives. These are: Te Wānanga o Raukawa, Te Whare Wānanga o Awanuiārangi and Te Wānanga o Aotearoa.

Chapter 2 Decolonising education

Moana Jackson

This chapter was developed in conversation with Moana Jackson and shares his thoughts and words on the topics of decolonisation and Māori education in Aotearoa. Formerly a secondary school teacher of te reo Māori, Moana is a lawyer and a guest lecturer in the Ahunga Tikanga (Māori Laws and Philosophy) programme at Te Wānanga o Raukawa. He is well known throughout Aotearoa by whānau, hapū and iwi and is an international champion of indigenous peoples' rights.

The impact of the 'education' system

It is important to begin by being clear about what we mean by the word 'education' and to keep the education 'system' as it currently exists in context in terms of its history and the role it has played in our lives since 1840. To do that we need to temper any enthusiasm for the often-repeated claim that "education is the key to our people's success" with a willingness to define what we mean by education and, indeed, what we mean by success.

It is, of course, well known that education is fundamental to the colonising process, because in order to dispossess us of our lands, lives and power, the colonisers had to educate us to think that what we already knew, or might know from our own traditions, our own education and our own cultural understanding of the world, was not worthy. We had to be taught to think that we did not possess 'real' knowledge or even a real intellectual tradition. Colonisation had to change our minds until we believed that knowledge and education only resided in the systems and pedagogy that had been brought here from somewhere else.

I think the evidence of the effects of that education system on our people is beyond dispute. It ranges from the deliberate physical punishment of our people for speaking the reo, to the kinds of deliberate policy decisions made in the early 20th century to prepare our boys to be labourers and our girls to be domestic servants. But there were much more insidious effects in what I call the psychological and intellectual subversion of what it meant to be Māori and what it meant to know and learn in Māori terms. In a way, colonisation may be defined as a deliberate process of re-education, and the imported education system was inevitably one key factor in that overarching process. It was one instrument through which our minds were colonised to accept a particular political and social order where all power (and, therefore, all valid modes of thinking) is vested in the colonisers.

That still manifests itself today. One simple but telling example that I often refer to is the everyday language that we have been taught (and colonised) to use. We have been taught to talk about Pākehā law, the law imposed from somewhere else, as *the* law, as if it is the only law. We have also been taught to talk about Pākehā systems and institutions as the mainstream, again as if they are the only ones. This language actually privileges the colonisers and dismisses our law as irrelevant or non-existent, and our systems as unimportant as a little muddy creek. Similarly, when we talk about education or the education system, we can also too easily assume it is the one that colonisation brought. We may do so because that seems to be the only reality (which, in itself, is a construct that colonisation defines and controls). But, in effect, we are also privileging that system and consequently running the risk of forgetting or not properly recognising what that system has been and still is about, let alone forgetting the ways of learning and knowing that are integral to our world.

So, if we are going to talk about the impact of that system on our people, then, in my view, that can only really be done by always positioning it within the colonisation that introduced and sustained it. In that context there have been two major and inter-related impacts. The first may be called the *educational or pedagogically specific impacts* that result in the 'failures' of too many of our mokopuna at school and so on. The second are the *culturally deliberative impacts,* which are the broader ways that it has redefined or diminished our knowledge, and thus our sense of self. Together they are fundamental parts of the whole colonising process that has dispossessed us.

The failure of the education system for Māori learners

The education system still continues to fail so many of our mokopuna because that's what it was designed to do. Times have changed since its imposition, of course, but much of its underlying ethos remains the same, just as colonisation itself still remains. Indeed, the fact that any of our mokopuna manage to achieve any success in its terms is due more to the efforts of our people and many dedicated teachers over the years to make it more responsive and accountable, rather than to any intrinsic or universalist aspirations it might systemically have about our achievement.

In many quite fundamental ways, that educational 'design' has always been related to the kind of social and economic order that colonisation introduced. It was necessarily hierarchical and had to 'educate' children to fit within the accepted hierarchy. As recently as 30-odd years ago it was based around the School Certificate examination system, where 50 percent had to pass and 50 percent had to fail. It was deliberately structured to fail a certain number of people in order to maintain the classes of that particular social order. That blatant pass/fail dichotomy is now gone, but the idea of structuring education to serve a particular social order is still there. In fact, the current neo-liberal emphasis on the need for education to be market sensitive by reducing the number of programmes in the humanities and so on in favour of more 'practical' programmes is really just the latest attempt to make education serve the dominant social and economic order. It is the 19th century notion of preparing our mokopuna to be labourers and servants, brought up to date in a new jargon of efficiency, teacher accountability and market need.

In that sense it actually attacks the very purpose of education, which, in all enlightened societies, has always been about encouraging children to think, to be creative and to question. In the education system that our people had before 1840, the aim was to do just that and to preserve, develop and enhance our view of the world, a view in which people didn't 'fail'. It was structured to transmit knowledge to all. Some people may have been more capable of absorbing particular knowledge than others; some may have been identified to go on to the whare wānanga, the schools of higher learning, but it was understood that everyone had the right to know, because the need to question is fundamental to being human.

In Ngāti Kahungunu, for example, we had what are called whare purokuroku or outreach centres, where everyone was able to access specific or specialised knowledge, because to learn and to know were integral parts of maintaining relationships with other people and, indeed, the world and the universe. In that sense, the idea of education was woven around an all-embracing whakapapa-based transmission of knowledge. When the colonisers came, they destroyed that education system and even physically destroyed the institutions of wānanga. For example, at Waikawa, the site of the first wānanga in Kahungunu, they actually burnt and tore down the buildings. Once they had established their own education system and began to teach our children, they also began preparing them for a world that they, the colonisers, would control.

I believe that the long, slow battle to remove that control remains a major challenge for our people, and that until that is achieved and education is seen as something more than a kind of glorified preparation for one's place in a market-defined hierarchy, the current education system will continue to fail our mokopuna. It will fail them because it will not enable them to think critically, to ask questions, or to recognise the fullness of who we are and might be: that we are more than just potential class ciphers, and more even than just experts in waiata or wonderful myth-tellers, important though those things are. In the end, it is not designed to empower our mokopuna to be decolonised, to know that we are entitled to determine our own destiny and to make our own political and constitutional decisions. Educating them in the skills, and giving them the courage, to once again exercise our rangatiratanga are simply not parts of its core curriculum.

Decolonising education and the education system

A number of things need to happen, which many of our people have been working on for a long time. They include the wider and eventually universal availability of good-quality teaching in the reo, the establishment and adequate funding of more kura, restructuring non-kura to be whānau-inclusive, and so on. They are really important and address what I earlier referred to as the pedagogically specific impacts of that education system. We have many committed whānau, teachers and academics doing ground-breaking and brave work in that area, and that should—and obviously will—continue.

What I would like to focus on are the culturally deliberative impacts and the need for ongoing discussion among our people about what we mean when we say, for example, that our mokopuna must get a good education. How can we find Māori ways, if you like, in which they can achieve all they wish in career terms while also ensuring that they are educationally and politically astute enough to be self-determining in the broadest possible sense of that term? How do we educate for rangatiratanga rather than just equating success with a university degree, and so on? That necessarily means asking two questions: How does, or how can, this education system prepare our people to do that? And how can, or should, that be related to the important cultural questions of keeping them safe and enabling them to be proud, confident and capable young Māori, able to live in the 21st century? The second question is more complex, but in my view also needs discussion. If we conclude that the current education system cannot, or will not, do that, what options are available to us to ensure the sort of colonisation-free rangatiratanga-embracing education that our tamariki are entitled to?

As with any complex question, the answers are complex too and require the sort of imaginative courage that inspired those, for example, who first advocated for the establishment of kura. Perhaps one way to have that discussion is to look honestly at where kura are at and what they are doing at the moment. I, personally, get real joy going into kura and hearing tamariki confident in the reo. However, I have been concerned on some occasions when I have observed lessons on the Treaty, for example, that are in the reo, but the content is actually an unquestioned version of the colonising story, complete with assertions that we ceded sovereignty and that the Crown was motivated by good faith. In essence, they are transmitting in the reo a Pākehā view of the world. That may be the version of the Treaty required by the national syllabus, but I'm not sure it's consistent with Te Aho Matua. I'm certainly sure it's not the story of our tīpuna, and I would have hoped it is that truth that our mokopuna would be learning.

Perhaps the central part of challenging or decolonising the current system, then, is to ask the sort of question that was often asked during the drafting of the United Nations Declaration on the Rights of Indigenous Peoples: How can we free our people's minds to tell and be inspired once more by our own stories? If that is through kura, then how do we support them to get syllabus changes or other initiatives that will enable them to be the Māori story-tellers and the kaitiaki for rangatiratanga-based change? And what do we need to do beyond the kura gates to address the broader culturally deliberative issues that are the core papa, or base, for all the educational issues that we actually face?

Visioning a decolonised education system

It is important to always try to understand the existing Pākehā education system in its colonising context, and it is equally important to see decolonising that system within the context of how we can once again be self-determining; that is, how can we more fully and sensitively make our own decisions about education? Decolonising education, then, is part of decolonising everything else that has damaged and controlled our world since 1840, because in the end the only education system that will ultimately serve our people well is one that flows from and is guided by decisions made by our people.

I really admire the efforts over the years of many Māori teachers and educationists to critique and remedy many of the more obvious faults and shortcomings in the current system. It was no small achievement to get kura; it was no small achievement to get wānanga; it was no small achievement to have the reo more acknowledged in other schools. But there is still more to do. As brave and even noble as those efforts have been and still are, they don't address the final issue of the power that determines the course and content of education. Just as there is more to do beyond the Treaty settlements process, because they do not settle all that colonisation has done—and especially what it has done to effectively render our people politically and constitutionally powerless—so there is more to settle in education.

While there are many steps involved in that settling, I believe that it will only come from what is called constitutional transformation: the process of actually transforming power so that we can at last say this is the education we want for our mokopuna in the 21st century; these are the institutions through which we want that to happen; these are the things we think our tamariki should know in order for that to happen. In the work I am currently involved in with Matike Mai, the iwi-led Constitutional Transformation Working Group, these are just the sorts of questions our people are asking. We are aware that answering those questions will not be easy, but I think our people are on a journey, and the reclaiming of that authority—the reclaiming of what rangatiratanga means in its fullest political and constitutional sense—is an inevitable part of that journey. When that eventually happens, and it will happen because justice must always come to those who have been made powerless, then all the issues to do with changing the educational paradigm will inevitably happen as well. In the Working Group we have set 2040 as our goal for trying to implement substantive and substantial constitutional transformation.

In the meantime, I hope that we will keep having kōrero among ourselves and with others about what that means. At the same time, I am hopeful we will keep doing what we have got very good at since 1840, which is making the best of a bad situation: making the best of an education system that is there, and continuing to work out what we can do to protect our people within it, how we can ensure our mokopuna learn all they are entitled to learn, and how we can continue to advance our longer-term goals with whatever skills we might take from it.

I know that will be done, and I am also optimistic that the broader constitutionally based change will come, because that is what our people have always strived for. The only thing that gives me pause in my optimism is that the current political ideology of the Crown, driven by neo-liberalism and the cult of the individual, is even changing the purpose and face of education that Pākehā know. In many ways the ideals that Pākehā society once had about education are being driven back to an older and even more hierarchical and business/market-focused endeavour. In colonisation, indigenous peoples were automatically seen as an inferior lower class in that system, but now even many Pākehā are being 'educated out' of real opportunity and 'educated into' inequality.

Our people, of course, continue to be more adversely affected than Pākehā, so that even as we try to advocate or agitate for something that is uniquely ours and wonder how we can decolonise that existing system, the system itself is being manipulated and changed to serve narrow ideological purposes. In that context, the New Right that the neo-liberals promote is actually an old Victorian Right, where education and *laissez-faire* economics determined and sustained the dynamics of the class system and the hierarchies of wealth and power, and now we are having to confront a new yet old colonisation that necessarily complicates the process of decolonisation.

This new yet old colonisation is particularly insidious and powerful, because one of the things that neo-liberalism has got very good at doing is reframing Māori aspirations to fit within that market model. For example, in the area of prison reform the dominant dialectic is no longer about Māori reforming or even abolishing prisons, but how Māori can manage them as an expression of rangatiratanga. This might seem a tempting offer, and many of our people may think we would do a better job running them, but the fundamental question is not being asked: Is the whole idea of prisons, of incarcerating our people, actually consistent with rangatiratanga? Is it consistent with our notions of how to deal with wrongdoing by our mokopuna? A private prison, by its very nature, is designed to make a profit, and the only way this can be done is by having more inmates, which would mean our people locking away more of our own mokopuna. That seems to me to be really worrying and problematic in many ways, especially in tikanga and whakapapa terms. It certainly doesn't address such basic questions as why do prisons exist, why are so many of our people in there, and whose interest do they serve?

I think there are similar problematic issues with the neo-liberal push in education that I mentioned earlier. It may be tempting to see charter schools, for example, as an exercise of rangatiratanga, and many of our people would certainly do a better job running a school than others have done for over a hundred years. However, I think it would be wise to consider the ideology behind that suggestion. Is it actually a chance for us to exercise rangatiratanga as an effort to educate our mokopuna in Māori terms, or is it, like the prisons, a chance to exercise something in the name of rangatiratanga that is actually a Pākehā ideologically driven goal of educating people for the market, if you like? Will it free the minds of our mokopuna, or only make them more 'successful' in Pākehā terms? Those are questions that we have always had to ask when confronting colonisation, and what we now face is a particularly difficult form or variant of colonisation that is much more subtle and pervasive, and therefore much more difficult to deal with.

Conclusion

In conclusion, if we're going to talk about the notion of education, then part of what we need to do is look critically at the existing system in a way that actually helps our people understand what it is. I also think it's important that a lot of the really good thinking that's been going on around education gets out to our people, because that idea of wanting our mokopuna to have a good education is a really powerful driving force.

If in, say, 5 years' time we have 1,000 mokopuna with PhDs, that will be cause for some celebration, but if they have no critical understanding of the education system they've graduated in—if they have no political analysis that enables them to use whatever they have learnt in a way that advances the journey of our people towards self-determination—then all of that learning will really be to no avail, because little will actually change in the lives of most of our people. One of the great strengths of the concept of *kaupapa* Māori research is that it is based not just in a rigorous intellectual framework, but in a critique that might then lead people to think through change. In a way, I guess, that's what I'd hope a book like this might contribute to as well.

Chapter 3 Te Harinui: Civilising the Māori with school and church

Ani Mikaere

1. Not on a snowy night
   By star or candlelight
   Nor by an angel band
   There came to our dear land ...
   Te Harinui
   Te Harinui
   Te Harinui
   Glad tidings of great joy.

2. But on a summer day
   Within a quiet bay
   The Māori people heard
   The great and glorious word ...

3. The people gathered round
   Upon the grassy ground
   And heard the preacher say
   I bring to you this day ...

4. Now in this blessed land
   United heart and hand
   We praise the glorious birth
   And sing to all the earth ...

Described as "New Zealand's best-loved iconic Christmas carol",[1] Te Harinui was penned by Willow Macky in 1957. It commemorates the arrival of Samuel Marsden to the Bay of Islands, where, on 25 December 1814, he gave what is said to have been the first sermon delivered in Aotearoa, preaching from Luke 2:10: "Behold! I bring you glad tidings of great joy". Marsden later wrote, "When the service was over, we could not but feel the strongest persuasion that the time was at hand when the Glory of the Lord would be revealed to these poor benighted heathens" (Elder, 1932, pp. 93–94).

During the late 1970s the Anglican boarding school that I attended considered this an appropriate song to be performed at its end-of-year functions. No doubt the fact that the school bore the name of the preacher whose actions we were singing about added to the sense of occasion. Needless to say, pupils were never told about Marsden's nickname in Australian circles, "the flogging parson" (he earned the reputation among the convicts of being a particularly severe magistrate); nor were we taught the Ngā Puhi waiata "He Waiata mō te Mātenga", which commemorated Marsden's first sermon with the now well-rehearsed witticism that while Ngā Puhi looked up, Marsden looked down—a cynical reference to the Pākehā obsession with obtaining land (Te Reo Rangatira Trust, 1998, p. 26).

As a quietly rebellious teenager I balked at the suggestion that my tūpuna had been uplifted by "the great and glorious word", and regarded with disbelief the idea that Māori and Pākehā had been united in common worship ever since that fateful day. Needless to say, the ear-grating mispronunciation of the only two Māori words in the song (three, if you include the word "Māori") merely served to exacerbate my irritation. (I should note that the school roll was overwhelmingly Pākehā and that te reo Māori was not included in the school's curriculum offerings.) I had little understanding, at age 16, of why I disliked the song so intensely or why I found so galling the incessant obligation to bow our heads in prayer to the ultimate white male authority figure. But I instinctively mistrusted the messages being conveyed and deeply resented having to conform to the school requirement of participating in these activities.

Despite the passage of many years, the experience of being forced to sing this song has remained with me. I have often wondered how I could possibly have failed to voice my concerns about it at the time. I would have struggled to articulate my position, but how could that excuse my silence/complicity? The fact that challenging each and every expression of racism that I encountered while at that school would have been a pretty tall order (and the knowledge that I did frequently confront staff and students) does little to allay my sense of guilt.

Aside from being credited with the introduction of Christianity to Aotearoa, Marsden was also responsible for the establishment of the first mission school in 1816, thereby signalling the start of a lengthy missionary campaign to 'civilise' Māori through a zealous combination of schooling and church. While the first school, based at Rangihoua and headed by Thomas Kendall, was not particularly successful, by the 1830s Māori enthusiasm for literacy had translated into significant growth within the mission schools. Keith Sorrenson describes the Māori demand for the printed word as "insatiable", noting that by 1845 approximately half of all adult Māori had acquired a degree of literacy (Sorrenson, 1981, p. 168).

The conflicting goals of missionaries and Māori led to inevitable tensions. Motivated principally by a desire to convert Māori to Christianity, the missionaries limited their instruction to Christian texts that had been translated into Māori. While the language was Māori, the values being conveyed were distinctly European. Particularly significant was the corrosive influence of missionary beliefs about the inferiority of Māori philosophies and practices (Simon, 1998).

For their part, Māori parents saw no reason to limit their children's education to Christian texts or to te reo Māori. On the contrary, they were anxious for their children to acquire European knowledge and fluency in English so that they would be better equipped to deal with the threats being posed by a rapidly increasing Pākehā population and its obvious hunger for land. It is important to note, too, that the parents saw the acquisition of such abilities as complementing Māori language and knowledge rather than replacing it (Simon, 1998).

When Governor Grey extended state subsidies to the mission schools in 1847, he attached the condition that instruction should be in English, but it is clear that he was more interested in assimilation than in equipping Māori to better resist the expansion of Pākehā control. He also made industrial training compulsory, a move that caused considerable dissatisfaction among Māori parents, who were rightly suspicious of a policy that seemed designed to turn their children into servants (Simon, 1998). At about the same time as the state began to subsidise the mission schools, several church boarding schools were also established. These provided secondary education for those pupils deemed more promising and were aimed at removing them from "the Māori environment" of the village day schools (Sorrenson, 1981, p. 171). They included St Stephen's in Parnell (established in 1846) and Te Aute (established in 1854).

During the land wars of the 1860s Māori enthusiasm for Pākehā education plummeted, leading to the collapse of many of the mission schools (Simon, 1998; Sorrenson, 1981). In their place a national system of village primary schools was established. The Native Schools endured for over a century, from 1867 to 1969. However, it was not until 1941 that the first Native District High School was established to meet the needs (as judged by the Department of Education) of Māori secondary school students. Until that time, those who could not afford to attend the denominational schools took their chances at state schools or simply stopped attending school altogether.

For a lengthy period, then, aside from those who attended the denominational schools, all Māori students received a secular education. It should be noted, however, that by this time schools were no longer required as tools for conversion. Sorrenson notes that by the early 1840s most Māori had become, at the very least, "nominal Christians", adhering more strictly to Christian obligations (such as observing the Sabbath) than their Pākehā neighbours and frequently assembling in large gatherings for worship (Sorrenson, 1981, p. 171). So pervasive was the influence of Christianity that, over time, Christian principles became heavily intertwined with tikanga. A contemporary example of this phenomenon is the surprisingly common practice of opening a pōwhiri with a Christian karakia, after which the whaikōrero is allowed to begin.

During the 1980s Māori rebelled against the assimilatory thrust of the state education system, setting up kōhanga reo, kura kaupapa Māori and wharekura. The Education Act 1989 eventually caught up with Māori demands, providing for kura kaupapa Māori (section 155) and also for kura-ā-iwi (as special character schools under section 156). As state schools, kura kaupapa and kura-ā-iwi are obliged to offer a secular education at primary level. This does not mean a complete ban on all forms of religious observance or instruction, but there are conditions that must be met. While stating that teaching must be secular during the hours that a school is open for instruction (section 77), the Education Act 1964 also allows a school to close for up to one hour a week for religious instruction or religious observance (section 78). During such times, children must be free to opt out of these activities (section 79). Boards of trustees may choose to include religious instruction at secondary school level (section 72) but the obligation to comply with the New Zealand Bill of Rights Act 1990 means that any such activity must be offered in a non-discriminatory way, with students free to opt out if they wish.

These provisions suggest that Christian religious observance should play a minimal role, particularly at primary school level, within kura kaupapa and kura-ā-iwi. They would also indicate that at secondary level students should be made aware of their ability to absent themselves from any religious observance or instruction. However, as a parent with some 25 years' experience of children attending kura kaupapa, kura-ā-iwi or belonging to whānau units within Pākehā secondary schools, it is clear to me that Christianity masquerading as tikanga has pervaded these spaces to an alarming degree.

In all of these environments Christian prayer formed part of their everyday routines, opening and closing all gatherings and events. Not only were my children in attendance during such rituals, but they were regularly expected to participate in the recitation of lengthy prayers and the singing of hymns. All of them performed in school kapa haka groups, whose brackets typically began with a suitably Christian song as the choral item. My daughter was even corrected by her teacher when she suggested that their karakia should be addressing "ngā atua" (the gods) rather than "Te Atua" (God).

I'm ashamed to say (more guilt—an inevitable corollary, it would seem, of my every entanglement with Christianity) that I never challenged the privileged position that Christian ritual appeared to occupy within these various 'Māori' educational spaces. The most that I could manage was to reassure my daughter that I agreed completely with her analysis of what Māori karakia should be about. Showing extraordinary maturity for someone still in primary school, she appreciated that the kaumātua who had corrected her was genuine in his belief and, out of respect and affection for him, she had determined that the best approach was to hold to her personal view but to refrain from upsetting him by arguing the point.

Why didn't I question the prominence of Christianity within these Māori educational environments? In retrospect I think that my expectations of the education on offer for my children had been heavily influenced by the constant, grinding racism that had characterised my own journey through the education system during the 1960s and 1970s. If I'm honest, I was simply grateful that my children were able to attend primary schools where being Māori was the norm: where te reo Māori was spoken; where they would not have to cringe every time a person in authority butchered the pronunciation of their names; where they would be cushioned, for a few years at least, from the full force of having to deal with multiple expressions of racism on a daily basis. The fact that they might have to play along with the odd bit of Christian observance seemed a small enough price to pay.

Moreover, my older children started at primary school early in the 1990s, a time when kaupapa Māori options were still very much in their infancy. It was a struggle to gain support from Māori parents or from the state. In such circumstances, mounting a challenge against the credibility of the tikanga that was being practised within kura would have risked creating divisions in an environment where unity was crucial. As a strong advocate of kaupapa Māori education, it was almost inconceivable to consider raising a voice in protest against the uncritical way in which Christian ritual was being inflicted upon our children in the name of tikanga.

Unfortunately, it is still extremely difficult to raise such issues. Given the unyielding determination of the missionaries to destroy and supplant our 'heathen' practices with their own moral and religious code, the extent to which Māori society as a whole has succumbed to Christian teachings over time is probably not surprising. Moreover, in view of the constant need to defend any ground that we may have managed to win back from the assimilatory apparatus of the state, it is understandable that we should have become fiercely protective of the tikanga that we practise within kura. We have become highly sensitised to criticism, regardless of where it might come from: two centuries of being told that you are worthless will do that to a people. Understanding all of this, however, does nothing to detract from the perfect irony of finding Christianity, a force that is inherently destructive of tikanga, now flourishing within the kaupapa Māori spaces that we have fought so hard to create.

Something that has changed since my children began their journey through the compulsory education sector is a revival of interest in karakia Māori: it has become increasingly common to hear karakia Māori used as part of the daily routines within kaupapa Māori educational spheres. While this renewal of enthusiasm is encouraging, caution is still called for. I fear that many of the assumptions underpinning Christianity have become so deeply ingrained in our thinking that we are at risk of reinventing karakia Māori in a way that simply reinforces some of the most harmful aspects of Christian thought.

The main tension, as I see it, stems from the fundamental clash between, on the one hand, a theory of existence that is centred on whakapapa and, on the other hand, the dictates of monotheism. Reliance on whakapapa as a central organising concept means conceiving of the whole of creation as an intricate system of relationships. These relationships must constantly be negotiated, nurtured and developed to meet changing circumstances. Whakapapa is dynamic, flexible, complex and non-hierarchical. Monotheism, on the other hand, is rigidly hierarchical and compartmentalised. It is dogmatic, asserting one truth and permitting no other. It normalises the concepts of dominance and subservience, ranking the whole of creation in relation to the supreme power of the One God, who sits in divine isolation, demanding obedience from his subjects and punishing those who err.

In seeking examples of the contemporary practice of karakia Māori having become contaminated by Christian perceptions of religion, it is hard to go past the Io cult. *The Lore of the Whare Wananga* (Smith, 1913) has been subjected to over a century of rigorous critique: from Percy Smith's own contemporaries, such as Bishop Herbert Williams (Sorrenson, 1979); throughout the 20th century from scholars such as

Te Rangi Hīroa (Hīroa, 1952) and Keith Sorrenson (Sorrenson, 1979); and into the current century from Hirini Moko Mead (Mead, 2003) and Ross Calman (Calman, 2004). Despite this formidable array of doubters, the notion of a Māori religious code that apes Christianity in so many respects has proven to be remarkably tenacious. With its insistence on the existence of a supreme male god who created the world by force of his willpower, with its obsessive categorisation and ranking of all 'lesser' gods and other entities, with its rigidly tiered priesthood, and with its unbridled misogyny, the Io cult is fundamentally at odds with the whakapapa theoretical framework that our tūpuna devised in order to make sense of their existence. That it is so often accepted uncritically as authentically Māori is as profoundly illogical as it is disturbing.

This is just one example of the way in which colonised mutations of karakia Māori are sometimes perpetrated within kura. There are other practices that are equally dubious; for example, the ludicrous assumption that recitation of karakia is a peculiarly male activity. For those of us for whom decolonisation of the way we understand and acknowledge our place in creation is a priority, practices such as these are no less appalling than the unthinking adherence to Christian ritual that has pervaded kaupapa Māori educational environments during the past 25 years.

This decade marks two centuries of Christian influence in Aotearoa, and we are likely to hear the name of Samuel Marsden repeatedly during this period. It is interesting to ponder what he thought he was achieving when he delivered his Christmas Day sermon to a group of people who had no idea what he was talking about, a fact of which he was well aware (Elder, 1932). We know that the sight of the Union Jack flying above the congregation greatly pleased him: he later noted that he considered it "the signal for the dawn of civilization, liberty, and religion in that dark and benighted land" (Elder, 1932, p. 93). It is also fascinating to note his assessment of Māori as "apparently prepared for receiving the knowledge of Christianity more than any Savage natives I have seen" (Orange, 2004, p. 9). In reaching this conclusion, it is likely that he was comparing us with the indigenous peoples he had encountered in Australia. The task of 'civilising' them he considered far more problematic, on account of the fact that "they had no wants, they lived free and independent" (Marsden, 1826, p. 68).

As these sentiments reveal, the missionaries regarded conversion to Christianity as essential to the successful assimilation of indigenous peoples, who were being targeted for colonisation. During the past 30 years, Māori have been resolute in pushing back against the assimilatory tide of the colonial enterprise, particularly in the field of education. It is curious, to say the least, that even as we have fought to reaffirm our tino rangatiratanga across numerous spheres of activity, the inherently and irredeemably colonising influence of Christianity has remained largely unchallenged. Within Māori educational environments—as elsewhere—the time for jettisoning Christian contaminations of karakia Māori, along with Christianity itself, as part of the journey to reclaim our freedom and independence is long overdue.

References

Calman, R. (2004). *Reed book of Māori mythology*. Auckland: Reed Books.

Elder, J. R. (Ed.). (1932). *The letters and journals of Samuel Marsden 1765–1838*. Dunedin: Coulls Somerville Wilkie. Retrieved from http://www.Gospel/2014.org/marsden/

Hīroa, T. (1952). *The coming of the Māori*. Wellington: Whitcombe & Tombs.

Marsden, S. (1826). *An answer to certain calumnies in the late Gov MacQuarrie's pamphlet, and the third edition of Mr Wentworth's account of Australasia*. London: J. Hatchard & Son.

Mead, H. M. (2003). *Tikanga Māori: Living by Māori values*. Wellington: Huia Publishers.

Orange, C. (2004). *The story of a treaty*. Wellington: Bridget Williams Books.

Simon, J. (Ed.). (1998*). Ngā Kura Māori: The Native Schools system 1867–1969*. Auckland: Auckland University Press.

Smith, S. P. (1913). *The lore of the whare wananga or teachings of the Māori College*. New Plymouth: Thomas Avery.

Sorrenson, K. (1979). *Māori origins and migrations: The genesis of some Pākehā myths and legends*. Auckland: Auckland University Press.

Sorrenson, K. (1981). Māori and Pākehā. In W. H. Oliver and Bridget Williams (Eds.), *The Oxford history of New Zealand*. Wellington: Oxford University Press.

Te Reo Rangatira Trust. (1998). He waiata mō Te Mātenga, *He waiata onamata*. Auckland: Te Reo Rangatira Trust.

Endnotes

1   According to sounz.org.nz/works/show/13893.

2   See, eg, the Hope Project, launched by a coalition of Christian churches, which opens its website with the statement: "In December 2014 New Zealand celebrated the bicentenary of the Christian gospel arriving in New Zealand and the beginning of a hope-filled bi-cultural partnership with Māori". Samuel Marsden is referred to regularly in the materials provided: hopeproject.co.nz

Chapter 4 Ko te mana motuhake, ake ake, ake!: Reclaiming education for Waikato-Tainui

Sarah-Jane Tiakiwai

Introduction

There are multiple spaces in which the decolonisation agenda continues and perseveres across Aotearoa New Zealand. This chapter talks about a tribal space and is primarily written as a story of reclamation. Smith (1999) writes about claiming and reclaiming as a methodological approach to establish or assert legitimacy of our rights as indigenous peoples. Reclaiming stories also provides us with the opportunity to tell our collective stories. This chapter, then, is a reassertion of how we as a tribe value knowledge and higher learning and tells the story of how we are reclaiming this in our own unique way.

This chapter is also a specific story. The history of Waikato-Tainui has been told and retold, and any efforts to summarise it in a few paragraphs in this chapter would be both woefully inadequate and disrespectful to the tribe's rich and long history.[1] Rather, the focus for this chapter will be on key elements of the tribe's history as it pertains to the reclamation of tribal knowledge through the construction and establishment of the tribe's Endowed College. This framing is akin to what

Attwood and Magowan consider to be indigenous acknowledgements that our histories or accounts are often "framed by a radically different sense of reality, causation and time" (2001, pp. xiv–xv).

The story as written in this chapter is also a personal one. As a tribal member, not only have I directly benefited from the tribe's investment in higher education through scholarships, but I have also been privileged to contribute—alongside many others—off and on over the last two decades to the tribe's reclamation agenda through the establishment of the College. This means that the chapter, in attempting to tell the story of the College, is the story told through my eyes and what I have been privileged to witness, experience and contribute to.

Waikato-Tainui

National attention focused on Waikato-Tainui in 1995 when it reached a settlement with the Crown over the raupatu, or confiscation, of tribal lands in 1863. As one of the first in the contemporary Treaty environment, the raupatu settlement was achieved during a period of wider discontent for Māori, especially with regard to the government 'fiscal envelope' approach to Treaty settlements (Gardiner, 1996). In his reflections on the raupatu settlement, the tribe's principal negotiator, Sir Robert Te Kotahi Mahuta, noted that "colonial impact did not change the direction of the destiny of Waikato .... What we lost was our land, not our mana" (cited in McCan, 2001, p. 327).

One of the outcomes of the raupatu settlement was the establishment of an endowed college which would contribute to the mana of Waikato standing again: "we shall govern ourselves, educate ourselves … we can attend to the needs of our people ourselves" (Mahuta, cited in McCan, 2001, p. 332).

Te Arikinui Dame Te Atairangikaahu officially opened the Endowed College in February 2000. At the opening, Te Arikinui, who was also founding patron, expressed her desire that the College would be the tribe's gift to the nation. The reality, however, has been more of a long-haul challenge. One major challenge has been gaining the trust and confidence of the tribe to believe in ourselves and to reclaim how we as a tribe value higher learning. Aligned to this has been reconciling the notion that the inspiration for the College was in part premised on the very models of colonial thought that we revile in our reclamation of the indigenous thought and knowledge space. Sir Robert's vision for the College was based on his own Oxford experience—a combination of its intellectuality and the way in which it supported students through its College system. However, he felt that this combination was not alien to our own learning systems, which he described as being akin to a "mini marae" (Mahuta, 2001, p. 6). The mini marae concept has been reclaimed at the College and reframed into a noho wānanga, or living and learning environment, a concept similar to contemporary whare wānanga approaches to teaching and learning.

Part of this reclamation can be seen in the way the College itself has been built. As Mahuta notes, the College is "on the crest of a hill in the centre of returned lands", built as "our own permanent memorial to raupatu" (p. 331). Guiding the driveway leading up to the College are eight pou, or pillars, that refer to the traditional whare wānanga or houses of higher learning that used to exist around the Tainui region prior to colonisation. They are deliberately positioned there to remind us and all our visitors that higher learning has always been a part of our history as a tribe; the College simply represents the reclamation of that history and provides a platform from which the tribe can envision, plan for and develop its future.

Underpinning the College's living and learning environment is its commitment to being the memorial to raupatu and maintaining the values of Kingitanga. What this means is that the College buildings have been designed to reflect the history of raupatu, and within that the history and values of the tribe and of Kingitanga. This is integral to the College's story for a number of reasons. Firstly, we and all visitors to and students of the College are visually reminded on a daily basis of our history and thus, more implicitly, of the values we are expected to uphold, especially for those of us who are privileged to work at the College. Secondly, the buildings have embedded across them—both subtly and unsubtly—cultural symbols that as a learning institution remind us that higher learning and research have always been a part of us. These symbols represent a decolonising and reconceptualising of terms such as 'research' and 'higher learning'.

One example of this is a carving we have of Māui, which is a contemporary interpretation of him fishing up Aotearoa. Māui is often referred to in our stories, with his achievements and exploits being well recorded and which still hold value and place in our present. For the College, Māui exemplifies our approach to research. His exploits and achievements are the outcomes of research, beginning with asking questions like, How come the sun moves so fast?, Why can't we have fire?, and so forth. The process of search and discovery as told through the carvings and associated stories attached to them outlines for us the methodological frame and methods used. The findings or outcomes of these searches is the new knowledge, the new technologies that are, in contemporary Western settings, celebrated as the innovative, on-the-edge technological advances the world is looking for. Thus our reference to Māui is not simply as a symbolic or romantic representation of our historical and cultural or mythological past. Rather, it serves more as a reminder that we have always been innovative, at the forefront, and that the process of questioning within culturally contextualised settings has enabled us to make those on-the-edge advances.

So the presence of Māui as a carving in our College enables us to reclaim our traditional practice of being innovative and of having always embraced the concept of research. Extending this concept further, in the context of the research work that we do we retell the final act of Māui and his attempt to attain immortality by defeating Hine-nui-te-pō (Goddess of Death) through the ethical lens of what happens when one pushes the boundaries too far. The notion of research is always risky, and even when guided by our cultural underpinnings and ways of knowing, there are consequences for us to consider as we move within the research space. This is particularly important, for the reclamation of research within a kaupapa Māori and tribal research space does not mean that we can act without due consideration for those with and for whom we research. It serves to remind us of the consequences when we may not appropriately consider or apply ethical practices or considerations in our work as educators and as researchers and it requires us to be ever more vigilant. Thus Māui and his presence as a strong physical symbol within our College reinforces the need for vigilance and due consideration in our work.

A more subtle symbol is the portraits of our past ariki from the Kingitanga movement. The five portraits of the Māori Kings—Pōtatau, Tāwhiao, Mahuta, Te Rata and Koroki—together with the portrait of Te Arikinui Dame Te Atairangikaahu, speak to notions of resilience and a commitment to and strength of purpose in the Kingitanga, and then, following raupatu, in the resolution of the illegal confiscation of tribal lands. As symbols of resilience they remind us not to be so impatient in seeking quick-fix answers to the many challenges facing our people today. Instead, they remind us that a commitment to purpose, grounded in cultural values, principles and philosophies, will enable us to find solutions that are appropriate and will take our people forward.

The portraits represent six generations of resilience, perseverance and commitment to a kaupapa, such that each generation has built upon the achievements and advances of the previous generation. Indeed, any of our achievements must be connected to previous achievements. This layering of achievements, generation after generation, provide for us some pointed but subtle expectation that we will leave a contribution for the next generation to build upon. More importantly, our contributions then cannot stand alone, but instead seek to strengthen and add value to those whose contributions came before us.

Understanding this from a conceptual perspective is the easy part. As in an art gallery, we can look at the images and portraits as abstract concepts and try to make sense of them from our own frames. We can easily glide past the portraits and carvings as static symbols of a forgotten past, but to do so would undermine the commitment and the sacrifices of those who have gone before us and thus render our efforts empty and meaningless. One of the challenges, then, is how we can bring to life our history, make our contributions relevant and meaningful for our present and, more importantly, for the future. How do we reclaim our knowledge and practice, as encapsulated in the walls and through the building of our College, and bring them to life in our everyday work? This, to me, is the essence of decolonising ourselves, because it requires us to move past the romanticising of our past and, through a process of reclamation, focus not just on the nostalgic 'good bits' but draw deeply from the lessons learnt and left by previous generations.

This is the layering I referred to earlier. Much of the work we do is focused on contributing to tribal wellbeing in its broadest context. The layering comes in the sense that this work is informed by the generations of knowledge already contained in our histories, our mātauranga and our practices. Our role is to ensure that any new knowledge builds on or adds another layer to our understanding of what it means to be us as a tribe, how we relate ourselves to others and to the changing world. More importantly, though, it requires us to have confidence in understanding and then advancing our own positions, reclaiming through knowledge and research our own sense of mana motuhake.

An example of this is engaging in work that seeks to develop our own measures of success, our own indicators of wellbeing, of what tribal identity and integrity mean to us and for us, rather than having these defined for us. While we are not opposed to drawing on, and indeed do utilise, information, programmes and research provided by others about us, we insist that the ways in which these sources of information are used and applied be defined by us. Much of this in practice means negotiation and, at times, walking away from projects, ideas and initiatives that in our view do not support our commitment to engaging in work that supports tribal advancement. This, to me, is the decolonisation agenda in practice and for us how we reclaim who and what we are.

While the concept of who we would be as a College was long considered and planned for, our reality is that we are still in our infancy, and these original concepts have shifted and changed in response to the new environment in which we now exist. Thus, much of our work has involved responding to needs (perceived and actual) rather than progressing in the more deliberate and planned, forward-focused way I have talked about in this chapter. This is our decolonising agenda: a constant challenge to ourselves that we don't get caught up in a no-man's land and no-win space of trying to be everything to everyone but ending up being nothing of relevance.

Conclusion

In writing this chapter I was challenged about how I might represent our College. As a new institution that does not have any comparable examples, we are forging a new sense of mana motuhake. So what we thought we were 5 years ago, while in principle essentially the same, in practice has flexed and been moulded and shaped by our realities. We are still learning and have yet to fully consider the ways in which we might add our own contribution or layer to the knowledge and practice that surround us in the portraits and carvings at the College. Part of the reclamation process, in my view, is as much about having the confidence to say what we won't do as it is about what we do, and we will have much to explore, debate and consolidate before we can settle on what that might look like for us as a tribal institution.

To that end, I am reminded and comforted by the words of our founding patron, Te Arikinui Dame Te Atairangikaahu, who wanted the College to be a safe place for open enquiry. For me, at this point in time, it allows us to explore, to challenge and to be challenged—to be the Māui for our tribe, but in ways that are guided and shaped by our unique tribal history and setting.

References

Attwood, B., & Magowan, F. C. (2001). Introduction. In B. Attwood and F. Magowan (Eds), *Telling stories: Indigenous history and memory in Australia and New Zealand* (pp. xi–xvii). Crows Nest, NSW: Allen & Unwin.

Gardiner, W. (1996). *Return to sender: What really happened at the fiscal envelope hui*. Auckland: Reed.

Mahuta, R. T. (2001). Foreword. In *Te Taarere aa Taawhaki*, 1: 5–8.

McCan, D. (2001). *Whatiwhatihoe: The Waikato raupatu claim*. Wellington: Huia Publishers.

Smith, L. T. (1999). *Decolonizing methodologies: Research and indigenous peoples*. London: Zed Books.

Endnotes

1   For readers interested in learning more about the tribe's history particularly in relation to the tribe's raupatu claim, refer to McCan (2001).

2   Robert Te Kotahi Mahuta was the tribe's principal negotiator and Kaahui Ariki representative on the Tainui Māori Trust Board and its successor, Waikato-Tainui Te Kauhanganui. He was Founding Fellow of the College and awarded a knighthood for his services to his people in 1997.

Chapter 5 Marae-ā-kura: A culturally specific decolonising strategy in schools

Jenny Lee-Morgan

Introduction

When I attended a large Auckland urban secondary school in the 1980s, the establishment of a marae-ā-kura (school marae) was part of the revitalisation of Māori language and culture in schools. I remember the many hui held in our homes. Outside the environs of the school grounds felt like a much safer and happier place to strategise, or what Māori teacher Maiki Marks might have called at that time "to plot revolution" (Marks, 1984). As a student I didn't understand the radical nature of what we were proposing. We spent much of our time and energy trying to convince, persuade and coax many of the Pākehā teachers at our school, in particular the senior management team, of the value of Māori language, culture and knowledge. Our Māori-language teacher, Whaea Awa Hudson (Ngāti Whātua ki Kaipara), the only Māori teacher in our school for nearly two decades, was at the forefront of this project. Her work extended far beyond the boundary of the classroom. At the end of my seventh form year (Year 13) we had secured an old double prefab building on the edge of the school to develop a marae-ā-kura.

I have written elsewhere about the whakapapa (genealogy) of marae-ā-kura in relation to the revitalisation of Māori language and culture, and the government's selective inclusion of Māori culture in the curriculum through policies of assimilation, integration and multiculturalism (Lee, 2013). However, here I want to foreground the development of marae-ā-kura as part of the wider Māori-driven political movement. Spurred on by the radicalisation of Black, feminist and indigenous activists around the world, the activism of the 1970s in Aotearoa was characterised by the formation of Māori groups (for example, Ngā Tamatoa), protest marches (such as the 1975 Te Hīkoi land march from Cape Reinga to Parliament, led by Te Matakite of Aotearoa), and occupations (including the 407-day occupation of Bastion Point by Ngāti Whātua in 1977). Māori called for a return of confiscated land, equal representation in Parliament for Māori, and the recognition of the Treaty of Waitangi. In education, kaupapa Māori initiatives such as kōhanga reo and kura kaupapa Māori were a response to the disillusionment and loss of faith in the New Zealand education system. Active disengagement with state schooling saw the establishment of independent kōhanga and kura based on Māori philosophies, pedagogies and practices. Māori educational aspirations were articulated in the reclamation and reassertion of 'space' outside the education system and in the pursuit of tino rangatiratanga. For many Māori, these kaupapa Māori initiatives had become a political movement for educational emancipation of Māori from Pākehā control (Walker, 1991).

Less well known, although sharing the same kaupapa Māori agenda, was the struggle for Māori space within 'mainstream' schools, usually led by Māori teachers, whānau and allies. While kōhanga reo and kura kaupapa Māori were celebrated as radical and exciting Māori educational developments for Māori whānau, the majority of Māori teachers, learners and whānau remained in the mainstream secondary schools. In state schools, Māori fought for te reo Māori to be taught in schools, for the scaling of School Certificate Māori to the lowest pass rates to stop, and for te reo Māori to have its own subject space—not subsumed within the foreign languages department (Hughes, 1983; Marks, 1984; Mitchell, 1984; Waitangi Tribunal, 1989). In my own secondary school, Māori fought for the Treaty of Waitangi to be recognised, including a space for Māori parents and whānau on the board of governors.[1]

Māori also fought for a physical space in the form of a marae-ā-kura. Today there are more than 100 marae-ā-kura in secondary schools throughout the country.[2] Pat Heremaia, one of the first Māori teachers to lead the establishment of a marae-ā-kura, at Green Bay High School, West Auckland, in 1978, described marae-ā-kura in the following way in the 1980s:

> The evolution of the school marae in our secondary schools has been one of the most significant developments since the introduction of Māori language in the promotion of bicultural and multicultural education. (Heremaia, 1984, p. 25)

I argue here that the significance of the development of marae-ā-kura has not been fully realised; in particular, the contribution of marae-ā-kura to decolonisation. In my view, marae-ā-kura were always politically charged to advance a kaupapa Māori agenda, which can also be understood as a culturally specific decolonisation strategy. This chapter also draws on the voices of Māori students, teachers and whānau interviewed as part of a 2-year (2010–2012) research project funded by the Ministry of Education's Teaching and Learning Research Initiative (TLRI), which investigated the pedagogy of marae-ā-kura. However, it is the potential of marae-ā-kura for decolonisation within the often monocultural institution of secondary schooling that I want to call attention to here.

The revolution

The revolution in schooling that Maiki Marks mentioned in her paper delivered at the landmark Māori Education Conference in 1984 referred to the racism inherent in the schooling system and called for major changes to ensure educational success for Māori. In the wake of kōhanga reo, begun the previous year, Marks's frustration and depth of feeling was indicative of many of the papers at the conference. The collective experiences and shared commitment to a vision for Māori education propelled the 300 conference delegates to "challenge Taha Pakeha social prescriptions and advocate radical changes" (Walker, 1984, p. 17).[3] It was a pivotal moment in Māori education: schooling was not only identified as overtly assimilationist and oppressive, but also as a site of struggle and potential.

In the mainstream secondary school sector, Māori teachers were highly engaged and active in progressing kaupapa Māori aspirations. However, in 1984 Māori teachers only made up 6.8 percent of total teachers in secondary schools (Renwick, 1984, p. 9), and the struggle for and reclamation of Māori space was often slow, difficult and frustrating. Marks describes the challenge and realities in relation to the implementation of the Māori education policy at the time, Taha Māori:

> To sum up, then, the Māori language teacher is likely to be feeling
> frustrated by being a member of a system she seems to be able to
> do little to change. And even where the school has a taha Māori, it's
> probably merely a Māori club or timetable periods for language and
> arts and crafts. But the school is most unlikely to have changed its self
> so that it actually FEELS good to Māoris and actually works to give
> them an equal chance. Not an equal chance at Pākehā education only,
> but the same chance that Pākehā students get for *their* culture for
> their *own* culture. (1984, p. 44, emphasis in original)

Marks was highly critical of the monocultural nature of the mainstream secondary schools and its inherent philosophy, pedagogy and practice, given powerful expression through monocultural teachers, such that the implementation of taha Māori seemed to be near impossible. In Wally Penetito's (1986) analysis of responses to taha Māori in schools, one (of four) that clearly fits with Marks's sentiments, Penetito described "Taha Māori as a catalyst for revolution". According to Penetito, such a response emphasised the political domination of Pākehā and was deeply critical of any initiative such as taha Māori that claimed to be of benefit to Māori when the power structures and unequal power relationships between Māori and Pākehā remained. Rather than becoming submerged in the detail and implications of taha Māori, I want to foreground the response; in particular, the collective critical consciousness expressed by Māori teachers—the groundswell for revolution.

The revolution that Marks and others referred to in schools was not merely criticising the status of Māori language or the ideologically flawed scaling system of School Certificate[4] that resulted in systemic disadvantage. The revolution was one of decolonisation that recognised the historical exclusion of the Māori language and purposeful selection of Māori culture into the curriculum by the government—the status of things Māori was clearly associated with unequal relationships of power. In relation to kaupapa Māori education, Graham Smith goes further to say that the revolution was about the rise of a new consciousness:

> The real revolution that has occurred in Māori Education was *not* the wonderful alternative schooling models—the real revolution was in our heads—it was a change of mindset of *not* waiting for education to be changed for us to getting up and doing it for ourselves. (Smith, 2015, emphasis in original)

It was this radical consciousness that also spurred Māori educators to reclaim and assert culturally safe 'spaces' within state schools. The marae-ā-kura would not only be a place to teach Māori, but could demarcate a space to be Māori and assert a level of Māori control. The development of marae-ā-kura had to be understood as a pedagogical–political project.

A pedagogical–political project

In a 2-year TLRI-funded research project that case studied three marae-ā-kura, our research found that while the aspirations for marae-ā-kura were pedagogical, Māori teachers, whānau and supporters also understood the project to be inherently political. This understanding was most apparent in the planning, fundraising and building stages of the marae within the mainstream cultural conventions and systems of secondary schools: it was never a straightforward technical exercise or neutral activity. The Māori teacher who initiated the plan for a marae-ā-kura in one school many years ago said,

> Kei te hiahia mātou ki te whakanui i tō tātou iwi—koia rā te mea tuatahi … Ko tō tātou marae kia whakanui te iwi Māori, whakanui i te reo, whakanui i o tātou tikanga. Koinā te take, kaore he take ko atu i tērā. (interview with Jenny Lee, 2010).

> (We wanted to acknowledge our people—that was the primary reason … our marae sought to value Māori people, value our language, value our customs. That was the purpose, there is no better reason beyond that.)

In broad terms, the purpose of creating a marae-ā-kura was a commitment to Māori cultural regeneration. In our research project (Lee,

Pihama, & Smith, 2012), marae-ā-kura were seen by Māori teachers, whānau and others alike as the most effective way to achieve the aims of Māori education (where Māori language, culture and knowledge is at the centre), for Māori and by Māori, in a mainstream school.

The establishment of marae-ā-kura as a highly political act is reinforced by Linda Smith's, experience as a Māori staff member working to establish a marae in a large urban girls' secondary school in the 1980s. She identified the resistance from the predominantly Pākehā staff at the school to be twofold: staff were opposed to the changing of the physical environment, and they feared the school would become a place of cultural and political activity. Smith writes:

> These staff denied that the school was itself a product and the producer of cultural meanings and argued for the school as a neutral site which should not be used by Māori interests or any other ethnic interests to teach 'culture'. (Smith, 1993, p. 64)

Confounding the issue of developing a marae or whare (in this case) was the government's educational policy of multiculturalism, which served to endorse the whare in an effort to acknowledge cultural diversity within the school and community. However, the discourse of multiculturalism placed competing demands on the focus of whare to include the wider interests of the school. As Smith points out, the challenge was largely ideological; it highlighted the cultural and structural norms in operation in the mainstream. Smith sums up by saying:

> developing the whare provided a specific symbol for a struggle over ideology. Almost everything pertaining to Māori issues within the school and in the wider social context was assembled into arguments over the validity of the whare. (Smith, 1993, p. 71)

These tensions were also experienced (at varying levels) at the schools in our aforementioned research project. In each of the three schools it took years of planning, strategising, meetings and fundraising before the whare or marae was officially opened.

For Māori students, the marae-ā-kura represent a powerful visible symbol of, and physical space for, Māori culture, knowledge and people. The students we interviewed (102 in total) were strong and clear in their articulation of the purpose and significance of the marae-ā-kura to them. The following quotes from students described marae-ā-kura as the "heart" or their bilingual or rumaki unit, and a "safe haven" in the school to be Māori:

> It's the heart, because it brings us together. If we didn't have a marae, it would probably be different—we wouldn't feel as safe. (Year 10 student)

> … with a marae in the school, we're not afraid to be Māori. (Year 11 student)

> It makes us feel more Māori, 'cause of the marae. (Year 12 student)

> If we didn't have the marae, I think there would be a lot of teens dropping out, Māori in particular … so to have a marae is a good thing. (Year 11 student)

The students' comments about the safety the marae-ā-kura provides show how the tensions and ideological clash regarding the purpose and culture of schools are played out for Māori students:

> 'Cause when you're in the mainstream you don't feel like you belong. Like when we're all together, we are friendly and happy— and don't get judged when you're down here [at the marae-ā-kura]. (Year 13 student)

> It [belonging to the marae-ā-kura] makes you want to come to school. I want to come to school. If I wasn't in Māori, then I would be gone! I wouldn't be at school. (Year 13 student)

> Like if we hadn't had the marae here, I reckon we would be little hoods running around going crazy. We would be heading towards nowhere pretty … because of the whare—the [reo rumaki] unit, it just gives us opportunities, opens up doors. (Year 13 student)

The students we interviewed were extremely positive about the cultural and pedagogical opportunities afforded by the marae-ā-kura and the bilingual or reo rumaki units they belonged to. They said that the marae-a-kura provided them with a strong sense of tūranga -waewae, pride, respect and support in a setting they often felt was isolating, hostile and irrelevant. Hence, while the students clearly recognised the advantages of the marae-ā-kura as part of their learning space, they were also inherently aware of the politics such a space created.

> Well first of all, we got a lot of support when we came into our marae. It's a lot of whanaungatanga, the whole sense of belonging. When you have people around you with the same outlook on things it helps you with your studies. (Year 11 student)

> It [marae-ā-kura] gives you a sense of belonging. It also gives you something to do in the morning so you don't get in trouble. You can catch up with friends. It's a happy environment to be in. (Year 11 student)

The positive experiences of marae-ā-kura inadvertently served to emphasise the deficiencies of the mainstream perceived by Māori students. Rather than focus on the pedagogical deficiencies and politics of mainstream schooling for Māori, familiar to Māori learners and experienced intergenerationally by whānau, I want to reiterate the point that marae-ā-kura provide a culturally specific and qualitatively different experience for Māori (as Māori) inside the environs of the school grounds. It is this difference that I will now address.

Decolonisation: Teaching, learning and living as Māori

In our research we found the marae-ā-kura (like tribal marae) were used for various functions that provided different experiences for Māori within the school setting. These included: hui, karakia, cultural performances, classes, wānanga, noho (overnight stays), celebrations, tangi, pōwhiri, formal farewells, and informal social occasions. While each of these marae-ā-kura were part of the wider school, they were considered the focal point of, and synonymous with, the school's bilingual or reo rumaki unit. It was the place that Māori students, teachers, parents and whānau gathered, and the location where Māori activities occurred. Rather than detail the various activities held at the marae-ā-kura, I want to argue that these activities provided distinct pedagogical experiences relevant to the project of decolonisation.

The students were most likely to talk about how the marae-ā-kura made learning te reo and tikanga Māori meaningful. In the students' words:

> I reckon if we didn't have a marae it wouldn't be so real ... we wouldn't take in what we are learning ... it [Māori] would be just another subject ... just another subject that goes in one ear and out the other. But because it's put in context, yeah, you're not just being a listener, you're actually doing what you are learning. (Year 13 student)

Having a marae-ā-kura is quite significant, and that's because I believe I have been brought up in my college years at school around tikanga Māori. So, if I was to go to another high school, I know I wouldn't be embraced in tikanga Māori, like coming to a kura marae taking your hat off, taking your shoes off, speaking te reo, taking karakia in the mornings, having carvings and tukutuku—all remind you that, you know, you are Māori—and yeah, of my nanny. (Year 13 student)

While the teaching and learning of Māori language and culture have always been central to the aspirations of Māori educators, the marae-ā-kura brings Māori language and culture to life within the school. This is not to say that te reo and tikanga Māori cannot exist or cannot be authentic without a marae, but rather that the marae itself creates another world. In reference to the last Māori student's comments, it is a world that reminds him of his tupuna.

The spiritual connectedness the marae-ā-kura engendered was highly valued by whānau and teachers, as well as by students. The following quotes portray the ways in which spirituality was lived through marae-ā-kura:

I think because we feel more comfortable and more relaxed, so that we will actually do it [work] … we don't feel so contained and so pressured as we would in the [mainstream] class … most of us, I reckon, need to be in the marae because it just gets rid of like bad wairua. (Year 13 student)

I just like sitting next to my pou … and spending some time with them. (Year 13 student).

This [marae-ā-kura] is like another home, a second home for us. This is the place where we can come back to … for spiritual reasons. (Year 9 student)

You know, for me sometimes, the marae is rejuvenation. Rejuvenation is to go back to the marae and sit there, and look at my maunga. So for me, education wise, it's really important to have that centre point, I guess it is what it is for my children. For me as a parent, it's easy for me to come here [marae-ā-kura]. I don't have to see a teacher or talk to anyone; I just come here, sit here, and wait for my children. So the marae is like their home base, you know? It is an easy way to put it. (Mother).

> I think it [marae-ā-kura] determines our operation every day … kua tau te wairua o ngā mātua tīpuna i waenga i ā tātou, you know? That there is that wairua Māori i tua atu i te reo me ōna tikanga. Kua tau tērā wairua Māori ki roto i ā tātou nei, ākonga, tauira – which is something I suppose we do because of the environment [marae-ā-kura] that we are in, where we live, and where we are placed, and where we teach. (Teacher)

The spiritual dimension of marae-ā-kura, indeed Māori education, has always been emphasised by Māori educators and leaders alike, and is only touched upon in the above quotes. Harry Dansey, Māori Race Relations Conciliator in 1975, encouraged the early establishment of marae-ā-kura and reinforced the importance of locating Māori education spiritually:

> On a marae [a-kura], they [Māori teachers and students] are hosts and teachers, accepting the responsibilities that these roles demand. Here they can learn of themselves and their own culture, gaining in addition to knowledge dignity and stature. Into this situation they can draw all others of goodwill. Then those values which are of the spirit—'te taha wairua'—can flourish because the material body—'te taha tinana'—is there for the spirit to inhabit and to enliven. (cit. in Heremaia, 1984, p. 72)

As intended, te taha wairua makes up a significant part of not only *what* occurs at the marae-ā-kura but *how* it occurs. The cultural protocols, practices and pedagogies are intimately interwoven with spiritual values, beliefs and knowledge that are part of the foundation of marae-ā-kura and decolonisation.

Decolonisation, as Linda Smith (2012) reminds us, is an approach that centres on "the survival of peoples, cultures and language; the struggle to become self-determining, the need to take back control of our destinies" (p. 142). As such, the marae-ā-kura are well placed to move this agenda forward. Marae-ā-kura is not just a Māori place to teach and learn, or to teach and learn Māori, but a highly significant and visible physical space for Māori. Marae-ā-kura are culturally and politically demarcated spaces to regenerate our language, culture, knowledge and spirit, and to ensure our survival as Māori.

Conclusion

I have argued in this chapter that marae-ā-kura have always been part of the political movement in Māori education that is characterised as kaupapa Māori, where Māori language, culture and people are at the centre. Ranginui Walker (1992) described the start of marae-ā-kura as symbolic of the urgent need for the "maintenance of culture, assertion of identity, and resistance to assimilation" (p. 72). Marae-ā-kura continue to be strong, visible representations of Māori culture, and have a powerful presence because they claim physical space, buildings and land. Furthermore, they are powerful because they create cultural boundaries and cultural expectations that demand that Māori language be heard, and Māori cultural protocols be adhered to, and Māori knowledge be valued within the environs of the monocultural school grounds. I have argued that Māori teachers, whānau and supporters who initiated marae-ā-kura as a kaupapa Māori project always intended these to be pedagogical but political places. This is played out in schools today as Māori students, whānau and teachers tell us that marae-ā-kura continue to create cultural safe havens that connect our past, present and future generations.

Indigenous academic Gregory Cajete (Tewa Indian from Santa Clara Pueblo) urges indigenous educators to understand the power in the decolonising process. He writes:

> A primary goal of indigenous education must be empowerment,
> which for indigenous people and communities must begin with an
> inward transformation, a kind of "in-powerment" that emphasises the
> internal work that each of us must do to "come back to our power".
> This type of empowerment leads to greater personal, interpersonal,
> communal, and political power and enables indigenous people
> and communities to transform oppressive situations into actions of
> healing and transformation. (Cajete, 2012, p. 147)

In my view, marae-ā-kura can also facilitate personal internal in-powerment of individual and whānau, as well as challenge the external wider school about 'power'. I encourage Māori learners, teachers, whānau and others to remember and understand the power inherent in marae-ā-kura for decolonisation, a critical component in pursuit of tino rangatiratanga and other kaupapa Māori objectives. The potential for marae-ā-kura to contribute to transformation lies within its inherent pedagogical and political nature, which requires the school itself to make structural and cultural change. Key to the politicisation is the notion of establishing Māori control, and engaging in a radical Māori—or in this case marae-ā-kura—pedagogy that challenges normative teaching, learning and classroom practice. Marae-ā-kura are a culturally specific educational intervention that resists mainstream conformity and begins to recover a core aspect of Māori identity for cultural regeneration. Marae-ā-kura as decolonising spaces have political intent, pedagogical purpose and transformative potential.

References

Cajete, G. (2012). Decolonising indigenous education in a twenty-first century world. In Waziyatawin and M. Yellow Bird (Eds.), *For Indigenous minds only.* Santa Fe, NM: School for Advanced Research.

Heremaia, P. (1984). Marae as a learning environment in secondary schools. In R. Walker (Ed.), *Ngatumanako: Māori Educational Development Conference, Turangawaewae Marae, 23–25 March 1984* (pp. 32–35). Auckland: Centre for Continuing Education, The University of Auckland.

Hughes, D. (1983). The examination system: The cause of unnecessary failure. *New Zealand Counselling and Guidance Association Journal, 5*(1), 30–36.

Lee, J. B. J. (2013). Marae ā-kura: Tracing the birth of marae in schools. *set: Research Information for Teachers, 2,* 3–11.

Lee, J., Pihama, L., Smith, L. (2012). *Marae-ā-kura: Teaching, learning and living as Māori.* Wellington. Teaching Learning Research Initiative.

Marks, M. (1984). The frustrations of being a Māori language teacher. In R. Walker (Ed.), *Ngatumanako: Māori Educational Development Conference, Turangawaewae Marae, 23–25 March 1984* (p. 43). Auckland: Centre for Continuing Education, The University of Auckland.

Mitchell, I. (1984). Māori examination failure. In R. Walker (Ed.), *Ngatumanako: Māori Educational Development Conference, Turangawaewae Marae, 23–25 March 1984* (pp. 53–55). Auckland: Centre for Continuing Education, The University of Auckland.

Penetito, W. (1986). Taha Māori in schools: Evolution, revolution or transformation. In G. Smith (Ed.), *Ngaketewananga: Readers in Māori education:* Māori perspectives of taha Māori (pp. 1–19). Auckland: Department of Māori Studies, Auckland College of Education.

Smith, G. (2015, April). *Transforming research: The indigenous struggle for social, cultural, and economic justice within and through education*. Presidential address, American Education Research Association, Chicago.

Smith, L. (1993). Getting out from down under: Māori women, education and the struggles for mana wahine. In M. Arnot (Ed.), *Feminism and social justice in education: International perspectives*. London; New York: Falmer Press.

Smith, L. T. (2012). *Decolonizing methodologies: Research and indigenous peoples*. New York, NY: Zed Books.

Renwick, W. (1984). Picking up the challenge. In R. Walker (Ed.), *Ngatumanako: Māori Educational Development Conference, Turangawaewae Marae, 23–25 March 1984* (pp. 6–15). Auckland: Centre for Continuing Education, The University of Auckland.

Waitangi Tribunal. (1989). *Report of the Waitangi Tribunal on the te reo Māori claim (Wai 11)* (2nd ed.). Wellington: Author.

Walker, R. (1984). The Māori response to education in New Zealand. In R. Walker (Ed.), *Ngatumanako: Māori Educational Development Conference, Turangawaewae Marae, 23–25 March 1984* (pp. 32–35). Auckland: Centre for Continuing Education, The University of Auckland.

Walker, R. (1991). *Liberating Māori from educational subjection*. Auckland: Research Unit for Māori Education, The University of Auckland.

Walker, R. (1992). The relevance of Māori myth and tradition. In M. King (Ed.), *Te Ao Hurihuri: Aspects of Māoritanga* (pp. 170–182). Auckland: Reed.

Endnotes

1   Boards of governors were the governance bodies for secondary schools. In 1989, under the Tomorrow's Schools reform process, these changed to boards of trustees.

2   The Ministry of Education was cautious about providing this statistic because the codes it uses to distinguish types of buildings do not necessarily mean that a whare or marae is not in operation in another building in the school. Furthermore, the Ministry of Education is not able to provide this information for state-integrated schools, private schools and schools on marae. Personal communication, research analyst, Demographic and Statistical Analysis Unit, Ministry of Education, 26 May, 2006.

3   Taha Pākehā literally means 'the Pākehā or White New Zealander side' and refers here to dominant Pākehā culture, beliefs, practices and norms.

4   School Certificate was the national examination system usually given to Year 11 students, replaced by the National Certificate of Educational Achievement (NCEA) in 2002.

Chapter 6 Reflections from the trenches: Decolonising hearts and minds in Aotearoa

Takawai Murphy

Introduction

> *Ehara taku toa i te toa takitahi engari he toa takitini.*
> *(My strength was not mine alone. There were many others involved.)*

This is a narrative of my journey as a decolonisation seminar facilitator, a journey that began more than 25 years ago in the 1980s. In that time I have facilitated more than a thousand decolonisation seminars.

Rethinking education

So, how did it all begin? At the Catholic boarding school I attended my first choice of subjects would have been te reo Māori, learning my language, but that wasn't an option in the 1960s, unless I learnt it from the caretaker! If I had been more mature I would have taken that option in place of the double dose of French and Latin I learned instead. I've since realised that the desire to reclaim the language must have been intrinsic because I wasn't aware of the importance of te reo Māori at all back then.

Fast-forward to the mid-1970s, teaching in a small rural school. My daily greeting to my class was "Tēnā koutou tamariki mā." The instruction from the school committee to stop saying this unless I included greetings in other languages as well reflected the views of the dominant system entrenched within mainstream education. It reinforced the longtime view that things Māori were less important, and even undesirable, and that there was no place for te reo Māori, even though it was the language of the land.

Standing up to the school committee at a meeting with the other teachers and principal (all Pākehā) in support was a great experience. School committees were very powerful: they were the school governors, like boards of trustees are now. When they spoke, teachers and principals listened. I felt that it was a personal triumph because the other teachers supported me and recognised the pettiness of the request, and I knew that it was right to be able to speak even a little of my language in the school. It was also good to be able to challenge their cultural arrogance, and it allowed them to see that not all Pākehā held their racist views.

Interestingly enough, two of the school committee members, whose children I taught at the time, were Dutch. They couldn't see anything wrong with what I was doing so they supported me as well. The original complainants were left isolated. It was an experience that really made me aware of the difficulties many Māori were facing in the education system and wider society. My sense of the injustices began to grow.

Ironically, it was an issue concerning te reo Māori that finally drove me away from teaching. In the mid- to late 1980s, while a senior teacher in a Taranaki primary school, I was learning te reo at night class with my son Enoka and also learning te reo extramurally through Massey University. There was a big interest from teachers at that time in learning conversational Māori, so I was tutoring teachers after school as well. I became so busy tutoring teachers learning the reo that there was no time for me to expand on my own learning.

I obtained leave from school to attend language classes under the tutelage of two inspirational teachers, Huirangi Waikerepuru and Ruakere Hond, and also one of the Parihaka leaders of the time, Te Miringa Hōhaia. The three of them looked at the world differently to other Māori I knew. My world had been that of the majority, accepting what was, although I knew from my own experiences that there were enough community prejudices and judgements around to make life difficult for many Māori. I also knew that, generally, things pertaining to Māori were of no importance to most New Zealanders. The longer I spent with them, the more convinced I became that the counter-narrative they advocated made sense. I felt a greater connection to te ao Māori (the Māori world) and to myself. For the first time I felt a real need to find out more about my history and culture.

Reclaiming te reo Māori

On reflection, I had always believed that te reo Māori should have been mine as of right—as it was for other peoples in other lands, and it should be there for the Māori students I taught as a right also. I thought about options available to me to gain greater access to my language. I considered taking the Department of Education to court for denying me my language during my school years, or taking a case to the Waitangi Tribunal. But these options would be too expensive and drawn out.

My wife, Chris, helped me find a solution. Both senior teachers at different primary schools at the time, we had cared for her elderly parents, who died within 6 months of each other. Suffering from stress, Chris subsequently took a period of extended paid leave. During this time she asked me if living without my language and culture was stressful. Yes, that was the answer! So I went to my doctor, a young Pākehā guy, and talked to him about the stress I felt teaching in a system that gave no status, prestige or mana to anything Māori. Surprisingly, he recognised and understood the cultural vacuum I felt and connected that the stress this created could be relieved by taking time out to immerse myself in my language and culture.

During the lead-in to this, I had been completely honest with educational officials and I thought we had a sound, friendly and open relationship. But all that changed when they saw the doctor's recommendation of 3 months' stress leave—on full pay! Their letter in response demanded a second medical opinion and there was talk of referring my doctor to the Medical Council to be disciplined. My doctor referred me to a psychologist, Mike Nightingale (an Englishman), who also understood, based on his practical experience teaching in schools with a predominantly Māori roll. But he was an educational psychologist, not a medical practitioner, so I was referred on to a psychiatrist, an elderly Pākehā man. My first thoughts were that he would never understand. But again, surprisingly, he did.

When I returned to my employers with another medical diagnosis of stress and a recommendation of 3 months' leave, they were not pleased. No one had ever done this before and they could not understand why someone would do such a thing. "What has happened to you?" they asked in a perplexed manner. "What is the cause of this madness?"

My stand caused me to be unpopular with nearly everyone in the local primary school system, including Māori teachers. They claimed that I wasn't suffering from stress at all, that I was abusing the system, which was completely untrue. My stress was genuine, and so was my need to be immersed in my culture. They had adopted the hegemonic view that Māori language and culture didn't count. I could see that what I was experiencing in my life, in school and at home, was a deep disconnection. I had spent my whole life disconnected from my language and culture, from the things that shape a person at the deepest level and make them who they are. I am not sure whether I had gone looking for my culture or whether my culture had come to claim me and return me home to a true sense of self.

So, what had happened to me? I had been exposed to new information that was easily digestible and easy to understand. I was inspired to learn te reo and to learn more about Māori. I was encouraged to embrace who I really was. What those teachings really provided was a pathway home.

But perhaps I always knew that something was missing in my life, because whenever I went on to marae I felt inadequate. I couldn't fully understand what was happening and so was unable to participate. The new knowledge had helped me to join the dots. The time away from work became a time of transformation. It started me on a lifelong healing journey of decolonisation: stripping away the layers of colonial myths that have taught us as a people to dislike ourselves. It started me on a pathway towards cultural reclamation.

Returning to my work environment after taking stress leave presented difficulties. I had irrevocably changed. It became even more apparent to me that the 'Māoriness' of Māori students was not valued or even noted, and I was pretty sure that it was like that in the majority of other English-medium schools. Māori were being educated as Pākehā, as I was when I was a boy. Assimilation policies were operating strongly, albeit under other guises. I knew I had to do something and offered to teach a bilingual class. My offer was swiftly declined: the time was not right for such a venture, according to the school principal. I asked for a timeframe. There was none, so I left.

I realised that I now had no desire to continue battling for recognition for things Māori within the school and the system, which openly assimilated and colonised, so I ended my career as a primary school teacher. My ambition was to teach adults the knowledge I had recently acquired and to help facilitate transformation towards cultural reclamation in Māori people's lives. I wanted to facilitate decolonisation in the hearts and minds of the people, but I'm not sure that I was even aware of the term 'decolonisation' at that time. Fortunately, several events transpired that enabled me to do this.

An opportunity

Firstly, Te Ururoa Flavell, current co-leader of the Māori Party, had recently been appointed to the position of Māori Department head at the local polytechnic. In my view he was one of the most forward-thinking Māori tertiary leaders in all of the institutions, especially in terms of tino rangatiratanga and direct action. Secondly, the polytechnic had also appointed a new CEO, Errol Jacquiery, who was supportive of Māori and decolonisation education. Thirdly, cultural safety and decolonisation had recently become core components in the curriculum of trainee nurses, but because it was so new, the teaching staff had little knowledge of it or how to teach it.

Other Māori Department staff had reluctantly taught these subjects prior to my arrival—reluctantly because of the hostile reception they received from students. The country was in a state of denial regarding the history of Aotearoa, and so having the Treaty as a core component of many tertiary courses was a very new and challenging concept to many. I was pretty naive when I won that job teaching 'cultural safety' to all student nurses and 'decolonisation' to the Māori students. I had no clear picture of how to do it and was unaware that Irihapeti Ramsden had published a great book about it. So when Te Ururoa

Flavell and I met with the heads of the Nursing Department, and they showed me the brief of what I was to teach and asked me if I could I teach it, I had no idea what any of it meant. The terms were all new to me. But I could hardly say no and look like an idiot, so I nodded my head and said, "Yeah, I can teach that stuff". They looked at each other with relief, smiled and left. Te Ururoa looked at me with surprise—it was obviously all new to him as well!

"Are you sure you can teach this stuff?" he asked.

I should have been honest and admitted my ignorance, but he had only just hired me and he would have had thoughts about firing me, so I nodded confidently again. "Yeah. I can teach that stuff," I repeated.

Still surprised, he said "Okay", then chuckled and walked away.

What a fool I was! What had I done?

Designing the programme

Then inspiration struck. For nurses and their patients to be culturally safe, in my view, they needed to know what shaped Māori into what they are today. That was about teaching history so they had some understanding of what caused those inequalities in health and the other social indicator areas. That was colonisation.

The students also needed to know about the effects of assimilation in the schooling system, which had left most Māori bereft of their language and culture, as well as the role of the media in supporting and encouraging the colonisation process. Resistance strategies employed by Māori to counter colonisation needed to be there too, to counter the argument that Māori had done nothing to stop it then so why should they start now?

The final component of my cultural safety/decolonisation programme would be implementing the knowledge gained. The session would be about the strategies nurses could engage in to make a positive difference in their professional lives when working with Māori clients/patients/tūroro and their families. I was also aware that if it worked for Māori, it would work for everyone. So, within a minute I went from desperation to enlightenment. I was cultivating the seeds that would grow into the Te Pūmaomao Nationhood-Building learning experience, the decolonisation programme that would become such an important part of my life and my family's life in the years to come.

The first task was to determine the key components of the programme: the topics, what I wanted the programme to achieve, and the guiding principles and teaching strategies I would employ to facilitate a process of decolonisation of the minds and hearts of participants. My belief was that Māori, through no fault of their own, had grown up conditioned by the view that Pākehā ways were superior (including their language, norms, customs and protocols), and if Māori were to succeed in life, they would need to abandon everything Māori and embrace 'Pākehāness'. This was my upbringing and the upbringing of the majority of Māori of my generation.

Therefore, I wanted to design presentations that clearly demonstrated:

- how that had happened and was still happening
- resistance strategies employed by Māori from way back through to the present
- counter initiatives currently being undertaken
- further strategies.

The ideas came from a wide range of sources. In the early days a wonderfully diverse thinker, Dennis McLeod, from the local Te Puni Kōkiri office, would come along for an hour or two whenever the programme was being held locally. He would perform a simple demonstration where he would pace out the room to show the arrival of Pākehā and their thoughts about race, how their world view described themselves as 'civilised', while Māori were 'savages' and 'cannibals', thus Pākehā were superior, etc. This has since been developed into a powerful introductory session during the Te Pūmaomao learning experience.

Ideas also came from several other sources, including Te Ururoa Flavell, Toi and Maihi Berry, Ruakere Hond, Moana Jackson, and my wife, Chris. Others have also provided support (John Nīwa) and information, including Marlene Benson and Sister Genevieve, two wonderful Project Waitangi members from Taranaki.

I decided that I would employ an approach that would engage not only the mind but the heart as well. Decolonising minds, to me, is not enough. In my experience, in order to effect real change, we must also decolonise hearts. The programme must transform and stir the seat of emotions. I wanted to lift Māori pride and aspirations in being Māori.

I wanted to emphasise the importance of learning te reo and tikanga, and encourage the reclamation of traditional karakia along with the knowledge and philosophies contained within. I wanted to foster the support of kaupapa Māori events and initiatives and the important place of kaupapa Māori education.

A small but powerful initiative involved encouraging course participants to reclaim a Māori name. During the period of my own politicisation I had replaced Theo, the name I had grown up with, with Takawai, my middle name. At the time of my birth we had no doctors or nurses in Murupara, so Ngāti Manawa had its own wahine, Hine White, who birthed and sometimes named the tamariki—in my case Takawai, to commemorate the drowning of her own child. My father did the same to celebrate kōhanga reo, replacing 'Percy' with the name my mother had always called him, 'Marunui'.

Reclaiming a Māori name became a simple but powerful gesture, a symbol of commitment to the path of healing, decolonisation and cultural reclamation. Over the years, as I travel around the country, strangers have often approached me to tell me that they reclaimed their Māori name on a Te Pūmaomao course and have held on to it ever since. Others have told me similar stories about their children and grandchildren being given Māori names. Such a small gesture, but the impact, I believe, has been significant. My overall intent was to create a safe, empowering and engaging space for Māori and Pākehā to unpack tough issues around colonisation, power and identity.

Most importantly, I wanted to present and privilege a Māori perspective so that Māori could feel the excitement and empowerment of being Māori ("Being Māori is Choice!"), and so that they could feel increased optimism about their future, engage in the culture, and participate in reo acquisition as part of their normal lifestyle.

Long term, I wanted Māori to understand their responsibilities as Māori citizens and as members of whānau, hapū and iwi so that they, too, could pass on and preserve the taonga of the culture to their own tamariki and mokopuna. For the programme, my ultimate desire was to create an inclusive, 'flax-roots', paradigm-busting, heart-changing experience, one that no one could walk away from without being changed and inspired to act and create positive change. That was the real purpose of the Te Pūmaomao Nationhood-Building course.

Chapter 7 Matike Mai Aotearoa! The power of youth-led decolonisation education

Veronica Tawhai

This car is Aotearoa.

This person represents tangata whenua, Māori, and this seat is the driver's seat—the place of mana, of rangatiratanga.

This person represents the British Crown.

The driver of this car, Māori, invited the Crown to come and sit beside them. "Haere mai!"

So, the Māori and the Crown are in the front seat of this car:

Who decides where they are going?

Who decides how fast they get there?

Who decides which way they go?

What music is played on the way?

Along with the Crown, we welcomed all other people who came here. Consistent with our tikanga, everyone was offered a seat in our car. "Haere mai, haere mai ki Aotearoa nei".

So, again:

Who is in the driver's seat?

Who decides where they are going, and how fast they get there?

What music is played on the way?

So, is this how it is now? Are Māori still in the driver's seat? Really?

Where are Māori now?

Oh, OK.

Where is the Crown now?

That's right. They are in the driver's seat.

This is when our constitution changed...'

Introduction

Adult-led discussions about rangatahi Māori often revolve around two things: Firstly, that rangatahi are our 'rangatira o āpōpō', our leaders of tomorrow; secondly are the many challenges they face that threaten their ability to take up those leadership roles, and the support and intervention required (by adults) to help rangatahi to overcome them. What is less discussed, or acknowledged, is how rangatahi are leading today.

Between 2012 and 2015 my experiences as a co-ordinator for a national project about rangatahi views on the constitution transformed my understanding of rangatahi and their role in decolonising work. True, the rangatahi in this project were discovering and developing skills and abilities that would be beneficial to their future lives as adults. However, they also radiated a unique energy, positivity and enthusiasm that proved essential to the project's implementation. It was the 'secret ingredient' that saw the project explode into a national movement for transformation, built upon rangatahi connecting with one another to explore what their hopes and aspirations for our future constitution might be.

While my new insight into the rangatahi 'magic' was amazing, it was also a cause for personal alarm. I was meant to be a Māori development lecturer; a specialist in how to bring about positive changes for Māori and, with us, the rest of Aotearoa; someone who saw the many angles and layers in the bigger, longer-term decolonisation picture. How is it that I had come to see rangatahi as contributors-in-training as opposed to contributing right here and now? What opportunities were being lost by those such as myself applying an adult-centric, developmental lens to rangatahi and their initiatives? A quick look into the ages of some of our past leaders, Whina Cooper, Apirana Ngata and Hone Heke Ngapua when first embarking upon their political work, highlighted how our ancestors had valued and utilised rangatahi as a powerful force for change. I had to ask myself: When had my views of rangatahi become so colonised?

I became convinced I needed to decolonise my own understandings of rangatahi, including their role as decolonisation educators 'here and now'. This meant not engaging with rangatahi as I had been; an older educator/facilitator/community worker guiding rangatahi in their activities, with the added expectation that this would help develop their skills for future decolonisation work. Rather, I needed to acknowledge the powerful, creative force I had witnessed when rangatahi connected with each other for the purposes of their own learning and future-imagining. 'Matike Mai Aotearoa', the name given by Koro Huirangi Waikerepuru to the working group from which our project had emerged, was adopted by the rangatahi to reflect their ultimate desire for their peers to awaken, arise and answer the call to engage in constitutionally transformative work. From my co-ordinator's perspective, however, it also symbolised the rising of this powerful rangatahi decolonisation movement which had succeeded in overcoming the barriers to youth political engagement, through the development of a rangatahi-focused constitutional transformation education workshop, its implementation with thousands of young people nationwide, and the securing of rangatahi voices in contributing to the future of Aotearoa's future constitutional arrangements.

Matike Mai Aotearoa Rangatahi

In 2012 when I was first approached to co-ordinate the rangatahi project there were concerns worldwide over what seemed to be a growing apathy and disinterest among youth in political life (Cammaerts, Bruter, Banaji, Harrison, & Anstead, 2014; Snell, 2010). Low socioeconomic status, poor health, unsatisfactory housing and educational under-achievement were factors known to negatively affect political participation (Campbell, Gurin, & Miller, 1954; Lindquist, 1964). Research with indigenous youth overseas showed that their likelihood of disengaging from mainstream politics paralleled the likelihood of their feeling alienated or marginalised within mainstream society (Alfred, Pitawanakwat, & Price, 2007; Elections Canada, 2004). Here in Aotearoa, evidence showed rangatahi were bombarded with messages (Kupu Taea, 2014) and experienced ongoing hardships (Statistics New Zealand, 2013a) that told them they were destined for a life of struggle. They were not among those whose language, culture and identity were reaffirmed, or who had their health, welfare and wellbeing prioritised, by wider society. It was of no wonder to me that many rangatahi were choosing to disengage politically.

Through my own research I had also learnt that attempts to connect with and garner support from rangatahi only every election cycle were seen by rangatahi themselves as tokenistic and proof of why they should 'turn off' from politics (Cheyne & Tawhai, 2007). The near absence of political education curricula in our schools also meant rangatahi were less likely to be familiar with the technical details of our political system. Rangatahi I had engaged with knew that our current electoral system was Mixed Member Proportional (MMP), for example, but not how MMP differed from other electoral systems or what the implications were for Māori representation (Tawhai, 2011). This was despite rangatahi identifying Māori representation as something important to them and to their sense of contributing to political decision-making. It was therefore of no surprise to me also if terms such as 'constitution' seemed foreign and irrelevant to the lives rangatahi lived.

This was the first challenge identified by rangatahi when asked to take up the Matike Mai Aotearoa work in March 2012 at Waipapa marae, Auckland. The Independent Working Group on Constitutional Transformation, led by Moana Jackson and Professor Margaret Mutu, had been tasked with developing "a constitution for our country based on our tikanga and fundamental values, He Whakaputanga o te Rangatiratanga o Nu Tireni and Te Tiriti o Waitangi" (Jackson, 2011, p. 11). However, it was acknowledged that rangatahi participation in developing a constitution would only be achieved with rangatahi support. At Waipapa marae the challenge was extended to the rangatahi present to create something to engage other rangatahi nationwide on the topic of the constitution, with my assistance as a co-ordinator. While the rangatahi eagerly accepted the challenge, they also identified several barriers. Rangatahi voiced that many of their peers would never have heard the term 'constitution' and, due to the exclusionary nature of anything political, may not be interested in participating. Any project to engage other rangatahi in exploring the constitution would have to be educational. The goal would be to decolonise rangatahi understanding of politics, introduce them to the idea of a constitution and, having done that, draw out their thoughts and aspirations for the future. Here is where the idea of an interactive, educational workshop to connect to rangatahi and engage their dreams and hopes for a future constitution was born. Forming a small group of six to 12 rangatahi aged between

17 and 27 from across Aotearoa, we met for a further three weekend-long hui[2] to design the workshop. After only 2 months, the rangatahi created what would become the flagship of the Matike Mai Aotearoa Rangatahi project, the Rangatahi Constitutional Transformation Workshop.

The Rangatahi Constitutional Transformation Workshop

By 2012 and the creation of the rangatahi workshop, my experiences as a Tiriti o Waitangi educator had taught me that I would feel frustration, distress and deep sadness nearly as often as I would feel joy, laughter or a sense of satisfaction that I had managed to 'get through'. I had learnt that the knowledge of what happened to our ancestors was heavy to bear, as was the angst of trying to capture people's minds and hearts to a new way of being. Like others, I was propelled in the work by my love for my tīpuna, whānau and future tamariki mokopuna, but that did not make it easy work. I understood why so many educators, including my mentors, were susceptible to feelings of isolation, exhaustion and negativity.

That the creation of the rangatahi workshop would be challenging, weighted with the details of injustice and oppression that characterise our constitutional history was something I had just assumed. As co-ordinator I had prepared myself to help those rangatahi creating the workshop to channel their anger, work through their sadness and try to see the positive side; that they had been presented with an amazing opportunity to do something about it. That simply wasn't necessary. As a first step to creating the workshop we had shared our knowledge of the struggles of our tīpuna, the effects upon our whānau today and the ongoing injustices we experienced,[3] but the rangatahi did not dwell. Instead they moved naturally on to the next step of sharing their dreams and aspirations about what our constitution could be like. They were extremely positive, passionate discussing the reconnecting of humankind to atua (the divine/god entities), upholding laws to ensure we live in harmony with the environment and each other, and re-establishing processes for relationship-building with the end goal of all being looked after and cared for based on kotahitanga (unity) and aroha (love and care for one another). There was also no doubt that such a constitution could be achieved!

It was from this point that the rangatahi considered what form the workshop needed to take. Reflecting on the process they had just undergone, they asked themselves what was needed to get other rangatahi to share their aspirations and how that might most effectively be done. By the end, what they had created was a 90-minute workshop utilising digital media, spoken-word performance, audience-participatory drama and small-to-large-group activities. It had a DVD, a long list of resources,[4] and a run-sheet complete with video clips, dialogue, activities, timing and props. It radiated the positivity and beauty of the rangatahi's aspirations and their desire to connect with their peers, focusing upon five phases:

1. Te Ao Mārama
2. Hapū Authority
3. Arrival of Tauiwi
4. Today
5. Our Future.

In phase 1 of the workshop, "Te Ao Mārama", the rangatahi facilitators explore with rangatahi participants what a 'constitution' means to them from a Māori world view. This include the atua and Ngā Kete o te Wānanga (Baskets of Knowledge) as the sources of our constitution—kawa and tikanga (indigenous laws and protocols). In smaller groups the rangatahi then look at different scenarios, identify what tikanga they reflect, and discuss what the role of those tikanga might be in upholding our wellbeing. Discussion is then presented back to the wider group. This gives rangatahi participants an opportunity to share the knowledge they have of kawa and tikanga, and build their confidence by reinforcing how much they do know about a constitution.

In phase 2 of the workshop, "Hapū Authority", the rangatahi facilitators revisit with their participants the constitution in the time of our ancestors before colonisation. This includes the authority to uphold kawa and tikanga lying with hapū, and the importance we have as members of hapū and iwi today to make decisions that ensure the wellbeing of our people. In smaller groups rangatahi imagine they are hapū and decided, along with their name and imagined territory, what their kawa and tikanga are. This includes deciding what the consequences are for the breaching of tikanga in their territory! With props such as korowai, they then present themselves as hapū to the wider group, offering a detailed explanation of their kawa and tikanga. This helps rangatahi to understand that we are the decision makers and, like our tīpuna, can come up with systems and laws for the wellbeing and prosperity of our people.

In phase 3, "Arrival of Tauiwi", the rangatahi facilitators introduce participants to the constitutional changes that occurred with the arrival of colonising powers. This includes the documents signed by our tīpuna to protect kawa and tikanga, the 1835 He Whakaputanga o Te Rangatiratanga o Nu Tireni (Declaration of Independence) and the 1840 Te Tiriti o Waitangi (Treaty of Waitangi, Māori-language texts), and the eventual disempowerment of hapū as the number of colonial foreigners increased and these documents were ignored. The large-group exercise "Dude, Where's My Mana?" enables the rangatahi to explore together the change in the constitution when kawa and tikanga (the Māori in the driver's seat) were overridden by British systems and laws (the Crown's moving into the driver's seat, and the Māori being moved on). For rangatahi this is a powerful representation relevant to them and needing no further explanation as to what our tīpuna experienced and the consequences for our constitutional arrangements today.

Following on from phase 3 and the change in the constitution, rangatahi facilitators in phase 4, "Today", explore with rangatahi participants the consequences for Māori of decision making by others. Each workshop's examples draw upon the local region, such as the Rena oil spill for the hapū of Tauranga-Moana[5] and the police terrorist raids for Tūhoe.[6] The use of local examples help rangatahi connect deeply to the constitution and its effects on their own lives and whānau. In a large-group activity, "A Better Aotearoa", the rangatahi then reflect upon the different elements essential to Māori wellbeing such as language, knowledge, our own spiritual beliefs, land and authority, and the importance of restoring those elements as constitutional foundations for today.

In the final phase of the workshop, "Our Future", the rangatahi facilitators call upon their participants to take up the ultimate challenge of helping form a new constitution for Aotearoa. This involves the banner exercise "Matike Mai Aotearoa!", where pens were distributed and a large banner was rolled out for rangatahi to share visually their ideas and hopes about what a future constitution should focus on. After closing acknowledgements and the sharing of koha (gifts), the banners were given to rangatahi participants for them to keep and remember their hopes for constitutional transformation.

In May 2012 at Tapu Te Ranga marae, Wellington, a national hui was held for the rangatahi workshop design team to train a wider group of regional rangatahi representatives in the workshop's delivery. The task of these representatives was then to return home and form local teams to deliver the workshop to rangatahi in their region. By the end of 2014 there were 12 regional teams and over 80 rangatahi educators nationwide who had served as workshop facilitators. They had visited secondary schools, kura and wharekura (Māori language and learning philosophy-based schools), marae, alternative and community education centres, tertiary institutions, youth justice facilities and teen pregnancy units across Aotearoa. The constitutional transformation workshop had therefore been a success! Thousands of rangatahi engaged nationwide in exploring our constitutional history and a future reflective of rangatahi values, hopes and aspirations. Additionally, however, was the unexpected emergence of a national team of rangatahi workshop facilitators, committed to decolonising the political perspectives of their peers.

Rangatahi as transformation, decolonisation agents

As stated earlier, our history shows that it has been rangatahi who have fronted many of our challenges to the Crown's assumption of absolute constitutional power. Whina Cooper of Te Rarawa was 18 when she first led protestors against the government's leasing of local kaimoana (seafood) mudflats for farming while her father fought the issue through the courts (King, 2013). Hone Heke Ngapua of Ngāpuhi was in his early 20s when elected into Parliament as the Northern Māori representative and tasked by his people with introducing the Native Rights Bill, seeking constitutional recognition of the Te Kotahitanga movement's Paremata Māori (Kawharu, 2013).

Apirana Ngata of Ngāti Porou was also in his 20s when elected travelling secretary of the Te Aute College Student's Association, beginning his work with Sir James Carroll on legislation to secure Māori rights to control Māori affairs (Sorrenson, 2013). In more recent history, Ngā Tamatoa epitomised the revolutionary power of rangatahi to demand changes on issues such as Māori land, language, recognition of Te Tiriti o Waitangi and the need to address Treaty grievances.[7]

On 6 February 2015, as part of the 175th commemorations of the signing of Te Tiriti o Waitangi at Waitangi, representatives of the 12 Matike Mai Aotearoa Rangatahi regional teams added their names to our history of rangatahi leadership, presenting the findings of their project. Photos, videos and written accounts of the messages shared by rangatahi with them nationwide were presented to Pāpā Moana and Whāea Margaret of the Independent Working Group, wrapped within two banners—one from the rangatahi in the youth unit at Ngāwha prison (who had not been allowed to keep their banner) and another from the Matike Mai Aotearoa Rangatahi themselves. Ranging from 13 to 27 years of age, the Matike Mai Aotearoa Rangatahi had given their time on a volunteer basis while also studying, working and caring for whānau; some had their own young children, and many were fulfilling other roles and responsibilities within their community, hapū and wider iwi.

Led by Hilda Halkyard-Harawira, an original Ngā Tamatoa member, the wider community at Waitangi witnessing the presentation responded with a haka. They acknowledged the rangatahi for all the work they had done over the previous years leading up to that day, and the contribution that work would make to the benefit of us all in future. With the exception of the submission of a final project report to those who had supported the project financially,[8] this presentation was my final task as the national project co-ordinator. That evening during our poroaki (group farewell) at Rawhitiroa marae, Ohaeawai, I relinquished the co-ordination to the rangatahi themselves. The activities of the 3-year project I had been brought on for were essentially concluded. What was to become of Matike Mai Aotearoa Rangatahi lay with the rangatahi themselves.

Conclusion

Half of our Māori population is currently under the age of 23 years (Statistics New Zealand, 2013b). Knowing that makes me smile. Examples such as Matike Mai Aotearoa Rangatahi, now a growing national youth movement for constitutional transformation led by a national team of young, talented decolonisation educators assure us that positive change is ahead. The creation of the Rangatahi Constitutional Transformation Workshop, the forming of a national educator team and the engagement hui held by Matike Mai Aotearoa Rangatahi are testament to the phenomenal feats rangatahi can achieve when given the space and support to do so.

Adult-governed spaces however, such as in education, are drenched in our politics. The strict controlling of young minds in terms of space, time, curriculum and the maintenance of 'order' characterises much of the educational environment. After all their efforts to create, train and then prepare to deliver the constitutional transformation workshop, when it came to entering their local educational institutions many of our rangatahi teams were denied entry. Information on the project and my contact details as the national co-ordinator were provided should they have any questions or wish to discuss the project. However, many schools, centres and other learning institutions would simply not allow our rangatahi entry, or access to their peers, while others would cancel after scheduling a time with no explanation, sometimes on the same day the workshop was meant to take place. I was shocked at the mistreatment of the rangatahi, whereas the rangatahi themselves lamented the number of their peers who were not given the opportunity to hear about or share their thoughts on constitutional transformation and their future.

Using our positions as adults to ensure rangatahi have access to each other and the space to make those powerful decolonising connections is a primary way we could be better advancing the decolonisation of education in Aotearoa. In the delivery of the constitutional transformation workshop, I needed to have seen more clearly my power and privilege as an adult to ensure a space for rangatahi to make those connections in what are predominantly adult-governed spaces. Unfortunately, that realisation came too late for me to make any significant changes while co-ordinating the Matike Mai Aotearoa Rangatahi project. In many ways the full potential of the project during those years between 2012 and 2015 was never realised, due to the discrimination of those in power against things that are Māori and challenging of the political status quo. However, the experience and learnings were powerful ones, providing invaluable insight into how things might be better achieved in future. This includes the planning and implementation of ongoing constitutional transformation education by those rangatahi now driving the Matike Mai Aotearoa Rangatahi movement, and those of us supporting them into the future.

Acknowledgement

Thanks to Professor Margaret Mutu, Chair of the Independent Working Group on Constitutional Transformation, and three of our project rangatahi, Karena Karauria, Kiriana Hakopa and Pania Newton, for their review and feedback on the draft of this chapter. Thanks also to members of the Independent Working Group, particularly Moana Jackson, Mereana Pitman, Bill Hamilton, Hone Sadler and Kayleen Neho, and to Te Pūtahi a Toi School of Māori Art, Knowledge and Education at Massey University and Te Ata Kura (Society for Conscientisation) for their invaluable support of the rangatahi project.

References

Alfred, T., Pitawanakwat, B., & Price, J. (2007). *The meaning of political participation for indigenous youth*. Ottawa, ON: Canadian Policy Research Networks.

Cammaerts, B., Bruter, M., Banaji, S., Harrison, S., & Anstead, N. (2014). The myth of youth apathy: Young Europeans' critical attitudes toward democratic life. *American Behavioral Scientist, 58*(5), 645–664.

Campbell, A., Gurin, G., & Miller, W. E. (1954). *The voter decides*. White Plains, NY: Row, Peterson and Company.

Cheyne, C. M., & Tawhai, V. M (2007). *He wharemoa te rakau, ka mahue: Māori engagement with local government: Knowledge, experiences, and recommendations*. Palmerston North: School of People, Environment and Planning, Massey University.

Elections Canada. (2004). Roundtable on Aboriginal youth and the federal elections process. *Electoral Insight, 6*(1), 40–43.

Jackson, M. (2011). *The Independent Constitutional Working Group: Panui.* Unpublished paper.

Kawharu, F. R. (2013). Ngapua, Hone Heke. *Dictionary of New Zealand Biography, Te Ara—The Encyclopedia of New Zealand.* Retrieved from http://www.TeAra.govt.nz/en/biographies/2n12/ngapua-hone-heke

King, M. (2013). Cooper, Whina. *Te Ara—The Encyclopedia of New Zealand.* Retrieved from http://www.teara.govt.nz/en/biographies/5c32/cooper-whina

Kupu Taea: Media and Te Tiriti Project. (2014). *Alternatives to anti-Māori themes in news media.* Retrieved from http://trc.org.nz/alternatives-anti-maori-themes-news-media.

Lindquist, J. H. (1964). Socioeconomic status and political participation. *The Western Political Quarterly, 17*(4), 608–614.

Snell, P. (2010). Emerging adult civic and political disengagement: A longitudinal analysis of lack of involvement with politics. *Journal of Adolescent Research, 25*(2), 258–287.

Sorrenson, M. P. K. (2013). Ngata, Apirana Turupa. *Te Ara—The Encyclopedia of New Zealand.* Retrieved from http://www.TeAra.govt.nz/en/biographies/3n5/ngata-apirana-turupa

Statistics New Zealand. (2013a). *New Zealand General Social Survey: 2012—Tables.* Retrieved from http://www.stats.govt.nz/browse_for_stats/people_and_communities/Households/nzgss_HOTP2012.aspx

Statistics New Zealand. (2013b). *2013 Census QuickStats about Māori.* Retrieved from http://www.stats.govt.nz.

Tawhai, V. M (2011). Citizenship education: Rangatahi electoral engagement. In H. T. Jahnke and M. Mulholland (Eds.), *Mana tangata: The politics of empowerment* (pp. 65–96). Wellington: Huia.

Endnotes

1 Dialogue for the "Dude, Where's My Mana?" a large-group exercise, phase 3 of the Matike Mai Aotearoa Rangatahi constitutional transformation workshop, adapted from Moana Jackson's Tiriti o Waitangi chair exercise.

2 Held on 10–11 March at the Te Aroha Noa Centre in Palmerston North, 24–25 March at Kokiri marae in Wellington, and on 14–15 April at the Waimana Kaaku Executive Office, Waimana. The families and communities of these places and the other places that hosted us during our project are very much thanked for their support.

3 Specifically the rangatahi had brainstormed: Why do we need constitutional transformation? and Why can't we get what we need through the current system?

4 Including a laptop and projector, video camera and tripod, still camera, projection screen, sound system and mics, the photos of tikanga scenarios, dress-up korowai and a crown, elemental signs, pads of A1 paper, marker pens, a 3-metre banner and a koha (in the form of a book) for each workshop.

5 For information on the Rena disaster, see http://news.tangatawhenua.com/2011/10/lastest-news-on-the-rena-disaster/

6 For information on police handling of the Tūhoe Raids, see http://news.tangatawhenua.com/2013/05/ police-heavily-criticised-for-2007-tuhoe-raids-police-actions-contrary-to-law-report/

7 As stated by Rawiri Paratene, Nga Tamatoa: 40 years on, aired by Māori Television, Saturday 15 September 2012; see http://www.maoritelevision.com/tv/shows/ pakipumeka-aotearoa/S01E001/nga-tamatoa-40-years

8 Including J. R. McKenzie Trust, the United Nations Trust Fund on Indigenous Issues Small Grants Programme. These monies have been kindly administered for us for the duration of the project by Ngāti Kahungunu Inc. and Te Rūnanga-ā-iwi o Ngāti Kahu. We are also grateful for the guidance and support of the Independent Working Group's Finance Committee, Pā Bill Hamilton and Matua Hone Sadler.

PART 2: MĀORI IN RESEARCH

Māori in Research introduces into the discussion the key themes of:
colonisation and the resulting imperialism of Western knowledge and
approaches to knowing, indigenous standpoints, and the positioning of
ourselves as insiders within research, along with practical examples of
kaupapa Māori research in action.

Chapter 8 Positioning ourselves within kaupapa Māori research

Leonie Pihama

Whāia! Whāia!
Whāia ki te uru-tapu-o-Tane
Tāne te waiora
Tāne te pūkenga
Tāne te wānanga
Tāne te whakaputa nei
Ki te whaiao, ki te ao mārama
Tū te ngana
Tū ka maranga
Te tuhi, te rarama
Tēnei au e noho mataara nei
E rongo whakairia ake ki runga
Tūturu whakamoua ki a tina!
Tina! Hui e! Tāiki e!

Introduction

Like the karakia that opens and clears the way for this writing, kaupapa Māori is grounded within the deep knowledge of our people. It is of Aotearoa. It is of our tūpuna. It is ancestral knowledge. The challenge to current and future generations of whānau, hapū and iwi is to draw upon this knowledge as a basis for positioning ourselves as Māori in a contemporary context. This is a context that is affected daily by ongoing processes of colonisation. The act of colonisation itself is an act of violence. Colonial ideologies and practice are embedded politically, socially, economically, culturally and spiritually. Education is one site where contestation between colonial ideologies and indigenous struggle play out. That has been the case since the establishment of the first mission school in Rangihoua in 1816 (Pihama, 2001; Simon & Smith, 2001).

Pākehā-defined education has been in existence for close to 200 years in Aotearoa. The underpinning approaches to schooling and the broader education system in Aotearoa were defined through notions of racism, sexism and classism (Pihama 2001). It is well documented that the intention of both mission and Native schooling was to align with these imported colonial ideologies (Binney, 1968; Jenkins, 1991; Simon & Smith, 2001; Smith, 1986; Te Whaiti, McCarthy, & Durie, 1997). Schooling has been identified as a key mechanism for the assimilation of indigenous peoples (Hohepa, 1990; Pihama, 1993). A key underpinning assumption of assimilation policies was the notion of the existence of a hierarchy of civilisations, which located the coloniser as superior and the colonised as inferior. Such assumptions, supported by dominant scientific ideologies of the time, maintained the rationale for both imperialist expansionism and acts of both genocide and ethnocide upon indigenous people. Schooling has been a significant contributor to the ongoing reproduction of such beliefs. Schooling has been instrumental in the development and entrenchment of discourses that promote the domestication of Māori.

As a system founded on the ideological belief that Māori people required both civilising and Christianising, schooling was viewed as instrumental in bringing about the desired change. What this has meant in Aotearoa is the suppression of Māori world views and ways of living, and the development of a determined effort by the colonial forces to replace those with what was deemed appropriate for the 'Natives' of this country. The Pākehā education system has been instrumental in these processes. It has been constructed to facilitate the maintenance and reproduction of selected knowledge. This has occurred through the fashioning of particular forms of pedagogy, curriculum, methods and content of examinations, credentials, etc.

Colonising research

Schooling could not have achieved its colonising objectives without colonial research narratives that located Māori as inferior, savage, and uncivilised, and that both constructed and maintained hierarchies of oppression. Western colonial research provided both the rationale and the justification for the invasion and illegal occupation of indigenous lands across the world (Smith, 1999). It also provided the scientific rationale for the oppression of indigenous peoples.

Modes of 'scientific' legitimation emerged to justify race hierarchies. Colonial research undertaken by the likes of Francis Galton provided the rationale for the creation of early testing regimes such as intelligence testing, which has the assumption of racial hierarchies as its fundamental underpinning (Pihama, 1993). Another example is the research practice of craniology. Craniology incorporated the study of the size and shape of the skulls of different races as a means to relate superiority to brain size. The movement to identify physical differences between races as a means of determining positioning in the order of things was highlighted even further through processes such as craniometry (Pihama, 2001).

Craniometry was utilised in Europe and America as a means to determine physical differences as a basis for classification. What is clear is that such research was underpinned by a colonial imperialist desire to justify White superiority. What was presented as 'pure' and 'neutral' scientific research was in fact a process through which colonisers could assert their own racial superiority as a justification for oppression and colonisation (Gould, 1981). Furthermore, it is clear that such research included both incorrect calculations and conscious manipulation of data in order to confirm ideologies of race that were shaped by prior racial prejudices and conclusions (Gould, 1981). As Linda Tuhiwai Smith (2015) notes:

> The nexus between cultural ways of knowing, scientific discoveries, economic impulses and imperial power enabled the West to make ideological claims to having a superior civilization. The 'idea' of the West became a reality when it was re-presented back to indigenous

nations through colonialism. By the nineteenth century colonialism not only meant the imposition of Western authority over all aspects of indigenous lands, indigenous modes of production and indigenous law and government, but the imposition of Western authority over all aspects of indigenous knowledges, languages and cultures. (p. 67)

As Māori, our experiences of research have been dominated by being the 'object' that is studied and theorised about. Our lives, our whānau, our culture, our language, our entire being has been theorised by Pākehā academics and researchers over the past 200 years. Our world has been theorised through paradigms that bear no resemblance to the ways in which we would explain and understand ourselves. Sarah-Jane Tiakiwai (2015) highlights the ongoing struggle for a space for Māori within the research domain:

> The battle for legitimation and of 'finding a space' from which to resist the dominant constructs of what 'counts' as knowledge has been ongoing for indigenous and minority researchers. (p. 77)

The dominance of colonial research approaches within Aotearoa highlights why decolonising theory and research have been a focus for many Māori researchers (Lee, 2008; Mahuika, 2015; Pihama, 1993, 2001; Smith, G.H., 1997; Smith, L.T., 1999). Kaupapa Māori theory and methodologies have been central to that process and have provided powerful cultural frameworks through which Māori knowledge and approaches are able to be utilised and validated.

Kaupapa Māori theory

Kaupapa Māori has been a significant development in the area of Māori research and practice for the past 25 years. As a cultural construction, the term 'kaupapa Māori' has become one that is utilised to describe a range of initiatives that include the inclusion of tikanga and te reo Māori along with key cultural principles within the theory and practice of Māori researchers. Kaupapa Māori has had a significant impact on the education sector, transforming the way in which theory and research are articulated in Aotearoa, particularly with regard to Māori educational provision.

Māori education initiatives such as te kōhanga reo, kura kaupapa Māori, whare kura and whare wānanga have been hugely important to how kaupapa Māori theory has been framed (Pihama 1993, 2001; Smith, 1997). Kaupapa Māori theory, having originated in these Māori community initiatives, provides us with a theoretical process that ensures those struggles, and the inherent power relationships within those struggles, are a conscious part of our analysis. Given the unequal power relations that exist between Māori and the state, the recognition that such developments are the outcome of Māori aspirations and a subsequent struggle for the realisation of those aspirations means there is a clearly articulated political agenda that sits alongside cultural aspirations for te reo and tikanga Māori.

Linda Tuhiwai Smith notes that "The concept of kaupapa implies a way of framing and structuring how we think about those ideas and practices" (cited in Smith, 1996). With regard to kaupapa Māori within the Māori education sector, this way of framing and structuring is distinct in that its basis is within mātauranga Māori, and the philosophical underpinnings are Māori (Māori Education Commission, 1998). Taking this further, Smith (1997) has identified six elements that are evident in kaupapa Māori education: tino rangatiratanga, taonga tuku iho; ako Māori; kia piki ake i ngā raruraru i te kainga; whānau; kaupapa. Smith (1997) argues that these elements provide a solid basis for kaupapa Māori theory. Within Māori educational developments, kaupapa Māori initiatives are held together by collective commitment, philosophies and visions.

The naming of kaupapa Māori theory indicates an explicit acknowledgement of the theoretical approach being undertaken. The multiple layers of meaning within te reo Māori mean that the term 'kaupapa' has many possibilities. Kaupapa relates to notions of foundation, plan, philosophy and strategies. Kaupapa Māori, therefore, indicates a Māori view of those things. It relates to Māori philosophies of the world, to Māori understandings upon which our beliefs and values are based, to Māori world views and ways of operating. As such there is a clear cultural and political intent. The political intent of kaupapa Māori is described by Sheilagh Walker (1996) in her statement that "our struggle becomes our Theory" (p. 119). Kaupapa Māori provides a combined structuralist and culturalist approach to Māori issues, thereby enabling the development of interventions and transformation at the level of both 'institution' and 'mode' (Smith, 1997). As Smith (2015) indicates, engaging both culturalist and structuralist concerns is essential to understanding the various explanations for issues that have an impact upon Māori:

> In order for theory to have relevance and to impact meaningfully on Māori education crises, structuralist concerns which produce these factors, also (as well as culturalist concerns) need to be understood, consciously resisted and transformed … the dynamics of thrust and parry of culturalist and structuralist levels, and the resilience of both interest groups in reforming and positioning themselves when their interests are thwarted. (p. 27)

The idea that theorists and researchers are acultural is directly challenged by the assertion of indigenous theories, such as kaupapa Māori, which are grounded within cultural frameworks and epistemologies (Smith, 1999). Kaupapa Māori theory is based upon and informed by mātauranga Māori, which provides a cultural template, a philosophy that asserts that the theoretical framework being employed is culturally defined and determined. This has been argued consistently by kaupapa Māori theorists as the organic nature of kaupapa Māori theory (Smith, 1996; Pihama, 1993, 2001; Smith, 1997). Kaupapa Māori is a "body of knowledge accumulated by the experiences through history, of the Māori people" (Nepe, 1991, p. 4) that is distinctive to Māori in that it derives fundamentally from Māori epistemologies that include complex relationships and ways of organising society.

Kaupapa Māori methodology

Part of the growth and development of kaupapa Māori theory and research methodologies has been an increased engagement by Māori in the assertion of research aspirations that align with a broader Māori agenda of transformation (Smith, 1997). Kaupapa Māori theory and research methodologies and approaches are inter-related. Like whakapapa, they are continually layered with each other. The catch-cry for kaupapa Māori research, "for Māori by Māori", signifies the aspiration which Graham Smith (1997) refers to as the "tino rangatiratanga principle". Māori researchers clearly voice the need for kaupapa Māori to be determined by our people (Smith, 1999; Tiakiwai, 2015). Linda Smith (1999) has strongly argued that kaupapa Māori research differs from other research approaches in that Māori have control over all aspects of the research process, from defining the issues to conceptualising and designing the methodological framework, through to determining processes of knowledge dissemination.

The centrality of tino rangatiratanga is critical. Researchers who are unable to 'check their ego at the door', so to speak—that is, those who believe they have the right to define research areas and research questions for Māori—have no place in a kaupapa Māori approach. The view that researchers 'know' what is important and what questions need to be asked for Māori communities is incongruent with kaupapa Māori methodology. As Sarah-Jane Tiakiwai (2015) reminds us, there is an increasing resistance to "traditional western research methods, which place control and power in the hands of the researcher" (p. 78). What this means is that there must be a significant shift in how research is developed, designed, produced and controlled, and that it is for Māori to maintain authority over all phases of the research process.

Kaupapa Māori research methodology locates Māori understandings as central to the research design, process, analysis and intended outcomes (Pihama, 2001; Smith, 1999). Māori researchers across Aotearoa have been actively engaged in developing what has become known as kaupapa Māori theory and kaupapa Māori research over a long period of time (see, for example, Lee, 2008; Pihama, 1993; G.H. Smith, 1997; L.H. Smith, 1999). This approach has been shaped by a deep knowledge of education and the design of interventions such as kura kaupapa Māori. The role of Māori educational developments in informing kaupapa Māori research methodologies has been well documented (Nepe, 1991; Smith, 1997). The kaupapa Māori approach has been widely utilised by academics and policy makers seeking to understand and influence wellbeing within Māori communities, and to support Māori aspirations within the education sector. A kaupapa Māori methodology emphasises collaborative research between the researcher and the research participants or community, and the de-centring of traditional power relations. This is a clearly defined process within kaupapa Māori methodology and sits beside principles identified by Smith (1997), such as whakapapa, te reo, tikanga, rangatiratanga, mana wahine–mana tane. Each of these principles aligns to those identified in relation to kaupapa Māori theory (Smith, 1997).

Kaupapa Māori methodologies locate Māori understandings as central to the research process and analysis. There is a critical political project as part of kaupapa Māori research, which is to develop Māori-centred, -defined and -preferred ways of research, and which seeks to intervene in our historical experiences of colonisation (Smith, 1999). Kaupapa Māori research alongside its theoretical counterpart, kaupapa Māori theory, has at its centre the validation and affirmation of te reo Māori and tikanga. This provides a foundation from which we as Māori researchers and academics can locate ourselves, and which supports a desire to undertake research from our own understandings. What it states is that there are clearly Māori ways of exploring and conceptualising issues that face us as Māori people. Kaupapa Māori research carries particular cultural expectations, including the active participation of, and control by, Māori within all aspects of the research and a focus on research as transformative. There is a range of elements noted within kaupapa Māori that are of direct significance to this project. In particular, tino rangatiratanga, whānau, whakapapa, taonga tuku iho, te reo, tikanga are all elements that are critical to the research approach in that each of these elements is directly linked to developing research that is transformative for our whānau, hapū and iwi.

Central to any form of kaupapa Māori research methodology is relationships. In kaupapa Māori research it is critical to prioritise whanaungatanga relationships, whakapapa relationships, iwi relationships and Māori organisational relationships. A kaupapa Māori methodology brings a process through which whānau, hapū, iwi and Māori organisations are engaged in ways that ensure their research needs and aspirations are central to all aspects of the research process. The ability for Māori to determine what research is important for ourselves is key to being self-determining in terms of the research process. A key part of relationships is knowing who you are and having a clear understanding of your own position and identity. It is about having a deep awareness of how being who we are comes to play a role in the research context:

'Insider' 'Participant' 'Researcher' 'Kura Kaupapa Māori parent',
Māori women with Nga Puhi and Pakeha genealogical connections
(to name but a few) are not hats that I put on and take off. They are

not different coloured spectacles, one of which I may choose to look
through at any given time. I do not see these as multiple positionings.
Rather, these are some of the facets or dimensions that make me who
I am. One or another dimension might come to the foreground or go
into the background, depending on the circumstance. But they are
facets of me as 'researcher'. (Hohepa, 2015, p. 110)

Ensuring that tikanga and te reo are affirmed in all aspects of the
research process is also central. Kaupapa Māori asserts the centrality
and taken-for-granted position of te reo and tikanga Māori within
any research that is related specifically to Māori. Tikanga provides not
only a cultural template and practice that affirms Māori participation
and voice, but also enacts Māori ethics in ways that both protect and
acknowledge the relationship between researchers and communities and
provide mechanisms of accountability and obligation to all involved.
Such an approach challenges both the historical and contemporary
experience of our people in relation to dominant research approaches
that have located being Māori as a 'deficit', and have framed research in
ways that fail to acknowledge and validate Māori aspirations. Kaupapa
Māori methodology seeks to ensure that whānau voices are privileged
in ways that ensure their aspirations and reflections are at the centre of
all aspects of the project.

As an indigenous research approach that interrogates and investi-
gates issues as they are contextualised within Aotearoa, kaupapa Māori
enables an analysis of issues from an approach that is distinctively
Māori. Kaupapa Māori methodology allows us, as Māori researchers,
to connect with and accommodate the complexity of diverse Māori
lived realities (Irwin 1992; Smith, 1992). As such, there is a range of
methodological approaches that fit within the broader definition of
kaupapa Māori research. For example, the work of Jenny Lee (2015)
is grounded within pūrākau. She highlights that the practices of
pūrākau enable Māori researchers to undertake innovative approaches
to research, where Māori voices and narratives are articulated through
a uniquely Māori approach. Another clear example is that of mana
wahine approaches, as articulated by a range of Māori women researchers (Irwin, 1992; Jenkins, 1992; Pihama, 2001; Smith, 1992; Te
Awekotuku 1991) who have advocated for actively engaging with the

issue of the imposition of gendered hierarchies alongside those of race and the impact of these upon our people. What is evident in the development of kaupapa Māori methodologies is the need to ensure that diversity within the Māori world is reflected in the utilisation of a range of methodologies and methods.

A key principle of kaupapa Māori methodology is a focus on transformation. It is about making change for our people and developing positive interventions in areas where such processes are required. Research that benefits Māori and is transformative is also viewed as critical to ensuring that kaupapa Māori research is beneficial to Māori communities. Transformation is multiple and can happen in a whole range of places along a research process. There are times when you can see the change that is about to happen—whether there is a new intervention developed, or there is a new practice, or whānau say to you, "It changed my life". But a transformative approach to research goes all the way through the process. The fact that we can define our own questions, the fact that we can assert our aspirations and say, 'This is what is important to us'—that is already a transformation; that is already about interrupting some kinds of power relationships that exist.

Transformation comes in many forms. Sometimes it takes the form of thousands of people on a hīkoi to assert Māori rights. That is transformation. On another level transformation can be in the form of whānau. For example, when a whānau that has been denied Māori-language speakers for three generations makes a decision to place their children in Māori-language immersion education such as te kōhanga reo and kura kaupapa Māori, the pathway for that whānau is transformed. For those whānau, embarking on a journey of revitalising te reo Māori can change the life pathways for all generations to come. The point is that transformation can come in many forms.

What is clear is that if research is not transformative, if it does not seek to create positive outcomes for Māori, if it does not seek to intervene in existing inequalities or provide knowledge and outcomes that inform us and answer the questions that we believe are important, then that research is of little consequence. Kaupapa Māori research is about transformation, creating change and supporting positive movements for Māori—and it is inherently empowering.

Some concluding thoughts

As a wahine Māori working in the area of kaupapa Māori theory and research for many years, I have found the development to be incredibly invigorating. The Māori educational movements of the early 1980s created a space not only for the revitalisation of te reo and tikanga Māori, but also for the fundamental ways in which we think as Māori—in how we understand our world—to be regenerated. What we consider to be kaupapa Māori is not new. It is ancient. It is of Papatūānuku and Ranginui. It is of Aotearoa. It is of our tūpuna.

The movements of te kōhanga reo and kura kaupapa Māori opened a journey that went well beyond the education sector. Kaupapa Māori is an influence throughout all sectors. Kaupapa Māori theory and research remain steadfast, irrespective of the fact that the struggle to maintain our validity continues, often in a daily way, for many of our people. We have much to be thankful and grateful for to those who took on the struggle against the government and a predominantly monocultural society in order to create Māori immersion education initiatives that would change the face of Māori education in Aotearoa.

The power of kaupapa Māori research lies in te reo, tikanga Māori, mātauranga Māori and the culturally determined principles that serve to ground it. As all research methodologies are sourced from particular cultural, social and political contexts, so too is kaupapa Māori. In being explicit about the cultural framework that informs our research methodology, kaupapa Māori researchers are interrupting the dominant ideology of research as 'neutral' and 'objective'. Our experiences as Māori and the ways in which colonial research was utilised to justify and rationalise colonial invasion and occupation of indigenous territories tells us that research is not neutral, nor is it objective. Research is culturally, socially, economically and politically bound. There are many examples of the use of research as a colonising tool (Pihama, 2001; Smith, 2015). To engage in kaupapa Māori methodology is to 'research back' to those dominant understandings and to do that in line with our own cultural frameworks. That is a powerful position to take, and it is one that I would highly recommend.

References

Binney, J. (1968) *The legacy of guilt: A life of Thomas Kendall*. Auckland: Published for The University of Auckland by the Oxford University Press.

Gould, S. J. (1981) *The mismeasure of man*. New York, NY: Penguin Books.

Hohepa, M. K. (1990). *Te kohanga reo hei tikanga ako i te reo Māori*. Unpublished master's thesis, The University of Auckland.

Hohepa, M. K. (2015). Kia mau ki te aka matua: Research, Māori development and learning. In L. Pihama & S. Tiakiwai (Eds.), *Kaupapa rangahau: A reader* (pp. 109-117). Hamilton: Te Kotahi Research Institute.

Irwin, K. (1992). Towards theories of Māori feminism. In R. Du Plessis, with P. Bunkle, K. Irwin, A. Laurie, & S. Middleton (Eds.), *Feminist voices: Women's studies texts for Aotearoa/New Zealand* (pp. 1–19). Auckland: Oxford University Press,

Jenkins, K. (1992). Reflections on the status of Māori women. In L. T. Smith (Ed.), *Te Pua 1* (pp. 37-45). Auckland: Te Puawaitanga.

Jenkins, K. E. H. (1991). *Te ihi, te mana, te wehi o te ao: Māori print literacy from 1814-1855: Literacy, power and colonisation*. Unpublished master's thesis, The University of Auckland.

Lee, J. (2015). Decolonising Māori narratives: Pūrākau as method. In L. Pihama & S. Tiakiwai (Eds.), *Kaupapa rangahau: A reader* (pp. 91-99). Hamilton: Te Kotahi Research Institute.

Lee, J. B. J. (2008). *Ako: Pūrākau of Māori secondary school teachers' work in secondary schools*. Unpublished doctoral thesis, The University of Auckland.

Mahuika, R. (2015). Kaupapa Māori is critical and anticolonial. In L. Pihama & S. Tiakiwai (Eds.), *Kaupapa rangahau: A reader* (pp. 34-45). Hamilton: Te Kotahi Research Institute.

Māori Education Commission. (1998). *Report to the Minsters of Māori Affairs: Report 2*. Wellington: Māori Education Commission.

Nepe, T. M. (1991). *E hao ne e tenei reanga: Te toi huarewa tipuna, kaupapa Māori: An educational intervention*. Unpublished master's thesis, The University of Auckland.

Pihama, L. (1993). *Tungia te ururua, kia tupu whakaritorito te tupu o te harakeke: A critical analysis of parents as first teachers*. Unpublished master's thesis, The University of Auckland.

Pihama, L. (2001). *Tihei mauri ora: Honouring our voices: Mana wahine as a kaupapa Māori theoretical framework*. Unpublished doctoral thesis, The University of Auckland.

Simon, J., & Smith, L. T. (2001) *A civilising mission?: Perceptions and representations of the New Zealand Native Schools system.* Auckland: Auckland University Press.

Smith, G. H. (Ed.). (1986). *Māori perspectives of taha Māori: Ngā kete wānanga: Readers in Māori education.* Auckland: Auckland College of Education.

Smith, G. H. (1997). *The development of kaupapa Māori theory and praxis.* School of Education. Unpublished Doctoral Thesis, Auckland: University of Auckland.

Smith, L. T. (1992). Māori women: Discourses, projects and mana wahine. In S. Middleton & A. Jones (Eds.), *Women and education in Aotearoa 2* (pp. 33–51). Wellington: Bridget Williams Books.

Smith, L. T. (1996). *Nga aho o te kakahu matauranga: The multiple layers of struggle by Māori in education.* Unpublished doctoral thesis, The University of Auckland.

Smith, L. T. (1999). *Decolonising methodologies: Research and indigenous peoples.* London, UK: Zed Books.

Smith, L. T. (2015). Kaupapa Māori research: Some kaupapa Māori principles. In L. Pihama & S. Tiakiwai (Eds.), *Kaupapa rangahau: A reader* (pp. 46–52). Hamilton: Te Kotahi Research Institute.

Te Awekotuku, N. (1991). *Mana wahine Māori: Selected writings on Māori women's art: Culture and politics.* Auckland: New Women's Press.

Te Awekotuku, N. (1992). He whiriwhiri wahine: Framing women's studies for Aotearoa. In L. T. Smith (Ed.), *Te Pua 1* (pp. 46–58). Auckland: Te Puawaitanga.

Te Whaiti, P., McCarthy, M., Durie, A. (1997). *Mai i rangiatea: Māori wellbeing and development.* Auckland: Auckland University Press & Bridget Williams Books.

Tiakiwai, S. (2015). Understanding and doing research: A Māori position. In L. Pihama & S. Tiakiwai (Eds.), *Kaupapa rangahau: A reader* (pp. 74–90). Hamilton: Te Kotahi Research Institute.

Walker, S. (1996). *Kia tau te rangimarie: Kaupapa Māori theory as a resistance against the construction of Māori as the 'other'.* Unpublished master's thesis, The University of Auckland.

Chapter 9 Native agents: Navigating indigenous research across the borders

Mera Lee-Penehira

Introduction

Notions and practices of indigenous research have been evolving since the early 1990s and we now have the privilege of working in a research context in which these things are relatively commonplace. This does not mean, however, that they are always accepted, nor that they go unchallenged. Rather, the indigenous researcher plays a significant role in the continued development of research ideologies and methodologies that ensure the safety and respect of the indigenous researcher, those researched, and the indigenous research outcomes. Most importantly, they are responsible for research processes and outcomes which see that the ultimate aim of self-determination of indigenous peoples is reached.

How, then, do we set about designing research in such a way that we become active agents in the struggle for indigenous self-determination? How do we articulate the importance of research to ourselves and others who have suffered at the hands of racist researchers using their research to further entrench colonising attitudes and practices? How do we organise ourselves as indigenous researchers in international collaborations while still developing independent indigenous research frameworks in our own lands? And what and how does kaupapa Māori research contribute to international indigenous collaborations? These questions are explored in this chapter, with a particular emphasis on kaupapa Māori theory and how it might be applied in an international context.

Colonisation and research

Researchers have a torrid history of using research as a tool for further oppression of indigenous peoples (Mead, 1997; Pihama, 2001). For many generations, non-indigenous researchers have entered our communities to glean information, collect data and then analyse it in ways that are devoid of indigenous ways of knowing and behaving (Kidman, 2007; Smith, 2007). The end results have been to produce decontextualised research findings that position indigenous peoples as victims of their own wrongdoing, thus justifying the continued role of the coloniser to teach us the 'right way'—their way—in order to save ourselves from our own destruction.

Colonisation is a process whereby indigenous peoples are systematically taught to do things according to the colonisers' view of the world (C.W. Smith, 2002; G.H. Smith, 1997; Pihama, 1993). In the process, indigenous ways of knowing and behaving are deliberately removed and no longer considered of any importance whatsoever. These are experiences that are shared among indigenous peoples from many lands. It is these shared experiences that "Indigenous communities associate with racism, with inequality and injustices" (Bargh, 2007).

The analysis presented here is multilayered and shares commonalities with that of many other indigenous writers, and with many other indigenous people with whom I have spoken and shared experiences. These layers include:

- how colonisation affects one's ability to think and speak
- how we view our position in the communities in which we have been raised, and those in which we now live
- how we view our freedom or our entrapment

- how we view our position in the environments in which we move (i.e., the academic institutions, the business world, the governance institutions, social institutions, sporting institutions).

The list is as broad as the lives we lead, and this is a critical factor.

Many have argued that the academic arena is treacherous ground in which to apply indigenous analysis (Battiste, Bell, & Findlay, 2002; Castleden, Garvin, & Huu-ay-aht First Nation 2008; Walker, 2003; Witt, 2007), and for a long time it has been. However, it could also be argued that there are many areas of academia in which it would now be considered treacherous for an indigenous person to do otherwise. This represents the ground-breaking work of the academics who have preceded us, and the foresight and bravery of activists who work outside of academia in order to create a broader context for the eventual transformation of our world. Admittedly there remain vast fields within the academic institutions yet to experience this. Nonetheless, the fields of health and education are well used to being viewed and 'shaken up' through an indigenous lens. Given this, as indigenous academics, we can challenge ourselves to move outside of that 'comfort zone' of the institution and start applying the indigenous lens to the rest of our lives—if, in fact, that is not what we are doing already, or what we were doing before we even learnt to apply it to the institution.

What I argue for is the need for us to apply self-determining ways of being, both to our academic work and to our everyday engagement within our communities and broader environments. The work of Linda Tuhiwai Smith, whose doctoral studies focused on decolonising research methodologies, speaks directly to being self-determining people, and to deeper levels of reflection. In order to begin this discussion it is necessary to consider firstly the converse of decolonising methodologies; that is, colonising methodologies. Colonising research may be considered, among other things, as that which privileges academic literature and empirical evidence over and above oral accounts (Pihama, Lee, Taki & Smith, 2004; C.W. Smith, 2002; L.T. Smith, 2007). This is not to say that decolonising methodologies counter this by privileging oral accounts over academic literature and empirical evidence. Rather, it is about giving voice to material previously not recognised as valid in terms of research documentation. This includes, but is not exclusive to, oral accounts. Decolonising methodologies also acknowledge, for example, the historical and contemporary narratives contained in traditional carving, song and performance. Pūrākau is but one significant example of the contemporary application of a traditional practice being applied as a research methodology (Lee, 2005).

It is important to note that it is not the sole intent of kaupapa Māori or other indigenous research to counter the research of colonisers, as could be suggested by the term 'decolonising methodologies'. Rather, it is about doing what is necessary to assist people to become decolonised, to become self-determining, and to be resistant to the forces of colonisation (Bishop, 2008; Durie 1998; Walters, 2006). Sometimes this results in direct challenges to past research. However, to solely focus a methodology or research theory on this task would be to fall short of the ultimate aim of self-determination. This aim cannot be achieved by simply deconstructing historical or recent research alone, given the narrow focuses of the majority of these works in terms of the dimensions of our lives that it has covered.

Globalisation, the neo-liberal agenda and activ(ist) research

Neo-liberalism in the research context has had an enormous impact on indigenous peoples, just as it has on every other aspect of our community lives. Before exploring this, it is important to first define the term. Neo-liberal practices and policies are those that

> seek to extend the market mechanism into areas of the community
> previously organized and governed in other ways ... free trade and free
> mobility of capital, accompanied by a broad reduction in the ambit
> and role of the state. (Bargh, 2007, p. 7)

In the research context this has the potential to manifest itself in a number of ways. Firstly, research is more likely to be seen as transportable from one land to another. That is, research designed and conducted in one country is, under a neo-liberal way of thinking, easily replicated in another, with little if any heed paid to the differences among the people and their communities or ways of being.

Secondly, the neo-liberal researcher may see little benefit in replicating studies in other parts of the world in order to justify a change in practice that might be concluded by the research. That is, when research in one part of the world determines that changes are required, or otherwise, the neo-liberal would see no reason why that would not be so elsewhere in the world. It works on the premise that there is, or needs to be, a uniformity of thought and practice among all peoples in order to progress humanity, ultimately progressing the general market good. Clearly this concept is at odds with indigenous ways of being, which acknowledge, celebrate and seek to fully ensconce diversity, tino rangatiratanga and mana motuhake among indigenous peoples in our own lands.

Kaupapa Māori and international research

Kaupapa Māori research largely began in the area of education, closely followed by the health sector. Currently, there remains a larger force of kaupapa Māori researchers in both of these areas than in any other. However, with the current drive to increase the number of Māori graduating with PhDs, there is a greater spread of Māori researchers throughout the various faculties of our universities in Aotearoa. Concurrently we have many researchers emerging from our own indigenous universities known as whare wānanga. It is important to note, however, that not all Māori researchers practise kaupapa Māori research. How, then, does one identify as a kaupapa Māori researcher? It is simply a matter of stating explicitly at the outset of the research that this is your position and providing the rationale for that. The methodology, and most importantly the analysis, will be further evidence for that claim. Ultimately, the findings of a kaupapa Māori piece of research will be such that they add to the self-determination of Māori and/or indigenous peoples.

The present discussion views the notion of kaupapa Māori research as being not just something we do in our work, but rather a way of life. Kaupapa Māori, by definition, is simply 'about Māori'. 'Māori' is defined in dictionaries as 'natural', so it could be theorised that kaupapa Māori is about 'what is natural' or about 'being natural'. It is my contention that it is a difficult task to purport to undertake kaupapa Māori research and therefore be working in a 'natural way' yet live everyday life in other ways. That is, if it is 'natural', then it will 'naturally' be a part of you and the way you conduct yourself, be it at work, in your writing, or in your engagements with family and community.

It could be further argued that neither kaupapa Māori research nor kaupapa Māori education, health, art or scientific endeavours can ultimately be achieved by approaching them as you might any other job. While in many other jobs it is quite acceptable that the job is a completely separate facet of one's life, in kaupapa Māori environments one is more likely to succeed in one's role if the values and underpinnings of one's work are generalised to other facets of everyday life. One could go further and suggest that conflict arises when we attempt to live our lives by one code, the coloniser's code, while working by another code, the kaupapa Māori code, and this is particularly so for Māori and other indigenous peoples.

The discussion of kaupapa Māori research ties in with and often overlaps that of kaupapa Māori theory. Theory is defined by the Encarta World English Dictionary (2004) as "a set of circumstances or principles that is hypothetical" (p. 1). Having experiences, and indeed a life centred on things Māori, gives the 'circumstances' and the 'principles' by which everyday life routines and events are carried out. It does not, however, feel in any sense of the word 'hypothetical'. How, then, does one who practises or lives in a Māori way come to have an understanding of kaupapa Māori theory? I argue that to develop theory from a lived base of understanding is simply to develop and undertake analyses of those circumstances and principles by which that living is framed. It could be concluded, therefore, that a Māori analysis of things Māori is one manifestation of what kaupapa Māori theory is.

By contrast, how does someone who has essentially grown up removed from Māori ways of being and doing in the world, but who is well versed in theory and analytical skills, develop and conduct work using kaupapa Māori theory? A number of kaupapa Māori researchers currently practising in Aotearoa fit this category. Indeed, their numbers are growing as the number of Māori achieving doctoral qualifications increases. Many of these graduates have discovered being Māori through their university studies. At the same time, the requirements of research funding bodies are such that it is the academic qualifications and experience of principal investigators that predominantly determine funding success, as opposed to their lived understanding and experience of kaupapa Māori. The circumstances and principles of kaupapa Māori in this instance might be almost solely those experienced inside the academic arena. For some, the experiences and discovery of being Māori, of identifying as Māori, have begun in a university setting that many would describe as being in direct conflict with being Māori. Educational institutions are, after all, a bastion of colonisation of indigenous peoples, and this raises an interesting, albeit contentious, opportunity for further discussion.

The previous paragraphs have begun to describe two distinct types of kaupapa Māori researchers: those whose Māori knowledge has come about through their academic experiences and endeavours, and those whose academic experiences and endeavours have come about from their lived Māori knowledge. The purpose of this discussion is not to privilege one over the other, but rather to acknowledge the differences so that any potential impact they have can be discussed and mediated in order to progress forward. How might an understanding of these differences assist in the development of international indigenous research protocols? Firstly, it may be that these differences among Māori researchers' experiences also exist within other indigenous researcher groups; secondly, these differences may bring with them different approaches to indigenous knowledges and practices within the research teams; and thirdly, these differences may therefore have an ongoing impact in terms of differing approaches across teams in international indigenous collaborations.

Exploring the differences in and similarities of indigenous approaches within and across all of the teams is a critical first step in the development of international collaborations. This cannot be done without being sensitive to the notions of identity that underlie the current discussion. The differences between Māori and indigenous researchers being explored are essentially differences of identity and, more specifically, the bases of identity. That is both the academic base of one's identity and the lived base of one's identity. Given the context of colonisation and the various stages that individuals might be at in working towards decolonising, this is a sensitive area. Many might be cautious about exploring such an area, but not to do so would be to miss an opportunity for both individual and systemic decolonisation. Referring to Smith's (1999) model of the indigenous research agenda, this would ultimately detract from self-determining research.

A self case study is one model that provides a safe way to begin the exploration. Implicit in my practice as a Māori researcher is the ownership of this model (the indigenous research model) for self. This ownership compels me to analyse my living and research practices at regular intervals in the research journey. For example, at a macro level I ask myself if the ultimate aim of the research is to assist Māori and other indigenous peoples to become self-determining. Then, how self-determining is the life that I live and the research that I engage in? Just as the research methods employed may need to be fine tuned throughout the process to ensure that I stay on the ultimate self-determining track, so too does my life—or rather, lifestyle—require intermittent 'tweaking'. This self-application of the ultimate aim of the research is perhaps one critical difference between the job of a kaupapa Māori researcher and any other researcher. It may also be a difference between the Māori or indigenous researcher who grows their identity through academia and the researcher who grows academically through their identity, as described earlier. That is, the academic Māori researcher may not be as likely to self-analyse, or to apply the self-determining research methods and purpose to their own lives, or might do so in a different way to the Māori academic.

This raises the notion of an insider–outsider researcher. Historically, much social research has centred on 'proper research' being considered as such when it is conducted in an impartial or objective way. Kaupapa Māori research, by contrast, actually requires the researcher to situate him- or herself in some way 'inside' the research and largely remove levels of objectivity. Being subjective—that is, to see oneself as a part of the subject or subject group—is advantageous in kaupapa Māori research because it implies one's accountability to the research group and the research outcomes. Subjectivity is indeed necessary in order for the research to be deemed valid under kaupapa Māori terms. This accountability and responsibility to the people are particularly important in the context of the historical injustices perpetuated by research on indigenous peoples, discussed earlier in this chapter.

The notion of insider–outsider research has differing levels of application. For example, some kaupapa Māori researchers (Smith, 2008) go so far as to state that the researcher should have direct genealogical ties to the group they are researching. The rationale given is threefold.

Firstly, it ensures that the same level of accountability to the group applies, due to the researcher's familial ties. Secondly, the researcher is much more likely to have a background and contextual knowledge of the research area because they know and are known to the community. Thirdly, the researcher remains tied to the community beyond the life of the research and is therefore able to be held accountable for both the research outcomes and the longevity of the impact of these outcomes.

The accountability that comes with familial ties goes beyond the obvious: that the researcher is one of these people and therefore has a stake in, and is, to an extent, responsible for outcomes in the community. The tribal nature of Māori communities involves a complex matrix of roles, positions and responsibilities. Many relationships exist within whānau; tuakana–teina is one such relationship. Tuakana Nepe (1991) writes about tuakana–teina as it relates to her personal knowledge of whānau, hapū and iwi, and the family relationships she has experienced:

> At my immediate whānau generation level I am teina to my older
> sisters and tuakana to my younger sister and two younger brothers.
> This information influences how we interact, in terms of our
> reciprocal roles and commitments, to one and other. By virtue of
> our standing as either tuakana or teina to each other these roles and
> commitments are binding and fixed. (p. 21)

This appears quite straightforward. At an iwi level, however, the complexities are increased:

> At the iwi level my tuakana–teina relationships are complex and
> are varied in relation to all my great grandparents, siblings, great
> grandchildren. The important fact to remember is that the tuakana–
> teina kin relationships are not restricted to immediate whānau of the
> generation level referred to, but are applicable too at the extended
> whānau, the hapū, and the iwi levels … these kinship complexities
> are applicable to all social relationships. (p.22)

Clearly, the more extended the interactions, the more complex the relationships. In terms of facilitating research, this raises interesting issues. How do the inter-relationships and whakapapa between different hapū and iwi affect the tuakana or teina status of the individuals participating in research? How do researchers mediate these relationships?

Do they have enough knowledge to determine the status of the participants, or is that the role of other members of the tribe or family? These questions stem mainly from a methodological focus. For Māori researchers they will be answered in the construction and use of kaupapa Māori methods and frameworks. Other indigenous researchers have developed and used their own research tools to answer a similar set of questions.

Linda Tuhiwai Smith (1999) introduced the notion of an indigenous research agenda that in essence highlights important contextual issues to be mindful of when conducting indigenous research. It provides a framework for mediating and traversing the complexities that arise in such research, ultimately aimed at bringing about self-determination in indigenous communities:

> The indigenous research agenda is broad in its scope and ambitious
> in its intent … some things make this agenda very different from the
> research agenda of large scientific organizations or of various national
> science research programmes. There are other elements, however,
> which are similar to any research programme, which connects
> research to the 'good' of society. The elements that are different can
> be found in key words such as healing, decolonisation, spiritual,
> recovery. (Smith, 1999, p. 117)

Smith (1999) summarises these concepts in a visual representation utilising the metaphor of ocean tides, with the processes of healing, decolonisation, transformation and mobilisation being indicative of the four directions of our world: the northern, the eastern, the southern and the western.[1] The research processes we engage in need to be mindful of these four processes. That is, from design through to outcomes, and everything in between, an indigenous researcher needs to be aware of the context in which the research is placed, and, more importantly, that the context is ever changing, like the tides. This means considering how the research aids or impedes the processes of healing, decolonisation, transformation and mobilisation. In this way, the 'research agenda' can be viewed as both a framework to guide research and a framework for analysing any aspect of it.

Survival, recovery and development, and self-determination are "the conditions and states of being through which indigenous communities are moving" (Smith, 1999, p. 116). The indigenous researcher is not exempt from this, and neither are the communities in which we work and live. Acknowledging our own position and that of our research participants at all points in the research journey will help us to fit the research to the community. This is important because when research 'fits', it is more likely to result in meaningful outcomes that can be immediately applied and taken up, adding to the transformation and self-determination of people as the ultimate aim of the indigenous research agenda.

International indigenous research collaborations are increasing the opportunity to work alongside our 'relations' from other nations and to progress our shared goals for positive transformation among our peoples. As we move into international collaborations with other indigenous researchers, however, we need to negotiate new ways of working that enable each collaborator to stay true to the indigenous values of their own country without impinging on those of their fellow collaborators. Each international research collaboration would do this in its own unique way to meet the needs of both the people involved and the research outcomes. The processes that many Māori researchers have created and employed in the development of kaupapa Māori research provide rich material from which we can contribute to the construction of international indigenous research protocols. For example, many of the questions we ask ourselves in creating our own research guidelines could be used as the basis for the development of shared protocols with our indigenous research peers:

1. What are the critical factors for self-determining research processes and outcomes for indigenous peoples?

2. What are the historical and contemporary research contexts that need to be accounted for?

3. What are the specific diversities that must be honoured and protected?

4. What are the common elements of indigenously correct research?

It is important to note that shared protocols are not intended in any way to detract from the diversities between countries, or, indeed, the diversities within countries. The point is simply that these differences may highlight the distinct tribal and/or geographical nature of indigenous peoples, and, as such, should be reflected in the protocols.

In order to engage in the necessary in-depth information sharing between collaborators required to construct protocols, further questions might be posed, as follows.

Establishing a rationale and the indigenous research context

- Why are indigenous research protocols important to you and your research team?
- What difference will indigenous protocols make to you, to the research and to the research participants?
- Is it important to have shared indigenous protocols in an international indigenous collaboration? Why? Why not?

Protocols and principles for inclusion

- What are the top three things to be covered in the development of shared indigenous protocols for this project?
- What, if any, are the key underlying principles that should guide the shared indigenous protocols for this project?
- Is language translation of the shared indigenous protocols a necessary part of this development? Why? Why not?

Research outcomes

- Do you see indigenous self-determination as a key goal of indigenous research?
- In what way might indigenous protocols contribute to the self-determination of indigenous peoples?

Researchers would be encouraged to give responses that reflect the specific indigenous research processes and context/s of their lands, as opposed to attempting to edit responses in order to ease the 'sharing and unification' of protocols for an international project.

Conclusion

This chapter has explored issues of colonisation and neo-globalisation in the indigenous research context, alongside the role of the researcher as 'activist' in responding to the effects of these in our communities. Finally, an examination of kaupapa Māori theory and research as it applies in the international indigenous research agenda has been presented. In conclusion, it could be posited that although indigenous peoples have much to gain from international collaborations, we have potentially as much to be cautious about in this part of the research journey. Those cautions centre on protecting the unique identity of the indigenous collaborator/researcher in the context of international research opportunities that abound. Awareness and protection are integral to researchers achieving ultimate aim of self-determination for indigenous participants and communities.

References

Bargh, M. (2007). *Resistance: An indigenous response to neoliberalism.* Wellington: Huia Publishers.

Battiste, M., Bell, L., & Findlay, L. M. (2002). Decolonizing education in Canadian universities: An interdisciplinary, international, indigenous research project. *Canadian Journal of Native Education, 26*(2), 82–95.

Bishop, R. (2008). Te kotahitanga: Kaupapa Māori in mainstream classrooms. In K. Denzin, Y. Lincoln, & L. T. Smith (Eds.), *Handbook of critical and indigenous methodologies* (pp. 497–510). Los Angeles, CA: Sage.

Castleden, H., Garvin, T., & Huu-ay-aht First Nation. (2008). Modifying photovoice for community-based participatory indigenous research. *Social Science and Medicine, 66*(6), 1393–1405.

Durie, M. (1998). *Te mana, Te kawanatanga: The politics of Māori self-determination.* Auckland: Oxford University Press.

Kidman, J. (2007). *Engaging with Māori communities: An exploration of some tensions in the mediation of social sciences research.* Tihei Oreore Series. Auckland: Ngā Pae o te Maramatanga.

Lee, J. B. J. (2005). *Māori cultural regeneration: Pūrākau as pedagogy.* Paper presented at Centre for Research in Lifelong Learning International Conference, Stirling, Scotland.

Mead, A. (1997). *Cultural and intellectual property rights.* Auckland: International Research Institute for Māori and Indigenous Education.

Nepe, T. (1991). *E hao nei e tēnei reanga: Te toi huarewa tipuna.* Unpublished master's thesis, The University of Auckland.

Pihama, L. (1993). *Tungia te ururua, kia tupu whakaritorito te tupu o te harakeke: A critical analysis of parents as first teachers.* RUME Masters Theses Series Number 3. Auckland: The University of Auckland.

Pihama, L. (2001). *Tihei mauri ora: Honouring our voices: Mana wahine as kaupapa Māori theoretical framework.* Unpublished doctoral thesis, The University of Auckland.

Pihama, L., Lee, J., Taki, M. & Smith, K. (2004). A literature review on kaupapa Māori and Māori education pedagogy, for ITPNZ. Wellington.

Smith, C. W. (2002). *He pou herenga ki te nui: Māori knowledge and the university.* Unpublished doctoral thesis, The University of Auckland.

Smith, C. W. (2008). In *Tikanga Rangahau* (DVD). Auckland: Māori and Indigenous Analysis Ltd.

Smith, G. H. (1997). *The development of kaupapa Māori: Theory and praxis.* Unpublished doctoral thesis, The University of Auckland.

Smith, L. T. (1996). *Nga aho o te kakahu matauranga: The multiple layers of struggle by Māori in education.* Unpublished doctoral thesis, The University of Auckland.

Smith, L. T. (1999). *Decolonising methodologies: Research and indigenous peoples.* London & New York: Zed Books; Dunedin: University of Otago Press.

Smith, L. T. (2007). Neoliberalism and "endangered authenticities". In M. de la Cadena and O. Starn (Eds.), *Indigenous experience today* (pp. 333–352). Oxford, U.K.: Berg.

Theory. (2004). *In Microsoft Encarta.* Redmond, WA: Microsoft Corporation.

Walker, P. O. (2003). Colonising research: Academia's structural violence towards indigenous peoples. *Social Alternatives, 22*(3), 37–40.

Walters, K. (2006). Indigenous perspectives in survey research: Conceptualising and measuring historical trauma, microaggressions, and colonial trauma response. In J. Te Rito (Ed.), *Matauranga taketake: Traditional knowledge: Indigenous indicators of well-being: Perspectives, practices, solutions* (pp. 27–44). Auckland: Ngā Pae o te Maramatanga.

Witt, N. (2007). What if indigenous knowledge contradicts accepted scientific findings?: The hidden agenda: Respect, caring and passion towards aboriginal research in the context of applying western academic rules. *Educational Research and Review, 2*(3), 225–235.

Endnotes

1 See Smith, 1999, p. 117, "An Indigenous Research Agenda".

Chapter 10 Ngā Whiringa Muka: Decolonising research in Whanganui Iwi

Āneta Hinemihi Rāwiri

Introduction

Research has been, and largely remains, an inherently colonising activity. Colonisation attempts to change indigenous peoples into something other than who we are. When we read research by others about us, we often don't even recognise ourselves in the descriptions of our lives. Our lives are often misunderstood and distorted; or worse, reconstructed in ways that are fundamentally dehumanising and disenabling.

In contrast, decolonising research affirms our ancestral belonging to kin and land and respectful relationships between peoples. It creates spaces for us to define who we are and what is important to us. I began as a researcher within my iwi, Whanganui Iwi. It was there that I was supported to think critically and embrace decolonising research practice.

The project Ngā Whiringa Muka is an example of decolonising research practice. Led by Whanganui Iwi, it is often described as an investigation into adult literacy within the iwi. More correctly, it was a study that explored what wellbeing and decolonisation mean for Whanganui Iwi, and how adult literacy can support and advance these aspirations.

In this chapter I will describe the decolonising methodologies applied in the project, along with the research findings. Firmly grounded in indigenous values and ways of life, decolonising research supports a fundamental aspiration of indigenous peoples: to live our ancestral heritage and pass it on to future generations in its full richness and vitality. This approach enables us to fully articulate our realities and needs, and to define truly decolonising pathways.

Ngā Whiringa Muka research project

Indigenous peoples acknowledge that English language literacy is critical for individual and community wellbeing in today's world. However, examining the nature and extent of the distinctive adult literacy issues facing indigenous peoples, from an indigenous standpoint, has received scant research attention. Whanganui Iwi instigated Ngā Whiringa Muka within a wider collaborative adult literacy research programme to meet this need.

Orthodox adult literacy research employs a deficit approach, where low literacy engagement is explained in terms of addressing inadequacies within indigenous communities. This approach aims to 'fix' our individual and collective failure to participate in narrowly defined literacy outcomes that, in fact, undermine indigenous wellbeing (Antone, 2003; Yates, 1996). Ngā Whiringa Muka was developed to address this by facilitating an approach firmly grounded in the distinctive values and aspirations of Whanganui Iwi. One of our kuia (senior female elders), Te Turi Julie Ranginui, named the study. Meaning 'the woven threads', Ngā Whiringa Muka expresses the inseparability between the Whanganui River and its descendants. It also describes learning as a lifelong process of weaving together many threads of knowledge and understandings to provide meaning, purpose and wisdom for river descendants.

Research methodologies

Methodology is the research theory or approach applied within a study. It is important because it determines research questions, method and analysis. Decolonising methodologies aim to facilitate respectful, meaningful and effective research outcomes for indigenous peoples. The following indigenous research principles were adopted to guide the applied methodologies within Ngā Whiringa Muka.

- *Elders mentor and guide the research project*

  Elders are highly respected within indigenous peoples (Cajete, 2000). They are often very unassuming, and outside people may have difficulty recognising or understanding the vital leadership role they play. Elders are both men and women, and their respective roles are held in equal regard. They are valued for the integrity and deep insights they bring to the research process (Smith, 1999).

- *Ancestral ways of knowing and understandings are brought from the margins into the centre*

  Respecting the rich interconnections between the physical and spiritual—as well as the past, present and future—is very important to indigenous peoples. One way to achieve this is by observing ancestral protocols. Not simply traditions from a time past, they express ancestral values that remain fundamental to the wellbeing of present-day and future generations (Smith, 1999; Cajete, 1994).

- *Ancestral ways of knowing and understandings are respected as not being open knowledge*

  Ancestral knowledge is treated with great respect by indigenous peoples. It has its own mouri (life force) and is the source of our humanity and dignity. It is not to be misinterpreted, or misappropriated from the indigenous people to whom it belongs for personal gain or prestige.

  This principle challenges the deeply held Western belief that researchers have an inherent right to ancestral knowledge in the pursuit of finding the 'truth' (Smith, 1999). There is no such automatic right. Authority remains with indigenous peoples over how our ancestral knowledge is shared, represented and published.

- *Interconnection and reconnection are emphasised*

  Within the research process, indigenous peoples are asked to express their experiences of living within a dominant Western neo-colonial society. With this come stories of dispossession, racism and cultural denigration. It is equally important to seek out solutions to rise above these realities. This approach openly acknowledges and integrates a process of healing, recovery and decolonisation (Smith, 1999).

- *Research theory and method are simplified and demystified (particularly language), and shared openly and generously*

Robust information-sharing and decision-making processes make space for our aspirations to be built into the research study in systematic and proactive ways. To indigenous peoples, this provides for a respectful, ethical approach. This principle seeks to reverse past negative experiences of research as "information mining" (Smith, 1999).

- *The project facilitates proactive processes of change that seek to reshape non-indigenous research understandings rather than fit indigenous peoples into a Western paradigm*

Within this principle, research projects take a critical approach, challenging the ideologies and assumptions underlying orthodox Western approaches (Bishop, 1994). This approach is difficult, firstly, because ethical and professional requirements exclusively reaffirm the validity of Western ideologies. They remain the dominant framework within which academic institutions and research funding agencies operate. Secondly, these ideologies are widely held as taken-for-granted, common-sense beliefs, reinforced by dominant Western social, economic and legal institutions (Deloria, 1995).

In applying this principle, indigenous peoples define the questions that are important to them, and then facilitate a systematic, respectful way to work through these questions to find the answers (Smith, 1999). We can give a voice to the things that matter to us, where others may dismiss their importance or validity. More importantly, we can explore and find solutions to the many real-life and pressing issues we face today—in real, meaningful and effective ways.

Research method

Ethics

Whanganui Iwi gave ethical approval for the study following an intensive 2-month process. Iwi representatives required us to seek feedback from elders and iwi members by way of project presentations at marae, other venues and sometimes in homes. We were also required to seek ongoing feedback throughout the study. The key terms of approval were that:

- the integrity of Whanganui Iwi would be maintained within the project
- the study would provide ongoing practical, positive and measurable outcomes for Whanganui Iwi beyond the end of the project.

The research team consisted of an iwi researcher (me) and two senior iwi researchers, who supervised the project. A non-iwi social practice literacy researcher became a senior adviser to the study. Iwi elders and representatives facilitated iwi discussions and the field work; and tikanga were observed throughout. I was often asked to reciprocate this assistance by providing advice or support to other iwi projects. We published two project reports, which were distributed widely, free to iwi members. The Massey University Human Ethics Committee also approved the study, as required by our research funding agency.[1]

Research method

A literature review found that indigenous peoples have distinctive English-language literacy experiences, impacts and understandings. The following broad questions were therefore developed for exploration in the field-work phase of the study:

- Is there a relationship between Whanganui Iwi's history of English-language literacy learning and current literacy practice within the iwi?
- What relationship do iwi members see between English-language literacy and individual wellbeing?
- What relationship do iwi members see between English-language literacy and iwi wellbeing?

Interview and focus group questions were developed to investigate these key research questions. Qualitative data were gathered from in-depth semi-structured interviews with 14 iwi members; of these, six were current or past adult literacy students. Despite a small sample size, the in-depth nature of the interviews, and the diversity in age, gender and hapū membership, provided in-depth narrative data. Each interview represents an individual case study of English-language literacy impacts. Data were also gathered from semi-structured discussions during a one-day focus group for iwi adult literacy tutors.

We analysed the data by applying decolonising methodologies and social practice theories. We also applied tikanga to enhance data gathering and analysis, and research reliability and validity. Where research findings resonate with the indigenous people whose experiences are being investigated, as this study has, this is a sign of high reliability and validity.

Findings

Wellbeing, tikanga and decolonisation

In the research study we asked river descendants what wellbeing means to them. They were adamant that continuing to live ancestral ways of life—known as tikanga—in today's world is critical to wellbeing. Tikanga are firmly grounded in the fundamental life principles of mouri, tapu (sanctity of life) and mana (inherent dignity and authority). These core principles maintain the natural cycles of all life.

All life is created via the natural cycles of life that are encoded within the whakapapa of creation, known as te orokohanganga o te ao. This whakapapa is looked after carefully by selected caretakers and never disclosed outside the iwi. When we live tikanga, we live according to this whakapapa and come to understand its depth and meaning.

Tikanga connects our individual wellbeing to a wider collective wellbeing of people and all things within the natural world. This collective wellbeing also extends to the past, present and future. Whakapapa expresses an interdependent, interconnected web of life, which is reaffirmed by tikanga. When we live according to tikanga, we gradually gain a deep understanding of life. Our old people describe this as a progression from knowing, to understanding, to wisdom.

River descendants of all ages spoke about a school curriculum which teaches that animate things are alive and inanimate things are not alive, whereas they learned from our old people that everything is alive and has its own mouri, especially water and land. The metaphysical and spiritual aspects of life are intrinsic to physical wellbeing, and are a natural part of everyday life.

They learned that being told about the whakapapa of the cycles of life is less important than living with them as our old people did, by living according to tikanga. Our old people shared a deep respect and reverence for the sanctity of life. They approached everything with great care, respect and good humour. They were, and are, strong, humble, loving people.

At the heart of wellbeing is a lived knowing that the natural cycles of te orokohanganga o te ao—the creation of life—are ongoing. With every new breath, with every new growth, with every new day, life is being created and recreated within and around us. In this way, tikanga affirm and sustain life, and connect us to a deeper wisdom and fulfilment.

Continuing to live according to tikanga is an immensely difficult challenge in today's world. We now live within a dominant Western society whose neo-colonial, neo-liberal ways of life are neither life affirming nor life sustaining. They do not respect the sanctity of life. They disconnect us from who we are, and the mouri within and around us. Neo-colonialism tries to change us into something other than who we truly are. It tries to make us less than who we are. All river descendants were adamant that wellbeing is about living a fully connected life, and it should remain this way into future generations. This is critical to creating decolonising pathways for present and future generations.

English-language literacy

We also asked river descendants what meaning English-language literacy holds for them. Elders told us that for them it means deceit and duplicity. They talked about literacy as a tool used to invade and dispossess us of our ancestral homelands. It was used to desecrate our revered sacred places and break down cherished ways of life. They spoke of the humiliation and deep hurt suffered from being hit at school by teachers for speaking their mother tongue.

Those in the following generations who are not able to speak te reo (our ancestral language) as a result of education policy told us of the shame they carry because of that. They spoke about how enriched their lives would have been had they grown up with te reo as their first language. They also spoke about the many difficulties they face in protecting and handing down our language and culture to children, grandchildren and future generations.

Experiences of racism in school continue to be widely experienced by younger generations. Because of this, most iwi members strongly associate English-language literacy with negative experiences of cultural denigration, assimilation and exclusion. Even where river descendants have had positive school experiences, they regard literacy as being mutually exclusive to the tikanga that provide the basis for living a meaningful and fulfilling life.

When talking about why tikanga are important, river descendants shared deeply meaningful things. They spoke about being a people woven together by whakapapa. There is a strong sense of belonging within river communities, which extends to past, present and future generations, and to our ancestral river and homelands. Moreover, ancestral heritage is understood not only to be a precious source of belonging and identity, but also a people and land management system; that is, a way to live one's life based on respectful relationships. The life principles that underlie these relationships are held in sacred regard by river descendants. They spoke about how it would be deeply wrong to lose these. The sense of loss already felt in the many difficulties we face to maintain tikanga today is profound indeed.

A defining historical experience of Whanganui Iwi is of literacy as a tool of colonialism and dispossession. The belief remains that English-language literacy essentially facilitates an adoption of outside individualistic, neo-colonial behaviours at the expense of ancestral relationships to kin and land. Because of this, there is a general inter-generational resistance to literacy participation within the iwi.

There is an acceptance that literacy in English is a necessity in today's dominant Western society, particularly to interact with outside people and gain employment. However, the prevailing view is that English-language literacy is mutually exclusive to the ancestral values that provide the basis for living a meaningful and fulfilling life. It should not detract from these fundamental iwi ways of life as it has in the past, and mostly continues to do so today.

Iwi members were adamant that the insights gained from observing tikanga—insights into the sanctity of life, and the mouri in all things—are critical to the wellbeing of people and the natural world, and this should never change. They spoke about ancestral literacies and literacy practices. These are ancestral practices through which river descendants understand our world and come to respect who we are, and our relationships to each other, to other peoples and to the natural world.

Yet we also found that iwi members willingly engage in English-language literacy practice that serves as a practical memory aid for carrying out valued iwi activities. This suggests that the meaning of English-language literacy directly relates to purpose, and if the purpose changes then so too does its meaning. When reading and writing activity is embedded in ancestral literacies and activities, it becomes personally meaningful. River descendants are then motivated to read and write, and to improve their literacy skills.

The findings reveal that it is not improved English-language literacy skills *per se* that support literacy participation, but rather the social meanings attached to them. Changing that meaning will change literacy practice. When iwi ways of life are removed from literacy practice, so, too, are the conditions needed for effective learning and participation. Equally, when English-language literacy is embedded in iwi values and ways of life, it becomes meaningful and motivates iwi members to use and improve their literacy skills. An orthodox Western approach to literacy will not facilitate this. At its best, literacy will continue to be overlooked as lacking relevance; at its worst, it will be actively resisted as being inherently assimilationist.

Discussion

Ngā Whiringa Muka provides an opportunity to understand English-language literacy from an indigenous standpoint. The findings reveal how river descendants' literacy experiences interact with the powerful impacts of a dominant Western, neo-colonial, neo-liberal society.

English-language literacy holds very little positive meaning and experience within Whanganui Iwi. Instead, it has played a significant role in the breakdown of rich ancestral ways of life. This has created a fundamental barrier to literacy participation. Simply providing more orthodox, inherently assimilationist programmes that treat literacy as decontextualised generic skills will not change this. An orthodox Western approach also attributes low literacy skills to a lack of cognitive ability. This, too, is neither useful nor applicable.

The findings reveal how different approaches to literacy shape indigenous peoples, and how context provides incentives or disincentives for literacy participation. English-language literacy meanings are not fixed and constant, and effective participation will occur only when literacy fits the meaning and purpose of community. Being literate is not simply about performing functional tasks: more fundamentally, it is about participating as indigenous peoples according to our ancestral literacies and values, and is embedded in sociopolitical relationships and experiences.

Indigenous peoples have distinctive English-language literacy experiences and realities (Kral & Falk, 2004; National Aboriginal Design Committee, 2002; Soler, 2000). For us, literacy is about exclusion and inclusion, resistance and participation, neo-colonialism and decolonisation. How these multiple meanings are addressed will determine the success or failure of raising low literacy participation and outcomes. The implications of these findings are not new. They resonate with a body of academic work and research that has consistently maintained that defining literacy is an inherently social and political act, determining what is valid and valued for today's society (Barton & Hamilton, 2000; Freire, 1972; Freire & Macedo, 1987; Hohepa & Jenkins, 1996; Jackson, 1992; Nakata, 2002; Street, 1984).

Orthodox Western notions of literacy are firmly grounded in eurocentric assumptions that have described indigenous ways of being in the world as preliterate, uncivilised and primitive. Notions of cultural superiority and cultural inferiority are strong recurring themes within this discourse, and have entrenched Western social, political and economic domination (Jackson, 1992; Roburn, 1994). Arguably, the rhetoric of this discourse largely persists today within a wider agenda of neo-colonial, neo-liberal globalisation. It reaffirms an orthodox Western view of what literacy should be, rather than supporting indigenous and other communities to self-determine our literacy needs (Darville, 1999; Hamilton & Barton, 2000).

Indigenous and non-indigenous scholars have promoted a reconceptualisation of adult literacy to embed it within a fundamental aspiration of indigenous peoples to validate cherished ancestral ways of life. Despite being now well established, it has yet to be meaningfully integrated into national and international adult literacy research, policy and strategy. This demonstrates how entrenched and pervasive Western orthodox ways of thinking are, and how difficult change is.

The Māori Adult Literacy Working Party encapsulated this discussion within the following definition of literacy: "Literacy is a lifelong journey of building the capacity to read and shape Māori, and other worlds" (Māori Adult Literacy Working Party, 2001, p. 13). Over the last two decades adult literacy has become framed within a narrowly defined human rights discourse. This approach now needs to be reconceptualised to embrace a discourse of indigeneity as a human right. The focus will then shift away from the limited notion of adult literacy as an individual human right, to a wider one where it becomes a collective human right for indigenous peoples to self-determine how to best provide for our distinctive adult literacy needs and aspirations.

The UN Declaration of the Rights of Indigenous Peoples promotes this kind of collective human rights framework and approach. Establishing new, decolonising adult literacy pathways will bring about the shift envisaged by the declaration. This will transform international and national literacy strategy and policy to affirm all humanity—not just some.

Conclusion

Ngā Whiringa Muka is an example of decolonising research.[2] It embeds adult literacy within a deep respect for the elders and descendants of the Whanganui River, and the spiritual, cultural, historical and natural values of our ancestral river and homelands.

The study found that, for Whanganui Iwi, adult literacy is about participation on our own terms in today's world. This is based on a desire to continue to manage our own affairs according to ancestral ways of life, as we have done for many centuries. It is about elevating and validating our distinctive aspirations and values. It is emancipatory and self-determining in its thrust, and is human rights-based. It is about cultural continuity and dynamism, and transforming outside institutions that have an impact on our lives.

The irony and inherent difficulties of seeking to change institutions that reinforce deeply entrenched monocultural beliefs are not lost on indigenous peoples. They influence the level of autonomy—or, conversely, the level of subjugation—within which we operate. As Martin Nakata has argued, for indigenous peoples English language and culture literacy is about improving our ability to shape, influence and reshape outside knowledges that seek to position us within a world view that is not our own (Nakata, 2000). He argues that this is as critically important for our survival as understanding and practising ancestral knowledge pathways.

Decolonising research firmly challenges the validity and reliability of orthodox Western approaches. By being grounded within indigenous values and ways of life, its focus is indigenous lives and communities as places where we live our ancestral heritage and pass it on to future generations. Arguably, this can be considered to be the only authentic basis on which to facilitate respectful, meaningful and effective research outcomes for indigenous peoples.

References

Antone, E. (2003). Aboriginal peoples: Literacy and learning. *Literacies: Researching practice, practising research, 1*, 9-12.

Barton, D., & Hamilton, M. (2000). *Situated literacies: Reading and writing in context*. London, UK: Routledge.

Bishop, R. (1994). Initiating empowering research? *New Zealand Journal of Educational Studies, 29*(1), 175-188.

Cajete, G. A. (1994). *Look to the mountain: An ecology of indigenous education*. Durango, CO: Kivaki Press.

Cajete, G. A. (2000). *Native science: Natural laws of interdependence*. Santa Fe, NM: Clear Light Publishers.

Darville, R. (1999). Knowledges of adult literacy: Surveying for competitiveness. *International Journal of Educational Development, 19*, 273–285.

Deloria, V. (1995). *Red earth, white lies: Native Americans and the myth of scientific fact*. New York, NY: Scribner.

Freire, P. (1972). *Pedagogy of the oppressed*. Harmondsworth, UK: Penguin Books.

Freire, P., & Macedo, D. (1987). *Literacy: Reading the word and the world*. London, UK: Routledge & Kegan Paul.

Hamilton, M. E., & Barton, D. P. (2000). The International Adult Literacy Survey (IALS): What does it really measure? *International Review of Education, 46*(1–2), 377–389.

Hohepa, M. K., & Jenkins, K. E. H. (1996). *Te ao tuhi: Māori literacy: A consequence of racism?* Joint paper presented to the Conference on Racism, Indigenous Peoples, Ethnicity and Gender in Australia, New Zealand, Canada. *Ngā Kete Kōrero: Journal of Adult Reading and Learning, 4,* 5–11.

Jackson, M. (1992). The Treaty and the word: The colonization of Māori philosophy. In G. Oddie & R. W. Perrett (Eds.), *Justice, ethics, and New Zealand society.* Auckland: Oxford University Press.

Kral, I., Falk, I. (2004). *What is all that learning for?: Indigenous adult English literacy practices training, community capacity and health.* Adelaide, SA: NCVER.

Nakata, M. (2000). Cultural diversity and English language teaching. In The New London Group (Eds.), *Multiliteracies: Literacy learning and the design of social futures.* New York, NY: Routledge.

Nakata, M. (2002). *Some thoughts on literacy issues in indigenous contexts.* Melbourne, VIC: Language Australia.

National Aboriginal Design Committee. (2002). *National paper on Aboriginal literacy.* Toronto, ON: Author.

Māori Adult Literacy Working Party. (2001). *Te kāwai ora: Reading the world, reading the word, being the world: Report of the Māori Adult Literacy Working Party.* Wellington: Te Puni Kōkiri.

Roburn, S. (1994). Literacy and the underdevelopment of knowledge. *Mediatribe: Concordia University's Undergraduate Journal of Communication Studies, 4*(1). Retrieved from http://cug.concordia.ca/mtribe/mtribe94/ native_knowledge.html

Smith, L. T. (1999). *Decolonizing methodologies: Research and indigenous peoples.* Dunedin: University of Otago Press.

Soler, J. (2000a). Literacy for the cultured individual 1900–1930. In J. Soler & J. Smith (Eds.), *Literacy in New Zealand: Practices, politics and policy since 1900.* Auckland: Longman.

Soler, J. (2000b). Māori literacy and curriculum politics: 1920–1960. In J. Soler & J. Smith (Eds.), *Literacy in New Zealand: Practices, politics and policy since 1900.* Auckland: Longman.

Street, B. (1984). *Literacy in theory and practice.* Cambridge, UK: Cambridge University Press.

Yates, B. (1996). Striving for tino rangatiratanga. In J. Benseman, B. Findsen, & M. Scott (Eds.), *The fourth sector: Adult and community education in Aotearoa/New Zealand.* Palmerston North: Dunmore Press.

Endnotes

1 This study was funded by the Foundation for Research, Science and Technology under grant MAUX0308 Literacy and Employment.

2 The report of this study was published as: Rāwiri, A.H. (2008). *Embedding literacy in a sense of community: Literacy and employment within Whanganui Iwi*. Whanganui: Te Puna Mātauranga o Whanganui–Whanganui Iwi Education Authority, on behalf of Whanganui Iwi.

PART 3: MĀORI IN PRACTICE

Māori in Practice talks back to colonisation. This part brings into the discussion the key theme of kaupapa Māori in action and makes visible diverse Māori practices and initiatives that have emerged from protest and struggle to honour ancestral practices amid the complexity of contemporary times.

Chapter 11 Ūkaipō: Decolonisation and Māori maternities

Naomi Simmonds and Kirsten Gabel

Ūkaipō:

1. Te wahine nāna i puta ai tētahi tamaiti ki te ao, nāna rānei ia i whakatipu (whaea).

2. Te wāhi nō reira mai te tangata, kei reira anō ētahi mea e arohaina ana e ia (kāinga).

(He Pātaka Kupu, 2008, p. 1030)

Ūkaipō is made up of three separate words: Ū—breast; kai—food or to feed; and pō—night or darkness. The term, therefore, has a literal interpretation of 'night-feeding breast'. As the meaning above, from He Pātaka Kupu, suggests, ūkaipō is much more than this. Firstly, ūkaipō is a term for mother, acknowledging her as the person who provides the 'night-feeding breast' and thus life and sustenance to a child. Not simply a reference to one's biological mother, however, the concept of ūkaipō includes those who are involved in raising children, whether biologically related or not. Secondly, it is a term that denotes a place or space to which a person feels a life-long physical and spiritual connection. Ūkaipō, we argue, is one of many concepts that serve to demonstrate the sanctity of the maternal body, the power and prestige accorded to mothers and mothering, and the empowering and collective approach to raising children within te ao Māori.

This chapter is based on our respective doctoral research, which examines Māori maternities—the ideologies, values, embodied practices and lived experiences of maternity, maternal bodies and maternal work (such as carrying, growing, birthing and nurturing a young child/children)—for Māori women and their whānau. It is our contention that reconceptualising maternities through a mana wāhine and kaupapa Māori lens serves to decolonise hegemonic discourses that continue to 'other' Māori maternal knowledges, bodies and the spaces (discursive, physical and symbolic) of pregnancy, birth and mothering. Further, we believe that the reclamation and revitalisation of uniquely Māori, iwi, hapū and whānau maternity knowledges and practices have the potential to transform and empower maternity experiences for women and whānau (see Gabel, 2013; Simmonds, 2014).

We write this chapter not only as academics but also as Māori mothers. In fact, it is our own respective pūrākau that have drawn us together in this work. Like many others, becoming mothers prompted us to deeply consider our own identities as Māori women and what it means to be a Māori mother in te ao hurihuri. We had to consider our own politics of decolonisation and self-determination in a very personal way. We had to consider how we make choices for our children so that the issues and struggles that consume us today will not consume the energies of our daughters and sons and generations to come. We had to consider and reconsider what it means to be hapū, give birth and mother as Māori. Ultimately, we had to consider the question: How do we provide a "decolonised pathway" (Simpson, 2006, p. 28) into and through this world for our children? It is this question that is at the heart of our journeys, our respective research and this chapter.

In what follows, we use the concept of ūkaipō to exemplify the possibilities of reclaiming Māori maternities in contemporary Aotearoa. First, we discuss the importance of pūrākau and mātauranga mana wāhine (Māori women's knowledges) in the maternity experiences of wāhine and whānau. We argue that there is a rich body of knowledges, stories, concepts, values and practices within our whakapapa that can empower women's maternity experiences. Second, we demonstrate how colonialism has caused significant disruption to the ways in which we come to know and perform maternities in Aotearoa New Zealand (and indeed for numerous other indigenous communities). Finally, we seek to demonstrate the potential within concepts such as ūkaipō to decolonise maternities and transform the individual and collective experiences of pregnancy, birth and mothering for women, whānau, hapū, iwi and Māori.

Ngā pūrākau mana wāhine

> Naomi: From the moment I found out we would be welcoming a new taonga into our whānau, my world, as I knew it, changed. Everything I was so sure of suddenly became uncertain. Everything that I had one day hoped to learn became all the more pressing. My longing to find my place in the world suddenly became a deep-seated need to weave a place for you. (Simmonds, 2014, p. 27)

> Kirsten: The clinical and medicalised nature of my first birthing experience was a significant catalyst for me to seek out some of these stories and knowledges. Much strength can be drawn from learning and re-learning the stories of our tūpuna and our atua wāhine.
> (Gabel, 2013, p. 161)

Growing, carrying, birthing and nurturing a child/children are profound and life-changing experiences. Numerous indigenous and feminist authors have reflected on their own experiences of pregnancy, birth and mothering, as we do above, and have discussed the transformations (physical, social and spiritual) that can occur as part of the maternal journey. For example, Kim Anderson, First Nations scholar, writes "as a new mother in the mid-1990s, I was overcome with a desire to learn about indigenous customs related to pregnancy, childbirth, infant care, and ceremonies that honour children's life passages" (Anderson, 2000, p. 6).

We argue that it is to the stories of our atua wāhine, our cosmological stories and the stories of our own whānau, hapū and iwi that we can look to find concepts, knowledges, practices and ways of being that serve to decolonise maternities in contemporary Aotearoa. Our ancestral stories speak strongly to the positioning and sanctity of the maternal in Māori society (Mikaere, 2003; Murphy, 2011; Smith, 2012; Yates-Smith 1998). These stories provide a rich, much-needed and empowering body of knowledge that can transform how the maternal body, maternal 'work' and maternities more generally are understood.

For example, if we are to look at the whakapapa of maternities from a mana wāhine perspective, there are multiple pūrākau that speak to the sanctity and power of the maternal body. The birth story of Papatūānuku, from Te Kore through Te Pō and into Te Ao Mārama (Mikaere, 2003); the pains similar to birth felt by Papa at the restlessness of her children as they lay in darkness between her and Ranginui; the creation of Hine-ahu-one from the clay found at Kurawaka (Yates-Smith 1998); the stories of Hine-nui-te-pō, who nurtures those who have passed away (Murphy, 2011); the karakia used to assist Hine-te-iwaiwa during the birth of her son (Yates-Smith 1998); all of these stories hold profound knowledges, messages and practices that can serve us in our maternity experiences today (Mikaere, 2003; Smith, 2012). Aroha Yates-Smith (1998, p. 271) comments that

> modern Māori women have inherited mana wāhine from ancient
> times … the fundamental role of women remains as creator and
> mother, thus fulfilling generative function previously carried out by
> Papa, Hineteiwaiwa, Hinekorako and many other Atua Wāhine.

The narratives within our whakapapa pertaining to maternities are replete with legacies about resilience and the capacity for resistance, the unique place of women, the tapu of women's bodies and the power of female sexuality, the complementary roles of men and women in maternities, and the central role of tamariki within communities (Mikaere, 2003; Murphy, 2011; Smith, 2012). Reclaiming and revisiting these narratives has incredible potential to decolonise maternities, where wāhine and whānau can find powerful concepts, values and practices that can enable them to make sense of their current realities and project them with confidence into the future. As Ani Mikaere (2003, p. 319) points out, "the logic of whakapapa tells us that in the final analysis, we are our atua and they are us." This on its own can radically transform the way in which maternities are understood and practised by women and whānau, as well as those who are charged with the responsibility to care for maternal bodies.

Our traditional pūrākau are not simply historical accounts; rather, they can be statements about our current realities. Further, our understandings of these stories are likely to be significantly different to what they were when we were children, and they can also change considerably when we become mothers ourselves. Therefore, we should not be afraid to reread our stories and histories as we move through our journeys as Māori women and as we become Māori mothers. We should not be afraid to grow into these stories in order to grow into our mana as wāhine.

Colonising te ūkaipō

Colonisation has always been about much more than simply the theft of land, the decimation of an indigenous population by introduced disease and the seizure of political power. It has always been about recreating the colonised in the image of the coloniser. Our colonisers regarded our collectivism as beastly communism, our language as inferior and our spiritual beliefs as heathen (Mikaere, 2011, p. 206).

Colonialism has undoubtedly transformed Māori maternities. There have been, and will likely continue to be, attempts to fragment our whakapapa as Māori women and to distort our pūrākau. Nearly all of the cosmological accounts have been subject to colonial retellings that marginalise the role of wāhine and distort the power and tapu of the maternal body (Mikaere, 2003). Further, the reconstruction of Māori maternities into what was perceived to be an ideal European model of pregnancy, birth and mothering began at the earliest point of European contact. The state failed to recognise existing systems of maternity already in place, and working well, within Māori society and subsequently launched a comprehensive attack on Māori maternities, the effects of which are still being felt by women and their whānau today.

Colonial and patriarchal interventions infiltrated almost all aspects of Māori maternities, resulting in the marginalisation of the maternal figure, the medicalisation and institutionalisation of the maternal body, and control over the rearing of our children being vested in patriarchal frameworks of Western education. For example, the policies of medicalisation and the disenfranchisement of tohunga and tāpuhi in the early 20th century, have seen pregnancy and childbirth, for most Māori women, relocated from home to hospitals (Simmonds, 2014). Maternal knowledges and practices have been moved away from the auspices of whānau, tohunga and tāpuhi to now be considered the domain of 'experts' trained within Western institutions. As Christine Kenney argues (2009, p. 63):

> if midwifery in New Zealand is largely a European dominated middle class profession then it is extremely unlikely that the profession will comprehend the nuances of mātauranga Māori and this appears to be reflected in the governance language of the profession.

Further, the systematic destruction of the collectivism of Māori society through land theft, the Native Land Court, policies of urbanisation and the imposition of colonial and patriarchal understandings of family has served to isolate Māori women in their maternity experiences. As Linda Smith (2012, p. 151) notes,

> family organisation, child-rearing, political and spiritual life, work and social activities were all disordered by a colonial system which positioned its own women as the property of men with roles that were primarily domestic.

This is a stark contrast to what our stories tell us about the diverse and powerful roles of women in Māori communities.

The marginalisation of te reo Māori, the misrepresentation of mātauranga and the attempts to 'sanitise' Māori spiritual knowledges and practices have all served to 'redefine' the maternal body and maternities within a narrow colonial and patriarchal framework. Legislation, in various ways, affirmed and supported these attempts to individualise and institutionalise maternities for Māori women and whānau. The effects of this are intergenerationally felt and embodied. As one woman in Naomi's research highlighted:

> I wish it was general knowledge that was passed down through the generations but somewhere along the way Western medical practice dominated and they [Māori maternal knowledges] got lost. When my Dad was growing up te reo wasn't respected, not at school or in society, so he lost his connection to the language, and in a way to his culture, his birth right and so he passed on as much as he could but much was lost. (cited in Simmonds, 2014, p. 119)

It should be remembered that we cannot talk about colonisation as something that has occurred in the past. Throughout the last century the state has continued to scrutinise, regulate and intervene in the realm of Māori maternities, from managing and surveying Māori birthing bodies, to prescribing and scrutinising how we raise our children. Current government policies and legislation continue to reinforce the nuclear family structure and to assert the state's expert authority over all aspects of our maternal journeys (Gabel, 2013).

Colonisation has constructed, and maintains, a conflicted space for Māori women and whānau within maternities. While our Pākehā counterparts navigate the challenges of motherhood within a society that is structurally favoured for their own cultural constructs, Māori mothers are caught in the contradictions between the Western and Māori maternal realms. The inherent need of Māori whānau to follow the maternal traditions of our tūpuna, while attempting to do so within a society that has consistently moved to undermine those traditions, has meant that Māori mothers are engaged in a perpetual process of survival, resistance and reclamation. As Kirsten (Gabel, 2013, p. 153) points out in her research:

> Our resistance to colonising entities and practices is not merely a
> product of contemporary enlightenment or conscientisation, but
> rather an unfailing and constant mode of action, characterised by our
> assertions of tino rangatiratanga, our absolute authority, autonomy and
> self-determination.

This was also understood by women in Naomi's research. Speaking of her experience during labour and childbirth in hospital, one wahine pointed out:

> They [the hospital] have specific protocols that they have to follow. That
> in many ways was like the sort of imposition of a system on me. I guess
> in a way similar to the way that the legal system has been imposed on
> whenua Māori and all these other systems imposed on Māori people. So
> my ability to resist that and to cut through that in some ways was because
> I was Māori and I share in an experience of having those things imposed
> upon you. (cited in Simmonds, 2014, p. 160)

Resistance is a reality for many Māori mothers. Maternities in Aotearoa represent a colonised space within which we find ourselves under threat of scrutiny, marginalisation and intrusion. There is a powerful body of literature by scholars such as Ani Mikaere, Ngahuia Murphy, Leonie Pihama, Linda Smith, Takirirangi Smith and Aroha Yates-Smith (to name just a few) that demonstrates the decolonising and transformative potential of our ancestral knowledges and specifically mātauranga mana wāhine. Other indigenous women around the world are actively engaging in the decolonisation of maternities (Anderson, 2000; Lavell-Harvard & Corbiere-Lavell, 2006; Simpson 2006). There are important connections to be made to wider indigenous maternities; for example, Oneida scholar Lina Sunseri (2008, p. 23) highlights that "Oneida women see mothering as a political act, as a way to participate in the sustainability of the self and the community." Ūkaipō is one such concept in the context of Aotearoa that can serve to decolonise and transform maternities for wāhine and for whānau.

He ūkaipō—repositioning the maternal

Ūkaipō is one of many concepts that can be found embedded and embodied in our stories, waiata, language and landscapes. It is thanks to the foresight of our tūpuna that we are able today, despite the fervent efforts of the colonial project, to find meaning and strength within concepts such as ūkaipō. Literally referring to 'the night-feeding breast', ūkaipō is reflective of a person's enduring and perpetual connection with the maternal (in both the physical and the spiritual sense). It is said that this concept was born from the words given to Tāne advising him to return to his mother: "kei wareware i a tātou te ūkaipō—lest we forget the mother who nurtured us at her breast" (Gabel, 2013).

The significance of ūkaipō to Māori maternities is multiple. There are the obvious references to breastfeeding, which serves as a powerful precedent set by Papatūānuku (Glover & Cunningham, 2011; Murphy, 2011). Ūkaipō also serves as a reminder of the significance and prestige that was accorded to maternities and mothering. Our traditional cosmologies reinforce the importance of ūkaipō, and the prominence of the maternal figure in the creation of the world, in the creation of humankind and in the finality of death: all involve the reiteration of the power of the maternal body and the recurring theme of returning to the night-feeding breast (Mikaere, 2003). The role of women as ūkaipō, as mothers and nurturers, contemporarily is, therefore

> assimilated and knitted to Papatūānuku … to Hine-hau-one … and Hinetitama … what is reciprocally significant too is that at the end of life, that is at death, the body of flesh and bone is returned back to Papatūānuku. (Nepe, 1991, p. 35)

There are a number of other concepts in te ao Māori, such as whare tangata, whenua, atua, hapū and whānau, that demonstrate the significance, prestige and sanctity of maternities. Currently, however, there is very little recognition and understanding within mainstream maternities of Māori concepts and their significance, such as ūkaipō and te whare tangata. A number of studies (Glover, 2008; Kenney, 2009; Rimene, Hassan, & Broughton, 1998) highlight an urgent need for culturally appropriate techniques and technologies within maternity services in Aotearoa that acknowledge and respect the mana and tapu of te whare tangata and the prestige of te ūkaipō.

Maternities currently represents a conflicting space for many Māori women and whānau. Decolonising maternities, therefore, must occur across multiple spaces, both discursive and physical. There are numerous examples of whānau who are working to decolonise maternities through the use of te reo Māori, the practice of tikanga pertaining to birth and mothering, and the reclamation of concepts such as ūkaipō. This is exemplified by one wāhine in Naomi's research, who reflects on her experience, saying:

> We used muka to tie the pito and greenstone to cut the cord and
> made ipu whenua. My boy went straight into a waha kura (woven
> basket) for sleeping. I went down to my sisters' antenatal class which
> was on the marae … at the class we made muka. We made our ipu
> whenua … I got a friend of mine to cut the greenstone. It makes
> sense because that's how they would have done it back in the day
> as well. All our terminology, as far as we would refer to our body
> parts and our baby and processes were all in Māori; little waiata
> and things like that … Also, it wasn't just me; the whānau were on
> board and they would actually just get things and do things. (cited in
> Simmonds, 2014, p. 209)

For the most part, however, the practice of tikanga continues to exist on the periphery with regard to dominant maternities in Aotearoa New Zealand. Perhaps one of the exceptions is the return of the whenua, the afterbirth, to perhaps *the* most important maternal figure, Papatūānuku. This raises the question: In all of the advice, information, checklists and guidelines that we are given as new and becoming mothers, where are the uniquely Māori, iwi, hapū and whānau ways of knowing and being? Where are our oriori, waiata, our language and our concepts? Kei hea te ūkaipō?

That being said, the creativity and pragmatism demonstrated by women and whānau in our research and beyond is inspiring. It is important to remember, too, that it is not just the material expressions of tikanga that are important; we must also look for and acknowledge those values that can inform and transform our maternity experiences. Reclaiming the collective approach to raising children, as affirmed in the concept of ūkaipō, is one such value that we can draw from to transform maternity experiences for women and whānau.

Traditionally, raising a child was a robust system that ensured the wellbeing of both mother and child, and, ultimately the wider whānau and community. This is reflected in concepts such as te pā harakeke (Pihama, 2012). This is especially apparent within the stories of Māui, where his care, education and socialisation were undertaken by a wide number of whānau members, male and female (Mikaere, 2003). The mothering of children was a role undertaken by many within the collective group and was not just restricted to the biological mothers of children. The principle of "he ūkaipō ... nānā i whakatipu" (He Pātaka Kupu, 2008, p. 1030) makes it clear that all women are mothers regardless of whether they physically give birth to children or not. Further, Māori maternities reflect a supportive and collective approach to the mothering of children with the involvement of men, wider family members and especially grandparents. Cheryl Smith (2012, p. 261) states that:

> For Māori, the task of raising grandchildren is considered an honour. It is generally considered that mokopuna raised by grandparents are treasured because they will learn the knowledge of the older generation.

In order to reclaim the full meaning of te ūkaipō, therefore, we must also reclaim the collectivism of Māori communities and raising children. We must decolonise Western patriarchal and hetero-normative conceptualisations of family that serve to isolate Māori mothers from traditional networks of support. As Kim Anderson (2007, p. 775) highlights, if we fail to do so we:

run the risk of heaping more responsibility on already overburdened mothers ... we must question the logic of asking mothers to 'carry the nations' ... we must ask ourselves: Where are the men? Where are the communities? Where is the nation and where is the state? And—not to forget—where are the children?

Reinstating the collectivism of maternities, of Māori society more generally, will more readily enable collective and empowered child rearing. By ensuring our children have access to other 'mothers' in their lives, we also ensure that as mothers, as ūkaipō, we are supported to mother, to teach and learn, to care and heal, to decolonise and reclaim.

He ūkaipō—He mana wahine

The birth stance
A haka of flexible dimension,
The posture of a woman entering an extending circle ...
A stomping, sure-footed woman, growing daily into the season of her own power. (Kahukiwa & Potiki, 1999, p. 30)

Ūkaipō is a term for mother(s) in the widest conceptualisation of the term, acknowledging those who provide the 'night-feeding breast', those who raise children and provide nurturing and sustenance to a child/children. Ūkaipō is one of many concepts found within our traditional pūrākau that speaks to the power, sanctity and prestige accorded to the maternal figure and to maternal bodies and knowledges. It provides an empowering conceptualisation of the maternal that exists outside of the colonial and patriarchal articulations that exist within mainstream maternities.

Ūkaipō is also a term that denotes a place or space to which a person feels a life-long physical and spiritual connection. It is a concept that is intimately entangled with this place—Aotearoa—its histories, geographies and politics. Decolonising Māori maternities, then, requires a reclamation of place, of those places that we as Māori, as iwi, hapū and whānau, consider our ūkaipō—those places and people where we as mothers and as whānau can go to feel supported and nurtured.

Decolonising maternities can take many forms, from protests and placards, political activism and other radical actions, through to the stories and histories of our ancestors; the words of songs, waiata, haka, karakia, poetry and plays; the images of artwork and moko; in the pages of books, journals and theses. Decolonisation is also found in the everyday experiences of women and whānau who are birthing, raising and nurturing their tamariki and mokopuna. Decolonising maternities is happening within whānau, in the choices they make in birth, mothering and education of their children, in the language they speak to their children and the names they bestow upon them. Decolonisation is born and reborn through the multiplicity of ways that women and whānau continue to sustain their position as ūkaipō, as mana wahine.

References

Anderson, K. (2000). *A recognition of being: Reconstructing native womanhood.* Toronto, Ontario: Second Story Press.

Anderson, K. (2007). Giving Life to the People: an indigenous ideology of motherhood. In O'Reilly, A. (ed.) *Maternal theory: essential readings,* Ontario: Demeter Press, 761–781.

Gabel, K. (2013). *Poipoia te tamaiti ki te ūkaipō.* Unpublished doctoral thesis, University of Waikato.

Glover, M. (2008). *Māori attitudes to assisted human reproduction: An exploratory study.* Auckland: University of Auckland, Department of Social & Community Health.

Glover, M., & Cunningham, C. (2011). Hoki ki te ūkaipō: Reinstating Māori infant care practices to increase breastfeeding rates. In P. Liamputtong (Ed.), *Infant feeding practices: A cross cultural perspective* (pp. 247-261)). New York, NY: Springer.

Kahukiwa, R., & Potiki, P. (1999). *Oriori: A Māori child is born: From conception to birth.* Auckland: Tandem Press.

Kenney, C. (2009). *Me aro ki te hā o hineahuone: Women, miscarriage stories, and midwifery: Towards a contextually relevant research methodology.* Unpublished doctoral thesis, Massey University.

Lavell-Harvard, J. and Corbiere-Lavell, M. (2006) *Until our hearts are on the ground: Aboriginal mothering, oppression, resistance and rebirth,* Toronto, Ontario: Demeter Press.

Mikaere, A. (2003). *The balance destroyed: Consequences for Māori women of the colonisation of tikanga Māori.* Auckland: The International Research Institute for Māori and Indigenous Education.

Mikaere, A. (2011). *Colonising myths: Māori realities: He rukuruku whakaarā.* Wellington: Huia Publishers and Te Wānanga o Raukawa.

Murphy, N. (2011). *Te awa atua, te awa tapu, te awa wahine: An examination of stories, ceremonies and practices regarding menstruation in the pre-colonial Māori world.* Unpublished master's thesis, University of Waikato.

Nepe, T. (1991). *Te toi huarewa tipuna: Kaupapa Māori: An educational intervention system.* Unpublished master's thesis, The University of Auckland.

New Zealand. Māori Language Commission 2008, *He pātaka kupu: te kai a te rangatira*, Te Taura Whiri i te Reo Māori/Māori Language Commission, North Shore; Raupo/Penguin.

Pihama, L. (2012). *Tiakina te pā harakeke: Māori childrearing within a context of whānau ora.* Retrieved from http://mediacentre.maramatanga.ac.nz/content/tiakina-pa-harakeke

Rimene, C., Hassan, C., & Broughton, J. (1998). *Ūkaipō the place of nurturing: Māori women and childbirth.* Dunedin: University of Otago.

Simmonds, N. (2014). *Tū te turuturu nō hine-te-iwaiwa: Mana wahine geographies of birth in Aotearoa New Zealand.* Unpublished doctoral thesis, University of Waikato.

Simpson, L. (2006). Birthing an indigenous resurgence: Decolonizing our pregnancy and birthing ceremonies. In J. Lavell-Harvard & M. Corbiere-Lavell (Eds.), *Until our hearts are on the ground: Aboriginal mothering, oppression, resistance and rebirth.* Toronto, Ontario: Demeter Press.

Smith, C. (2012). Tamaiti whangai and fertility. In P. Reynolds and C. Smith (Eds,) *The gift of children: Māori and infertility.* Wellington: Huia Publishers.

Smith, L. (2012). *Decolonizing methodologies: Research and indigenous peoples.* London: Zed Books.

Smith, T. (2012). Aitanga: Māori precolonial conceptual frameworks and fertility: A literature review. In P. Reynolds & C. Smith (Eds.), *The gift of children: Māori and infertility.* Wellington: Huia Publishers.

Sunseri, L. (2008). Sky woman lives on: Contemporary examples of mothering the nation. *Canadian Woman Studies*, *26*, 3–4.

Te Taura Whiri i te Reo Māori. (2008). *He pātaka kupu.* Auckland: Penguin.

Yates-Smith, A. (1998). *Hine! E hine!: Rediscovering the feminine in Māori spirituality.* Unpublished doctoral thesis, University of Waikato.

Chapter 12 Decolonising dreams and Māori Television

Jo Smith

Introduction

In the last 10 years Māori Television has dramatically increased the amount of te reo Māori programming on New Zealand television. It has also stimulated the growth of the independent Māori media sector and has attracted the admiration and approval of many politicians and media commentators (Mallard, 2013; Norris & Pauling, 2008; Turei, 2013). Yet, according to interviews conducted with a range of Māori Television stakeholders between 2012 and 2014 (including Māori Television employees, board members, independent Māori media producers, language advocates and academics), many want more from this indigenous media organisation.[1] This chapter argues that many of the aspirations expressed by those who have a commitment to Māori Television are dreams that align with a politics of decolonisation that helped fuel social and political change for Māori more than three decades earlier. I argue that such dreams could be the utopic horizon that Māori Television might aspire to in their day-to-day practices and in long-term planning processes.

By focusing on the aspirations and dreams of what Māori Television *could* be, I follow the decolonising logic of Hawaiian sovereignty activist

Pōkā Laenui (aka Hayden F. Burgess). Laenui describes five phases of the decolonisation process (Laenui, 2011), which include cycles of: rediscovery and recovery; mourning; dreaming; commitment; and action. These phases should not be understood as discrete and sequential, as they overlap, combine and are mutually informing. This is an iterative and dynamic model of decolonisation that has relevance to Aotearoa. Building on Laenui's model, I argue that the dreams and aspirations of those who have a stake in the work of Māori Television have a role to play in inspiring Māori Television's future commitments and actions. I argue that decolonisation is not a process that one eventually arrives at the end of, but involves an ongoing and dynamic relationship between dreams and actions. Such a politics involves a perpetual struggle to attain the political and cultural ideals and aspirations of a people in the face of persisting constraints.

The particular constraints facing Māori Television include a prevailing English-speaking public culture; a modest funding structure that makes the organisation dependent on the good will of industry practitioners (Debrett, 2010, p. 180); a dual governance model (between the Crown and Te Pūtahi Pāoho) that requires deft negotiation; a lack of industry professionals with te reo expertise due to the long-term impact of the loss of te reo Māori; and television norms that measure success based on ratings and audience share. While the focus of this chapter is on the dreams surrounding Māori Television as an ideal that might inspire new forms of commitment and action from the organisation, this chapter also acknowledges the larger challenges facing Māori Television given these constraints.

Māori Television's decolonising potential

Key characteristics of the shared aspirations found in kōrero with stakeholders reveal (a) a desire for greater integration of Māori language and culture across all aspects of Māori Television's organisational and programming practices; (b) greater links to, and engagement with, the diverse communities that make up te ao Māori; and (c) a desire to develop evaluative frameworks for the programming made by Māori Television that draw on Māori world views. These aspirations have direct links to a decolonising politics that can be broadly defined as focusing on achieving greater forms of cultural and political representation (Thiong'o,

1986); creating spaces to retell indigenous stories (Hutchings, 2002; Lee, 2009); enabling indigenous people to set their own agendas for social and political change (Smith, 2000); and as a form of anti-colonial struggle that grows from grassroots spaces (Zavala, 2013).

Māori Television's role in language revitalisation can be understood as a crucial cornerstone of a decolonising agenda. Since television's arrival in the 1960s, the "virtual absence" of te reo Māori broadcast content has been a significant factor in the decline of fluent speakers (Waitangi Tribunal, 1990, p. 36). The legislation governing Māori Television is designed to address this decline by contributing to "the promotion and protection of te reo Māori me ōna tikanga" (Māori Television, 2014, p. 11). Kōrero from Māori Television stakeholders remind us that the struggle for te reo Māori is a struggle waged on a daily basis and that wider social dynamics can frustrate language aspirations. For those who experienced childhood prior to the emergence of Māori Television, Aotearoa's media ecology was decidedly monolingual, with pockets of te reo Māori media content screened outside of primetime viewing or during Māori Language Week.[2] Eruera Morgan (Te Arawa, Tainui), Executive Producer of Māori Television's immersion channel, Te Reo, recalls the importance of having Māori-language content on television growing up as a second-language learner in the late 1990s:

> As a kid, I was learning, I was just picking up the language at college. I would run home to get my daily dose of language on air, on TV. Even though it was only a small dose of the Māori language on air, I would try and make those daily appointments to view. (Morgan, interview, 2014)

Morgan's comments underscore the rarity of te reo Māori programming prior to Māori Television, as well as the importance of daily viewing practices to improve his language skills.

More than a decade later, those children who have gone through kōhanga reo and kura kaupapa schooling systems still struggle against Aotearoa's pervasive monolingualism. In 2008 Māori independent producer Kay Ellmers (Ngāti Raukawa, Ngāti Tamatera) was inspired by her children's experience of schooling to create a children's television programme for Māori Television that was designed to promote te reo Māori:

> [M]y kids and all their peers were heading off to school where there was a world that was happening at school where everything happened

in te reo Māori and they talked about the world in te reo Māori and they did science and math and English and all of that in Māori. As soon as they stepped out the school gate that was not the world that they experienced inside the school gates. So my kids certainly started to think that te reo was only a language for school. It wasn't a real living language. (Ellmers, interview, 2012)

Ellmers's and Morgan's comments demonstrate how the struggle for the revitalisation of Māori language and culture is waged on a daily basis in the face of a pervasively monolingual public culture.

Acknowledging the challenge of promoting and protecting te reo Māori, former CEO of Māori Television Jim Mather (Ngāti Awa, Ngāi Tūhoe) describes his staff's investment in this kaupapa as "a crusade" (Mather, interview, 2012). One long-time crusader is Julian Wilcox (Ngāpuhi, Ngāti Tūwharetoa, Te Arawa). When asked about his start at Māori Television, Wilcox noted, "when I came into this job, it was all about reo, tikanga and getting into our communities and telling our stories" (Wilcox, interview, 2012). Alluding to the broader social environment out of which Māori Television emerged, Wilcox noted:

For me it was like "us against the world", and showing that not only should we have a place as an independent television service, we're the ones that have the responsibility of telling our stories to our people in *our* way. Because I think it is a different mode of journalism or television than the way mainstream tells our stories.

Remaining dedicated to this task until his departure in 2014, Wilcox's commitment to "telling our stories to our people in *our* way", while seemingly straightforward, encompasses a range of complexities that are still being negotiated by Māori Television. For how do you tell stories from the perspective of the diverse communities that make up te ao Māori, drawing on te reo and tikanga Māori, when the very media systems and structures you need to use have been established and shaped by non-Māori practices and values?

For example, Māori Television is asked by its stakeholders to provide the conditions necessary to tell stories on television in ways that align with Māori world views and practices. Yet, the constraints of entrenched television practices can get in the way of the cultural norms of te ao Māori. Orthodox presentations of news media include a bulletin format, which can restrict the kind of in-depth discussions that need to take place in order to understand the full weight of a story from a te ao Māori perspective. Funding constraints can restrict a broadcaster's ability to turn up to, and record, multiple community events occurring across the country. Flagship current affairs programme *Native Affairs* has been at the forefront of balancing the professional norms of journalism with Māori cultural practices, even as it attracted criticism in 2013 for its treatment of a story about te kōhanga reo and Te Pātaka Ōhanga, which for some Māori commentators was too "Pākehāfied".[3] In many ways the controversy surrounding *Native Affairs*'s treatment of a peer language organisation reflects the complex desires of many stakeholders for a more "Māori" form of Māori Television. These desires go beyond simply expecting Māori Television to provide quality te reo Māori media content: they extend to expecting the organisation to operate as an organisation where indigenous values prevail.

Māori Television, not television in Māori

The expectations placed on Māori Television outweigh those placed on national broadcaster TVNZ, or any other television provider in Aotearoa. Māori Television must provide quality programming content that can fill a weekly schedule on a very restricted budget, but the organisation is also expected to incorporate Māori values, practices and protocols into day-to-day work routines. To these ends, the guiding kaupapa of the organisation, "Kia tika; kia pono; kia aroha; kia Māori", are designed to help shape the organisation's practices. According to Māori Television board member and long-time language advocate Cathy Dewes (Te Arawa, Ngāti Porou), even though funding is an issue, one of the more important aspirations for the organisation is to have all staff using te reo Māori on a daily basis in the workplace. According to Dewes:

> I think that the ideal is to have the whole of Māori Television, in time, speaking Māori and by saying that I assume if a person is speaking Māori they have an understanding of tikanga Māori and te ao Māori which non-speakers don't have. And so ideally, the whole of Māori Television are Māori and everything they do, their thinking, their way of life, their ordinary daily being is Māori. ... [I]f we're all coming at it from the same perspective, the same rationale, the

same belief, the same values, it makes it easier to be the service for our people—for Māori. (Dewes, interview, 2012)

While there is much to say about this kōrero, one important aspect is the idea that if one has the capacity to speak te reo, then access to a Māori way of thinking and feeling behind the language will necessarily flow.

While an ideal that could be realised over time, kōrero from other stakeholders raise questions that challenge the natural link between te reo and tikanga suggested by Dewes. What of the shifting landscape of language acquisition, the many second-language learners within the broadcasting sector and the broadcasting imperatives that can have an impact on the thinking *behind* the use of te reo? Former general manager of programming at Māori Television and current independent producer/director Tawini Rangihau (Te Arawa, Ngāi Tūhoe) alludes to these issues when she emphasises the difference between "Māori news" and "the news in Māori":

> The big gap in all of that is that you do have trained journalists but from watching the news on both *Te Karere* and *Te Kāea*, [you can tell] their first language is English and that's the way they view all the writing of their stories. I think that if they started to look at journalism from a Māori perspective, in te reo, that is the real building stone to having Māori news, not the news in Māori. (Rangihau, interview, 2014)

Here Rangihau's emphasis on te reo as the pathway to producing news from a Māori perspective chimes with Cathy Dewes's comments, but also differs in terms of the attention she pays to the impact that entrenched (and non-Māori) broadcasting imperatives might have on te reo speaking journalists. Offering a form of journalism from "a Māori perspective" is, again, a seemingly simple aspiration which nonetheless throws up significant challenges to media-making practices that have been normalised, both nationally and internationally, by non-Māori practitioners.

Tawini Rangihau's desire for Māori news, not news in Māori, reflects the desire of other interviewees for a 'Māori' form of television, not television in Māori. One way of making Māori television would be to draw on the expertise, advice and talents of kaumātua in an extensive and daily way and to value the experiences of non-media professionals who nonetheless have cultural expertise. This is one of the aspirations of ex-Te Pūtahi Pāoho member and current Māori Television board member Piripi Walker (Ngāti Raukawa) when reflecting on the need for kaumātua within the institution who can offer guidance and advice to all staff:

> I always thought that a functioning Māori operating unit that was really truly Māori would have kaumātua right there in the centre. And it's easy to operate without them in the modern world that the young professionals want to live in. I suspect that it's like hospitality. We used to have this argument at the radio station [Te Upoko]. We had a kitchen going every day, you know, we had lunch together—a cooked lunch—and someone came in and said this place is for journalism, not for food. It was easy not to think about it, to discard that both in time terms and the fact that a few waifs and strays would come in for lunch every second day. But it was all part of it, you know. The place had a certain kind of lovely feeling and I would have thought that you'd try and recreate a sense of being a marae *within* the channel. (Walker, interview, 2013)

Piripi's comments address the day-to-day practices of manaakitanga that contribute to the overall ethos of an organisation as well as the need for regular access to the wisdom of elders to offer advice and guidance. While Māori Television has the Kaunihera Kaumātua, a council of elders representing iwi, which provides advice to some of Māori Television's practices (onscreen and within the organisation) on matters of tikanga, kaupapa and kawa, these elders are not usually available to all staff. According to Piripi Walker, the daily presence of kaumātua within Māori Television could be a step towards strengthening the organisation's cultural integrity.

While many of those interviewed expressed the desire for change *within* the organisation, other stakeholders emphasised the need for Māori Television to engage more consistently with the diverse worlds that make up te ao Māori. From some perspectives, Māori Television's start-up phase took a more conventional approach to television-making based on existing New Zealand broadcasting practices. Those who are passionate about Māori media's role in fostering language and cultural revitalisation imagine a form of television production developed from the flax-roots up.

Māori Television as conduit for the flax-roots

While the dual governance structure of Māori Television makes it accountable to both Crown and Māori (represented by Te Pūtahi Pāoho), kōrero from stakeholders expressed the need for greater connection with diverse Māori communities. For independent producer and Ngāpuhi language expert Quinton Hita, a more culturally appropriate form of Māori Television would be one that allowed for programming that reflected the rhythm, timing and pace of te ao Māori; a form of television that did not interrupt the immersive environment of te reo with Pākehā-speaking adverts; and a structure that connected to whānau in a way similar to the kōhanga reo movement. This is how Hita expresses his vision:

> The kōhanga movement became more than just a vehicle to teach our kids. It became a way of bringing us together as a community, enhancing us as a people. Māori Television does not achieve that in my opinion because it's centralised. They asked at the Rotorua meeting—that hui we had[4]—if you could reimagine Māori Television what would it look like. To me it would look something like that— devolving out to our communities and then you would end up with something far more meaningful. Devolve it to our communities and then the broadcaster becomes a portal that distributes that [content] to the country. (Hita, interview, 2014)

Hita acknowledges that such a devolved structure would include demanding learning curves built up over a long period of time.

Hita's comments also underscore the importance of a long-term vision, one based on getting things correct at the start:

> So going back to what I said before about when we start these ventures; we pick Pākehā structures because they give us credibility. But I think at some point Māori go; okay, let's review this. I think we are going into that stage right now with the call for the [new] Māori Language [Bill]. (Hita, interview, 2014)

Hita's vision for Māori Television involves a re-visioning of ideas about what constitutes good-quality Māori media. The focus is on imagining a form of television that is by Māori, for Māori and about Māori, and connected to whānau and communities.

The desire to improve community outreach is shared by many

Māori Television staff, including Julian Wilcox and Mahuta Amoamo. In a 2012 interview Julian Wilcox described one possible way forward for enhancing regional news media coverage that drew on the existing expertise and resources of iwi radio:

> We wanted to commit more regional reporters but one of the ways we were looking at was perhaps looking at Māori radio. [W]e give them a human resource and they provide the base. We [would] give them a Canon DSLR and train them up so they just operate at a Māori radio station. But the issue was in video transmitting everything back to base. The Punga Net is not ideal at the moment. (Wilcox, interview, 2012)

While the technological constraints of Te Punga Net may have been a key factor in this vision not being realised, the idea of harnessing the talents, resources and experiences of other Māori media broadcasters seemed to many interviewees a good idea in light of the under-resourcing, in general, of Māori media.[5] In addition, the missed opportunity for cohesion across the Māori media sector is perhaps compounded by the lack of a cohesive language strategy to support the first 10 years of Māori Television's existence.[6]

Another long-standing Māori Television staff member, Mahuta Amoamo (Whakatōhea, Ngāi Tūhoe), recalls the early days of Māori Television staff's efforts to forge relationships with communities:

> When Māori Television was fresh and new, with the news and governments going ra, ra, ra, iwi were very hesitant in letting us come to their events because they thought we were TVNZ and that's the way we were going to roll. So it was an achievement to get iwi like, say, Maniapoto—because this was my first event that I remember very well—[who] have a hunting competition every year. We went with a kaumātua and she [Tawini Rangihau] told them why we were there— we're here to make sure your people know what you're up to. They can hear your dialect, they can see you on television, they can find out why you do this competition. We'll be able to capture all of your rangatahi. (Amoamo, interview, 2013)

For Amoamo, as well as many other interviewees, Māori Television has the potential to build on its established reputation for telling stories about the successes of, and challenges facing, whānau, hapū and iwi.

So far the moemoeā expressed here for Māori Television have broadly included (a) greater integration of te reo and tikanga Māori at the level of the everyday in terms of institutional practices; and (b) greater outreach and responsiveness to diverse Māori communities. An additional moemoeā offers insights into how we might better understand the impact and significance of Māori Television, on *Māori* terms.

Taking a longer view

Following the logic of self-determination embedded in a decolonising political agenda, one could argue that any evaluative framework for assessing Māori Television's significance and impact must come from Māori communities. Key indicators of success in the television industry often draw on ratings and audience share, but, as minority language media experts argue, these measures are too crude given the very niche audiences such broadcasters attract (Cormack 2007; Bell, 2010).

Throughout my engagement with Māori Television stakeholders I noted ideas on how Māori Television successes might be evaluated using more appropriate measures drawn from the conceptual worlds of te ao Māori. This approach is inspired by the existing Māori education research of Te Wāhanga Research Unit, particularly the project Kia Puāwaitia ngā Tūmanako: Critical Issues for Whānau in Māori Education, which asks diverse Māori communities to identify the critical issues in education facing whānau and what their measures of success are (Hutchings et al. 2012, p. iv). While the scope of this chapter prevents a full account of how Māori Television might be understood *on Māori terms*, I outline below a recurring emphasis on the need for a longitudinal analysis of Māori Television's impact and significance.

Rather than ratings and audience share as indicators of Māori Television's impact and success, some interviewees discussed the longitudinal benefits of having a media repository of Māori language and culture for the generations to come. For example, Eruera Morgan invites us to imagine how Māori Television programming might function in the future when he states:

> Just imagine in say, five to ten, even fifty years time, this is a
> repository or an archive of how our people lived and how they spoke.
> Our language is moving very rapidly and for me, the classical Māori

is what I aspire to, in my quest for knowledge. And my quest for
the reo, is going back to the freshwater spring that provides us with
the foundation of the language and with the nuances that certain
people speak. (Morgan, interview, 2014)

Quinton Hita also discussed this kind of archival approach in relation to his series *Kōwhao Rau*. Hita sees this series as his life's work,
which is to create an archive of Ngāpuhi reo that can be handed
down for the generations to come. Another longtime broadcaster,
Whai Ngata (Ngāti Porou, Te Whānau-ā-Apanui), suggested a different approach when considering the quality of a programme:

I think Māori programmes should be judged on—maybe not all
the programmes—but they should be judged on whether they have
another life. ... Can they stand a repeat in a year, can they stand a
repeat in two years, can they stand a repeat in five? What about ten?
(Ngata, interview, 2012)

The moemoeā gathered here include the hope that Māori
Television continues to provide innovative and inspiring television
that contributes to the health and wellbeing of te reo and tikanga
Māori; that Māori values and practices might have greater influence over the workplace culture of the organisation; and that Māori
Television might be more responsive to the flax-roots and the needs
of diverse Māori communities. These dreams and aspirations align
with a decolonising agenda dedicated to achieving more potent
forms of representation, telling indigenous stories from indigenous
perspectives, making visible Māori political and cultural agendas,
and developing anti-colonial forms of resistance from the flax-roots.
Such changes can only come with time and must be nurtured over
generations.

This long-term perspective for change in the Māori media sector
also connects with changes in other sectors of society. Reflecting on
the future development of Māori Television, kaupapa Māori expert
Linda Tuhiwai Smith (Ngāti Awa, Ngāti Porou) states:

In the end, you know the kura, we had to train our own teachers
because the ones who are mainstream taught, in our view as
parents, brought into the classroom the colonising practices of
their mainstream education. It wasn't intentional, it just is. And so

now that we've got a generation of kura graduates returning to the classroom, that value system is already implicit in their practices and I think TV has to do the same. It has to produce in the end its own producers, directors, commentators. You know, it has to grow them up. (Smith, interview, 2013)

Smith's comments strike at the heart of the predicament of a state-, funded Māori media organisation that has had to build itself upon existing institutional practices, with few fluent Māori media professionals. More than this, Smith's comments invite the Māori media sector to look to the wider education sector when developing frameworks that can affirm Māori ways of thinking and doing.

Conclusions

In its first 10 years Māori Television has made important and significant contributions to protecting and promoting Māori language and culture. However, in this chapter Māori Television is discussed as an ideal and an aspiration for the various stakeholders interviewed. Pōkā Laenui's five phases of decolonisation include the important criterion of dreaming, which invites us to imagine the world in which one wants to live, and then, through actions, build this world. While there are counter arguments to the feasibility of the aspirations surrounding Māori Television, due to funding issues, institutional constraints and the long-term impact of the loss of te reo Māori, the focus of this chapter has been on the decolonising dreams surrounding Māori Television.

Māori Television has done much to change the media landscape of this country, but many of the decolonising aspirations surrounding Māori Television have yet to be achieved. Yet this is the nature of a decolonising political agenda. Rather than decolonisation understood as a process that one eventually arrives at the end of, Māori Television represents an opportunity to understand how such politics involves multiple sites of perpetual struggle that are ongoing and always in a state of renewal and negotiation. A crucial task ahead for all who care about the decolonising potential of Māori media is to dream into existence the kinds of structures, stories, sounds and images we would hope for in a Māori media organisation.

References

Bell, A. (2010). Advocating for a threatened language: The case for Māori on television in Aotearoa/New Zealand. *Te Reo*, 53, 3–26.

Cormack, M. (2007) The media and language maintenance. In M. J. Cormack & N. Lourigan (Eds.), *Minority language media: Concepts, critiques and case studies* (pp. 52–68). New York, NY: Multilingual Matters.

Debrett, M. (2010). *Reinventing public service television for the digital future.* Bristol and Chicago: Intellect.

Hutchings, J. (2002). Decolonisation and Aotearoa: A pathway to right livelihood. *Vimukt Shiksha: Unfolding learning societies: Experiencing the possibilities.* Retrieved from http://www.swaraj.org/shikshantar/ls3_jessica.htm

Hutchings, J., Barnes, A., Taupo, K., Bright, N., with Pihama, L., & Lee, J. (2012). *Kia puāwaitia ngā tūmanako: Critical issues for whānau in Māori education.* Wellington: NZCER Press.

Laenui, P. (Burgess, H. F.). (2011). Processes of decolonization. In M. Battiste (Ed.), *Reclaiming indigenous voice and vision* (pp. 150–160). Vancouver, BC: UBC Press.

Lee, J. (2009). Decolonising Māori narratives: Pūrākau as a method. *MAI Review*, 2, 1–12.

Mallard, T. (2013). Māori Television Service (Te Aratuku Whakaata Irirangi Māori) Amendment Bill. *New Zealand Parliamentary Debates*, vol. 688, p. 8792.

Māori Television. (2014). *Pānui whāinga: Statement of intent 2014–2017.* Auckland: Author.

Norris, P., & Pauling, B. (2008). *The digital future and public broadcasting.* Report for NZ On Air.

Smith, G. H. (2000). Protecting and respecting indigenous knowledge. In M. Battiste (Ed.), *Reclaiming indigenous voice and vision* (pp. 209–224). Vancouver, BC: UBC Press.

Thiong'o, N. w. (1986). *Decolonising the mind: The politics of language in African literature.* New Hampshire, NE: Heinemann.

Turei, M. (2013). Māori Television Service (Te Aratuku Whakaata Irirangi Māori) Amendment Bill. *New Zealand Parliamentary Debates*, vol. 685, p. 14921.

Waitangi Tribunal. (1990). *Claims concerning the allocation of radio frequencies: Wai 26 & 150*. Wellington: Department of Justice.

Zavala, M. (2013). What do we mean by decolonizing research strategies? *Decolonization: Indigeneity, Education and Society, 2*(1), 55–71.

Interviews

Amoamo, Mahuta, 25 January 2013.

Dewes, Cathy, 17 December 2012.

Ellmers, Kay, 1 August 2012.

Hita, Quinton, 7 February 2014.

Mather, Jim, 28 November 2012.

Morgan, Eruera. Interview. 13 June 2014.

Ngata, Whai, 5 November 2012.

Rangihau, Tawini, 19 February 2014.

Smith, Linda Tuhiwai, 2 July 2013.

Walker, Piripi, 27 March 2013.

Wilcox, Julian, 21 November 2012.

Endnotes

1 These interviews were conducted as part of a Marsden-funded project (2012–2014) entitled *Onscreen Indigeneity: The case of Māori Television*, led by Jo Smith (Victoria University of Wellington), with Sue Abel (University of Auckland).

2 Māori Language Week was established in 1975 and is intended to encourage New Zealand citizens to speak te reo Māori. New Zealand media outlets participate in this state-funded language week by including more te reo Māori in their on-air and online content.

3 See John Drinnan's opinion piece: Māori TV Probe Labelled Too Pākehā, *The New Zealand Herald*, 25 October 2013, retrieved from http://www.nzherald.co.nz/business/news/article.cfm?c_id=3&objectid=11145823

4 In October 2010 Te Māngai Pāho hosted Ihi, a Māori broadcasting summit in Rotorua.

5 Te Punga Net is the iwi radio distribution network which enables the exchange of programming across all iwi stations.

6 The 2014 Māori Language (Te Reo Māori) Bill is the most recent state initiative that seeks to repeal the Māori Language Act 1987.

Chapter 13 Bringing Māori food politics to the table: Decolonising food knowledge

Jessica Hutchings

Introduction

Our bodily and earthly landscapes have not benefited from colonisation. Two hundred years of disruption and change have left the water bodies and earthscapes of Papatūānuku (Earth Mother) polluted and our indigenous bodies lulled into lethargic complacency. Our ability as Māori to see our bodies, our minds, our energetic selves as nature, as Papatūānuku herself, was commonplace for our ancestors. However, this perspective is now hampered on a daily basis with the ingestion of neo-colonial[1] diets that do not draw directly from nature but rather provide food *products* that are grown for profit by corporations.

This chapter presents a way to decolonise food knowledge and calls for a decolonising learning and education system for how we approach, grow and think about kai (food). Developed by Te Waka Kai Ora (the National Māori Organics Authority of Aotearoa), Hua Parakore is one such system, which seeks to restore the connections between mind, body and nature. It is a kaupapa Māori food sovereignty and food-security initiative that has the potential to contribute, along with other kaupapa Māori initiatives, to decolonising education in Aotearoa with regard to food knowledge.

Motivation

As the indigenous storyteller of this narrative I am motivated to write about food because it is the essence of my being. It manifests in the vibration of who I am, how I move in the world, and how I interact with nature and the communities and whānau I am a part of. When I eat food from the māra (garden) that I have grown myself, in soil full of micro-organisms that I have nurtured and cared for, I can feel the nourishment in my mind, body and soul due to the connections between soil and me as a grower and consumer. The food is alive and is a part of me even before I eat it. My relationship with food begins with saving seed from previous seasons to plant out in the seasons to come. Like the moon cycles and the flows in my bodily landscape, the cycle of growing and eating my own food is a way to nourish my body and the traditions of our ancestors as food growers, gatherers and hunters.

Bringing kaupapa Māori to the māra empowers my identity as an indigenous woman and provides nutritious and pure food. I love exploring my practice of the Hua Parakore kaupapa; they are indigenous to this land and deepen my connection to the māra kai practices of our tūpuna.

Indigenous food knowledge is critical to a decolonising education and learning agenda for indigenous communities, because food connects us with the landscapes we eat, thereby forming a key part of our cultural, mental and physical wellbeing as indigenous peoples. This knowledge restores the holistic connection between our bodies and the earthy landscapes of Papatūānuku, which was decimated by the reductionist nature of Western knowledge systems that perpetuate the separation between 'Man' and nature.

Restorying the divide between humans and nature

The deep indigenous connection between ourselves as nature and nature as ourselves has been violently fractured by ongoing forms of colonisation. This is particularly true of the so-called Enlightenment period, when Western ideas were exported and imposed upon indigenous ways of knowing as part of the colonial project. This thinking proposed a separation between Man as rational and nature as something over which Man could dominate. This separation is also characteristic of certain modern reductionist sciences, such as genetics, nanotechnology and convergence technologies, which impede the perception of links and fragment knowledge into narrow disciplines and mechanistic categories. This is in contrast to a Hua Parakore approach, which trains the senses—the eyes, the mind, the body and soul—to restore the links across siloed knowledge domains.

The reductionist and mechanistic way of thinking pervades current global food systems, affecting how food is grown—usually in single crops, referred to as monoculture, and controlled by multinationals driven by a profit ledger rather than a connection with nature. The more I understand the global circuits of food production and the knowledge and politics that underpin them, the more determined I am to ensure that indigenous food security and sovereignty are legacies for our children. How do we, as whānau, disrupt this global multinational food system so that we can eat food that once again nourishes us as a part of nature? Asking and acting on this question is in itself is a decolonising act and a way to begin decolonising food knowledge for present and future indigenous generations.

Many indigenous communities and food growers urgently call for a decolonised form of food knowledge, and for people to resist neo-colonial food products that circulate globally, then land locally to line our local supermarkets shelves. In *For Indigenous Eyes Only: A Decolonisation Handbook,* Waziyatawin and Yellow Bird (2005, p. 67) remind us:

> Our colonisers taught us to believe that our health has improved
> because of western medicine, western foods and western technology.
> In a society that values progress, our colonisers taught us that
> conditions in the world are perpetually improving, that with each
> new technological advancement, each new discovery, each new way
> to utilise resources, each new way to utilise the environment, that the
> world is getting better, that it is advancing. These are all lies.

With the introduction of new food production methods and their claims of superiority over indigenous foodscapes and ways of life, indigenous diets were disrupted globally, fractured and destroyed in the early years of colonisation.

The impact of the Green Revolution on indigenous foodscapes

The 20th century saw the explosion of global foodscapes. The first flush of growth occurred during the Green Revolution of the 1970s, when industrialised agriculture, seeds, chemicals and fertilisers came to dominate world food production. The Green Revolution was established on the basis that it would solve world hunger by increasing global food supply. However, it was one of the least successful development projects in history, and its effects—which include displacing the traditional growing methods, crops and farming structures of indigenous communities, peasant and fisher peoples—are still widespread (Shiva, 2000).

The Green Revolution was a science-based agricultural transformation that capitalised production, leading to monocultures in both food and food production. It was the main contributor to a loss of biodiversity, both in nature and in the cultural food knowledge of indigenous peoples and Third World farmers (Hutchings, 2015). Furthermore, there was a symbiotic relationship between the inputs of the Green Revolution, and with chemical fertilisers becoming an essential part of the new seed technology package, which led to pest vulnerability by reducing resistance.

The package was built on the displacement of genetic diversity at two levels. Firstly, it stopped the rotation of crops and grains such as wheat, maize, millets, pulses and oil seeds, which had provided nutrition for indigenous and Third World communities for centuries, and replaced it with monocultures of wheat and rice. Secondly, the newly introduced wheat and rice varieties came from a very narrow genetic base compared to the high genetic diversity of traditional varieties.

Scholars such as Vandana Shiva (2000) have written about the correlation of the Green Revolution with colonisation and the notion of the empty earth:

> For five hundred years, colonisation has been based on the idea of
> the 'emptiness' of the earth and of other cultures. The assumption
> of the empty land leads to the denial of prior inhabitants and
> their prior rights. The idea of emptiness also leads to the notion of
> limitlessness—that there are no limits set by nature or other cultures
> to be respected, no ecological or ethical limits, no limits to the level

of greed and accumulation. The empty-earth hypothesis, in addition, creates a divided world—divisions of which still exist. (Shiva, 2000, pp. 25–26)

It is the politics of the Green Revolution, with its origins in Western science, along with the advent of genetically modified food and nano-based pesticides that are owned, promoted and delivered by the global food multinationals to our supermarket shelves in Aotearoa, that I refer to as neo-colonial foodscapes. It is this politics that provokes me as an indigenous woman to find other ways to produce the food I consume and to advocate for decolonised learning systems that can contribute towards educating indigenous communities about food and global food politics.

The importation of settler colonial diets into Aotearoa—character-ised by an over-reliance on whiteness, with white flour, white sugar and white fats, based on a global neo-capitalist food system dependent on oil, chemicals and uneven systems of distribution—is just one example of an unsustainable global food regime that will surely be one of the defining social struggles of our times. We now live in a world with unprecedented inequality in all aspects of our lives, and nowhere is the plutocratic inequality more profoundly illustrated than in food. Even though the world produces enough food, the United Nations Food and Agriculture Organisation (FAO) tell us that more than 925 million peo-ple in developing capitalist countries are "chronically malnourished", living on less than US$1 a day (FAO, 2011). Add to this the number of malnourished in developed capitalist countries, and the number of hungry worldwide is in the vicinity of 1 billion people. Around two bil-lion people regularly suffer from micronutrient deficiencies (Canadian International Development Agency, 2009).

Peoples and communities who face these food security issues are more likely to be hungry and to lack secure and stable access to suffi-cient, nutritious and culturally acceptable food. I argue that modern global food systems do not provide for a food-secure future, and that our wellbeing and even survival as indigenous peoples are at risk when we place all of our nutritional needs in the hands of the neo-colonial food multinationals. This chapter calls for flax-roots communities to challenge the multinationals and presents the Hua Parakore system as one alternative.

Hua Parakore

Hua Parakore is a kaupapa Māori food sovereignty and food security initiative that enhances the connections between our indigenous selves and nature by using indigenous knowledge about how we grow and consume our food. It is a response to the neo-capitalist global food crisis that treats food as a commodity, and nature simply as an input and a factor of production (Hutchings, 2015).

The result of a 3-year kaupapa Māori community research project, the Hua Parakore initiative validates Māori knowledge and is grounded in Māori cultural values and ways of knowing (Hutchings et al., 2012). Strongly supported by Māori growers, whānau and Māori communities, it is proving to be a way to ensure food security for indigenous communities in the future.

As a decolonised learning system, it is based on the richness of kaupapa Māori located within Māori tribal groups and whānau. It provides a basketful of knowledge on the Māori cultural practices and principles that constitute a product being defined as Hua Parakore. Sitting outside the neo-capitalist food system, Hua Parakore is about interconnected growing, where there is no division between people and nature. The system promotes six kaupapa Māori principles. They are not the only food-growing principles for growers, producers and whānau, but they have been identified as starting points to guide Māori communities and growers in their food production practices (Hutchings et al., 2012). The six Hua Parakore principles are: whakapapa (genealogical connections), wairua (spirituality), mana (authority), māramatanga (enlightenment), te ao tūroa (the natural world) and mauri (life force). Together they give rise to Hua Parakore food, which is a key contributor to a decolonising learning and education system.

Whakapapa is about the natural connections between deity, land, food and people. Wairua is the spiritual health and peace of the land (the māra, the kai it produces, and the people who work in the māra), while te ao tūroa is about maintaining the natural order of the world, reminding us to work in a way that enhances the natural interconnections of the earth where we can again see ourselves as part of and not separate from nature. Maintaining te ao tūroa means promoting a philosophy in the māra that is free of genetic engineering. Genetic engineering raises deep and serious issues, and Māori communities have strongly resisted it, both in the environment and in the food chain, due to the impact it has on tikanga (Māori cultural practices), human health and the environment.

It is through these Hua Parakore kaupapa that indigenous food security and food sovereignty kōrero and initiatives have emerged. Speaking about the kaupapa of whakapapa, Hua Parakore grower Geneva Hildreth (Ngā Puhi), from Pukerau Gardens in Kaikohe, says:

> I think [whakapapa] is all a part of Hua Parakore. Knowing about where the seed comes from so that it has some integrity in ensuring that they are safe seeds and that they're easily dependable and you know that the seeds are going to grow again ... it's about integrity and dependability in terms of sustainability. (Te Waka Kai Ora, 2011, p. 13)

Many Hua Parakore growers talk about the mauri or life force within seeds. They advocate both the philosophy and the practice of saving indigenous seeds from their own gardens to safeguard the diversity and vibration contained within indigenous and traditional seedlines. Seed saving is an essential requirement of any indigenous food sovereignty programme. Seeds hold the hope for future generations and their ability to feed and nourish themselves. Hua Parakore food politics resists the role of global food multinationals to corporatise, patent, own and profit from seed. The politics and practice of seed saving are key aspects of a decolonising learning system that seeks to decolonise food knowledge and bring indigenous food politics to the table.

The Hua Parakore kaupapa of mana is about the autonomy, self-determination and security of tribal collectives and whānau, as expressed through mahinga kai (food gathering and production). Unlike the insecure neo-colonial global food practices driven by multinationals for profit, bringing the kaupapa of mana to food production is about supporting cultural practices that strengthen communities and local Māori economies. It is not based on profit, or even money, but on relationships and reciprocity (Te Waka Kai Ora, 2011).

Exercising the kaupapa of mana brings into play the cultural practice of utu (exchange), as described by Rāwiri Richmond (Ngāti Raukawa, Ngāi Tai, Ngāti Tūwharetoa), Palmerston North:

I don't think it was exchange like if you give me two corn I will give you this ... you know someone sees you and says here is some fish. So I don't think it was trade a sack of spuds for something in return it was like here is some kai and later on it came back in another way, and that's like utu it will come back in some manner or form. And if you give me something then I am beholden at some stage to return the whakaaro [gesture]. (Te Waka Kai Ora, 2011, p. 17)

The Hua Parakore principle of mauri brings awareness to the life force, energy and vibrations needed to grow healthy kai. Making compost, planting by the moon and saving strong, vibrant seeds to plant out in the following seasons are all ways to enhance the mauri of the māra and the kai that is produced. Mana is about maintaining our autonomy, food security and self-determination through our māra practices. Finally, māramatanga is the insight and enlightenment that we gain through working in the māra. For me, it is when my vibration is strong, and bathed in light and energy that connect to the earth as soil and the planet and the cosmos.

Seed sovereignty is the basis for food sovereignty for the Hua Parakore food grower. Having an abundant and vibrant store of seeds collected from the māra is like having a pantry full of food. It gives us the means to grow food crops without having to buy seeds or seedlings from corporate seed merchants. Seed sovereignty coupled with healthy, vibrant, living soil is where my personal practice of food sovereignty begins.

The journey of Hua Parakore food growing is not only about the practice of growing food: it is also a political journey of asserting our sovereignty over food. For many of us who grow Hua Parakore food for whānau, it is a way of resisting neo-colonial food regimes and restoring the links and connections between our bodily and earthly landscapes.

A call to action: A decolonised learning system that promotes food security and food sovereignty

In this chapter I have told a story that I feel deeply part of. As an indigenous woman I see myself not as separate from nature but rather as part of her. The pūrākau I have told in this chapter has been about the ongoing assault on Papatūānuku and her abundant natural food systems that have germinated, generated and sustained thousands of generations globally. There is much to be done to halt the neo-colonial global food regime. A first step is to strengthen a decolonising education system by sharing food knowledge, such as the Hua Parakore system, which promotes indigenous food sovereignty and food security.

The Hua Parakore system talks back to the notion of 'emptiness' that is at the core of colonisation and clearly shows a grounded and living knowledge system that is connected to indigenous communities. Education is a powerful and potentially transformative tool, one that has been, and continues to be, used as a site of assimilation for indigenous peoples. In decolonising education in Aotearoa, it will be important for food knowledge to connect indigenous communities as nature and earth beings, to be practised and lived by schools, kura and across all learning communities.

I see an urgent need across all learning systems—Māori and English-medium schools, and tertiary and adult community education programmes—to engage with food politics and to work towards the decolonisation of our food knowledge. Reconnecting with our food systems, through kaupapa Māori initiatives such as Hua Parakore, provides nourishment for the mind, body and soul and connects us to the earth as earth beings. This initiative also heals the division between Man and nature prevalent in neo-colonial food regimes and rebuilds ways of knowing across knowledge domains, restoring the connections in a knowledge system that has become fragmented.

The Hua Parakore system is a tool for conscientisation. Learning communities, such as Te Waka Kai Ora, whānau, schools and kura, as well as other indigenous learners across other learning environments, can use the Hua Parakore to understand the impact that modern neo-colonial food regimes have on our health, our spirit and wellbeing, and on Papatūānuku. Building collective understanding of the circuits of neo-colonial food regimes provides a strong motivation to seek alternatives. The Hua Parakore system has been developed by Māori, for Māori, and is an alternative knowledge form that both restores and *restories* the connections between nature and people so that we can again feel and see ourselves as part of the interconnected web.

References

Canadian International Development Agency. (2009). *Micronutrients*. Retrieved from http://www.acdi-cida.gc.ca/acid-cida/acdi-cida.nsf/eng/FRA-4422402-563.

FAO (Food and Agriculture Organisation). (2011). *The state of food insecurity in the world 2011*. Rome: Author. Retrieved from fao.org/docrep/0140i2330e/i2330e00.htm.

Hutchings, J. (2015) *Te mahi māra hua parakore: A Māori food sovereignty handbook*. Ōtaki: Te Tākupu.

Hutchings, J., Tipene, P., Carney, C., Greensill, A., Skelton, P., & Baker, M. (2012). Hua Parakore: An indigenous food sovereignty initiative and hallmark of excellence for food and product production. *MAI Journal, 1*(2), 131–145.

Shiva, V. 2000. *Tomorrow's biodiversity*. London, UK: Thames & Hudson.

Te Waka Kai Ora. (2011). *Ngā kaupapa o hua parakore*. Wellington: Author.

Waziyatawin, A. W., & Yellow Bird, M. (2005). *For indigenous eyes only: A decolonisation handbook*. Santa Fe, NM: School of American Research.

Endnotes

1 Neo-colonialism is the geopolitical practice of using capitalism, business globalisation and cultural imperialism to influence a country. A neo-colonial critique can include colonialism and an economic critique of the disproportionate involvement of modern capitalist business in the economy of developing or colonised countries. This definition was drawn from https://en.wikipedia.org/wiki/Neocolonialism.

Chapter 14 Te Awa Atua: Menstruation, whakapapa and the revival of matrilineal Māori ceremony

Ngahuia Murphy

Introduction

Decolonisation to me is about healing, clearing, releasing, transforming, remembering, reviving and reasserting the pathways of our tīpuna (ancestors). It is also about confronting a continuing colonial agenda that manifests itself in myriad ways. These include the denial of our right to autonomy as indigenous peoples, the self-hatred that thrives in our communities as a consequence of ethnocidal policies that attempted to stamp out our philosophies and practices, and the relentless plundering of our elders—the land, the sea, the forests and rivers—under the banner of 'progress', 'civilisation' and 'development'.

Decolonisation is also about reclaiming and, where necessary, reconceptualising our sacred stories in ways that are more consistent with our own cultural paradigms (Mikaere, 2003; Smith, 2012; Yates-Smith, 1998). This is exciting and necessary work because our sacred stories are labyrinths that house our cultural identities, and they have been purged and modified, reinterpreted and retold by the coloniser in ways that demean and threaten our relationships between genders, across the generations, and to the taiao (the web of life) of which we are intrinsically a part.

This is especially true when it comes to our stories and tikanga (practices/customs) regarding women. Leonie Pihama (1994) details the marginalisation of Māori women's knowledge and roles in colonial ethnographic texts, stating:

> Māori women's knowledge has been made secondary to Māori men's
> knowledge and Māori women's roles redefined in line with colonial
> notions of gender relations. Information related to Māori women has
> been ignored or rewritten to become more conducive to colonial belief
> systems. (Pihama, 1994, p. 39)

Those redefinitions have been reproduced for well over 100 years and uncritically subscribed to by many of us in our quest for cultural recla- mation. Linda Tuhiwai Smith (1992) and the Crow wisewoman Pretty Shield (as cited in Allen, 1989) both point out that the power to control stories about ourselves is the power to control our own lives: "The one who tells the stories rules the world" (Shield, cited in Allen, 1989, p. 27).

The river of ancestors and descendants, the ancient matrilineal river that connects us to one another and to our atua (deities), pro- vides a potent example. In the quest to decolonise our stories this is a pivotal site, for it speaks to our very origins. For our tīpuna, the river of power—menstruation—was a symbol of whakapapa (genealogy), assuring the continuity of whānau (extended family) and hapū (a collec- tion of related whānau). It bound the genders by nurturing tikanga and it bonded the generations through simple ceremonies of celebration. Yet colonial ethnographers and historians (Best, 1924, 1929, 1941; Goldie, 1904; Shortland, 1882) have presented menstruation as a symbol of female filth and inferiority. Here, the political agenda behind 'storytell- ing' takes on a sharp edge.

Cosmogonic origins

Reclaiming our sacred stories is like gathering up the road maps that lead us to our own cultural wealth. Sacred stories house values, philosophies and strategies. Our tīpuna were philosophers, scientists, genealogists and metaphysicians. They were confidently navigating the most expansive ocean on the planet when Europeans thought the world was flat. They named and had stories for everything. Unlike Western colonial systems of knowledge whose foundations are based on a hierarchical polarity (that separates in order to dominate and rule), our knowledges lead us back to the centre, where all things interconnect.

So it is with our ancient stories regarding menstruation. According to our tīpuna, menstruation came from Papatūānuku, our beloved creatress mother earth as she ripened into her power within the cosmogonic womb of Te Pō (The Darkness) (Smith, 1913, p. 120). In an evolutionary quickening, the appearance of the sacred red river marked a pivotal moment in the unfolding cosmogonic cycle. Indeed, the blood that assures the procreation of humanity is the same blood that assured the conception of our pantheon of atua. All things are interconnected.

Ancient names for menstruation remind us of its cosmogonic origins. These names include:

- atua (deity/supernatural power)
- awa atua (river carrying a deity/supernatural power)
- rerenga atua (flowing deity/supernatural power)
- Māui (a Polynesian demi-god and cultural hero).

It is worth noting that only derivations of one term are used in the ethnographic texts: 'mate wahine', which colonial ethnographers have translated as a "sickness of women" (Goldie, 1904; Shortland, 1882). This term, however, is absent from the karakia (incantations), mōteatea (songs), and tribal and navigational histories that I surveyed.

Ikura (something precious, shades of red, incantation and sacred knowledge) is another ancient name with cosmogonic origins that recount the genesis of humanity. Our women's versions of this story have been ignored, censored and shunted to the margins. One example, based on oral traditions, is presented here.

> Long ago, before humans strode the earth, the atua Tānemahuta dreamed of the five fingered beings and sought to create them. In order to do so he had to find the mysterious and elusive ira tangata— the life principle that held the key to creating a new species of mortal beings. He hunted high and low and across the world, seeking, searching, but to no avail. All manner of creatures were created by his explorations but that is another story.

Finally, after exhausting himself in his pursuit, Tānemahuta decided to ask for his mother's advice. Papatūānuku, the mother of all things, directed Tānemahuta back to his own birthplace between her thighs. There at the centre of the world, at a place called Kura-waka, he found the secret ingredient capable of ushering in humanity. There he came upon the vibrant 'red clay' steeped in the menstrual river of Papatūānuku. There he finally encountered te ira tangata!

From the sacred 'red clay' Tānemahuta crafted the first human, a woman, Hineahuone. Brimming over with her own mana (authority) and tapu (sacredness), inherited from the divine river, Hineahuone met Tānemahuta as a beloved companion. We are their descendants, a living legacy of their love. And we carry the name ikura for the monthly flow, a name that reminds us of our lineage back to Kura-waka, through the blood. (Murphy, 2014, p. 25)

Hineahuone, by Regan Balzer, 2014. Reproduced with permission.

Colonial perversions

Few of us were raised with cosmogonic stories that vivify the power of our atua wahine (female deities) and the menstrual river. Rather, we were raised with the lacklustre, standardised reinterpretations of the colonial ethnographers, whose own Victorian beliefs warped their storying of 'the natives'. Below is a classic example:

> Tane the god created the first woman out of earth; he formed her by
> scraping up the earth into human shape and endowed her with life. He
> lay on her and breathed life into her and he called her Hine-hau-one
> [*sic*] ... he took her to wife (Cowan, 1930, p. 8).

This perverted version, faithfully trotted out for over a century, represents the antithesis of our cultural paradigms that celebrate the mana and tapu of our atua wahine and the whare tāngata (house of humanity/womb). Cowan's example completely silences the generative power of Papatūānuku and her status as an atua. Hineahuone (Hinehauone) is afforded the same mistreatment, finding herself relegated to a pile of dirt with language that erases the vocabulary of women's sexuality and power.

Colonial representations of this story, derived from biblical constructions of Eve, have been used to inform and perpetuate the myth that women are inferior to men "even as Hineahuone was inferior to Tane" (Best, 1924, p. 74). Here, at the genesis of humanity, what could be a story reflecting the intense power of women, sourced from the creative force of the earth, is instead a subdued story of female reticence. Translated in such a way, this story becomes the hook upon which to hang chronicles of masculine supremacy within the Māori world, chronicles that continue today.

Colonial fictions about the inferiority of women in the Māori world persist partly because they have been reproduced in print. Drawing heavily on Elsdon Best's work, Berys Heuer (1972) writes that Māori women are associated with misfortune, disaster and calamity, and that menstruating women are considered "unclean" and "defiling" (pp. 10–11). Salmond (1975), in her highly regarded *Hui*, presents the same tidy colonial rendition of gendered roles, stating that Māori men

> possess strong tapu qualities, as indeed does anything that enjoys great
> mana. On the other hand, women, the low-born, cooked food, water and
> the young all have noa (common) qualities. Thus women, the low born
> and the young will be prohibited from carrying out sacred rituals. (p. 42)

Drawing on Heuer, Kent and Besley (1990), in *He Whakamārama: Human Relationships: A Bicultural Resource for School and Community Workers*, proclaim that Māori women and girls feel shame toward their bodies (unlike the men) and are seen as a destructive force of low status and little power within Māori society (pp. 4–5).

Given this literary history of redefinition, it is not hard to understand why many people, including Māori, mistakenly assume that Māori women were (and are) accorded little status within Māori society. In contrast, Te Arawa tohunga (cultural expert) Hohepa Te Rake, whose teachings were recorded in 1926, asserts:

> Every Māori was kind and respectful to his mother, to his wife, to his betrothed, to his sisters, and the term sister covered all women excepting his mother and the mother of his children. Woman was not simply a creature of joy and beauty—she was the embodiment of all that was highest and most sacred in life, and her selective love was the purest and most wonderful force in nature: the only means whereby Mankind could improve itself. (Rout & Te Rake, 2003, p. 70)

Compare Te Rake's teachings with those of his Pākehā (non-Māori) male contemporaries of the time, whose deeply misogynist interpretations have been largely accepted as authoritative:

> This 'house' of misfortune, of ominous inferiority, is represented by this world, by the earth, by the female sex, and by the female organ of generation, which holds dread powers of destruction and pollution. (Best, 1924, p. 74)

This view is not derived from a Māori view of our cosmogonic origins, but rather from the Victorian patriarchal and misogynist cultural ideologies of the colonial ethnographers themselves. Understanding the lens through which they saw the world is critical to understanding how this redefinition took place.

The politics of domination

Colonial interpretations of Māori stories, values and beliefs are based on a hierarchical and gendered binary of opposites that underpins Western systems of knowledge. Examples include: male/female, superior/inferior, mind/body, reason/hysteria, civilised/wild, Christian/heathen, heaven/earth. These dualisms are purported to be neutral and natural categories, but one category becomes the privileged term and the other is positioned as its subordinate and negative counterpart (Grosz, 1994; Johnston, 2005). Christian doctrines have contributed to dualistic thinking, aligning men with morality, immortality and spiritual transcendence, and women with flesh, decay, mortality, the earth and sin (Blackford, 1999; Grosz, 1994; Ruether, 1996).

These dualisms and the philosophies that inform them are the lens through which colonial historians and ethnographers reinterpreted the Māori world (Pihama, 1994, 2001). Tapu and noa, for example, were redefined as a gendered hierarchical polarity rather than a continuum that men and women traversed throughout their daily lives (Mikaere, 2003; Pihama, 2001). Within the ethnographic records, Māori women are consistently categorised as inferior "daughters of the earth", aligned with mortality, the body and noa (which colonial ethnographers translated as profane). Men are posited as occupying a superior status as tapu (translated by them as sacred) "sons of the heavens" (Best, 1924, 1976). Best does concede that menstruating Māori women were regarded as tapu, but he retranslates 'tapu' in this one context as "unclean like in the Scriptures" (Best, 1924, 1929).

Such constructions deny our cosmogonic accounts, which describe the evolution of the earth mother Papatūānuku and the sky father Ranginui alongside one another within the womb space of Te Pō (Royal, 2003). Dominance and subordination are not characteristic of the primordial parents of humanity. Similarly, the presentation of Māori women as inferior through our matrilineal descent from Papatūānuku is incongruous with our conceptions of her as te ūkaipō, beloved nurturer of humanity (Stokes, 2002; Williams, 2004).

Introducing the politics of dominance and subordination to our sacred stories has distorted our gender relations and knocked out of kilter the balance our tīpuna strived for. Destabilising our whānau in this way has facilitated the success of colonisation and continues to do so. Likewise, narratives that present menstruation as something shameful and dirty progress a colonial agenda of cultural annihilation. We must ask ourselves: What does it mean to see the symbol of whakapapa, the blood of our origins, as something shameful, as something dirty?

Reclaiming our ancestral wisdoms

Rather than being seen as "defiling" and "demonic" (Goldie, 1904; Shortland, 1882), traditional Māori beliefs about menstruation present it as a medium connecting us to our "atuatanga, tangatatanga, whakapapa" (divinity, humanity, genealogy) (R. Pere, personal communication, 12 July 2010). When the river of ancestors and descendants arrived for the first time, marking puberty, it was greeted with celebration and ceremony. Examples include the ceremonial piercing of ears and cutting of hair, the taking of moko kauae (traditional Māori women's tattoo on the chin and lips), community feasting and gift giving (Murphy, 2013). Intergenerational teachings were an integral part of menarche ceremonies, binding the generations across time and space. When women bled each month, it was considered a time of rest in honour of the "house of humanity"—the whare tangata. Men took charge of the harvesting and cooking of kai (food) during this time (Murphy, 2013).

Below is an example of a traditional menarche chant.

He Whai Kanohi Me Ka Pohea
Te rā e hara mai rā,
Rere kura, rere toro hai,
Te marama e rere mai rā,
Rere kura, rere toro hai,
Ka whēkite,
Ka whēkaro, te kāhui tupua,
Nau mai ki waho;
Te ritorito,
Te wai whero;
Tupu te ora,
He ora, ora.

To Acquire Eyes Should One Be Blinded
The sun arising, coming forth
Flying red, seeking its journey
The moon arising, coming forth
Flying red, seeking its journey
One sees it dimly for the first time, dimly visible
Are the company of supernatural beings
Welcome come forward

The potential for life
The menstrual blood
Let life grow
Life itself, it lives.
(Grey, 1853, p. 281, translated by S. Ellison)

A symbol of the vivacity of life, menstruation in this karakia is no defiling source of female inferiority. When we examine our own oral literatures we discover that notions of female shame and insignificance are not a cultural inheritance, as some of us have been led to believe, but a colonial one.

Re-meshing the universe

Our myths are sacred stories that, in Oceanic philosophy, serve a critical purpose. The Hawaiian translation of myth is ka'ao, meaning the "meshing of the cosmos", the "netting of the universe" (Tangarō, 2007, p. vi). Our sacred stories carry the instructions of our tīpuna about proper conduct in order to maintain the balance. They are rituals that actively "net the universe", singing the strands that unite all things through whakapapa. As indigenous people in a process of decolonisation, if we find that our stories have been reinterpreted by others in a way that does not uphold the balance, then we must carefully re-thread the strands, always holding in sight that we are ourselves tīpuna. We have a responsibility to ensure that our stories and tikanga are tika (correct) *for us*. That is, they lead us to empowerment as a people and strengthen our whakapapa ties to one another across and beyond the human dimension.

What does this mean in terms of the river of ancestors and descendants? It means rejecting narratives that present it as dirty and shameful. It means rejecting terms such as 'mate' that reinforce colonialist Victorian beliefs. It means reclaiming traditional names for menstruation that remind us that it is an ancient river that flows across the generations connecting us back to our atua. It means re-envisioning ceremonies for today that empower our daughters, nieces and mokos and remind us that the matrilineal river of power assures the continuity of whānau and hapū. It means teaching our sons about the power of the blood so that respectful tikanga can, once again, foster a bond between men and women as tribal sisters and brothers.

All of these projects are decolonising in that they facilitate healing and transformation through remembering, reviving and reclaiming the wisdoms of our ancestors in the knowledge that they provide potential solutions to current challenges. To free ourselves from colonial representations and to trust our own intuitive knowing in the redesigning of our whānau rituals and in the reframing of our sacred stories is a political act. For, to trust and have faith in ourselves to reinvent, based on ancient teachings, is to honour our traditions as philosophers, scientists, navigators and knowledge seekers, extending ourselves beyond present limitations, constantly seeking new horizons.

References

Allen, P. (1989). *Spider woman's granddaughters: Traditional tales and contemporary writings by Native American women*. Boston, MA: Beacon Press.

Best, E. (1924). *Māori religion and mythology: Part 1*. Wellington: Government Printer.

Best, E. (1929). *The whare kohanga and its lore: Comprising data pertaining to procreation, baptism and infant betrothal*. Wellington: Government Printer.

Best, E. (1941). *The Māori*. Wellington: The Polynesian Society.

Best, E. (1976). *Māori religion and mythology: Being an account of the cosmogony, anthropology, religious beliefs and rites, magic and folk lore of the Māori folk of New Zealand: Part One*. Wellington: Government Printer.

Blackford, H. (1999). My lips, sealed for your protection. In C. Steele (Ed.), *Moon days* (pp. 12–23). Woodstock, NY: Ash Tree.

Cowan, J. (1930). *Legends of the Māori: Volume one*. Wellington: Harry H. Tombs.

Goldie, W. H. (1904). *Māori medical lore*. New Zealand: Southern Reprints.

Grey, G. (1853). *Ko nga moteatea me nga hakirara o nga Māori*. Wellington: Robert Stokes.

Grosz, E. (1994). *Volatile bodies: Toward a corporeal feminism*. Bloomington, IN: Indiana University Press.

Heuer, B. (1972). *Māori women*. Wellington: Published for the Polynesian Society by A. H. & A. W. Reed.

Johnston, L. (2005). Man: Woman. In P. Cloke & R. Johnston (Eds.), *Spaces of geographical thought* (pp. 119–141). London, UK: Sage.

Kent, J., & Besley, T. (1990). *He whakamarama: Human relationships: A bicultural resource for school and community workers*. Christchurch: Christchurch College of Education.

Mikaere, A. (2003). *The balance destroyed: The consequences for Māori women of the colonisation of tikanga Māori*. Auckland: The International Research Institute for Māori and Indigenous Education and Ani Mikaere.

Murphy, N. (2013). *Te awa atua: Menstruation in the pre-colonial Māori world*. Ngaruawahia: He Puna Manawa.

Murphy, N. (2014). *Waiwhero: He whakahirahiatanga o te ira wahine*. Ngaruawahia: He Puna Manawa.

Pihama, L. (1994). Redrawing the maps: The plural society and its futures. *Te Pua, 3*(2), 37–41.

Pihama, L. (2001). *Tihei mauri ora: Honouring our voices: Mana wahine as a kaupapa Māori theoretical framework*. Unpublished doctoral dissertation, The University of Auckland.

Rout, E. A., & Te Rake, H. (2003). *Māori symbolism*. London, UK: Stephen Austin & Sons.

Royal, T. C. (Ed.). (2003). *The woven universe: Selected writings of Rev. Māori Marsden*. Otaki: The Estate of Rev. Māori Marsden.

Ruether, R. (1996). Ecofeminism: Symbolic and social connections of the oppression of women and the domination of nature. In R. S. Gottlieb (Ed.), *This sacred earth: Religion, nature, environment* (pp. 322–333). New York, NY: Routledge.

Salmond, A. (1975). *Hui: A study of Māori ceremonial gatherings*. Auckland: Reed Books.

Shortland, E. (1882). *Māori religion and mythology*. London, UK: Longman & Green.

Smith, P. (1913). *The lore of the whare wananga: Te kauwae runga*. New Plymouth: Polynesian Society.

Smith, L. T. (1992). Māori women: Discourses, projects and mana wahine. In S. J. Middleton, (Ed.), *Women and education in Aotearoa 2* (pp. 33–51). Wellington: Bridget Williams Books.

Smith, L. T. (2012). *Decolonizing methodologies: Research and indigenous peoples*. London, UK: Zed Books.

Stokes, E. (2002). Contesting resources: Māori, Pākehā, and a tenurial revolution. In E. Pawson & T. Brooking (Eds.), *Environmental histories of New Zealand*. Auckland: Oxford University Press.

Tangarō, T. (2007). *Lele kawa: Fire rituals of Pele*. Honolulu, HI: Kamehameha Publishing.

Williams, J. (2004). Papatūānuku: Attitudes to land. In T. Ka'ai (Ed.), *Ki te whaiao: An introduction to Māori culture and society*. Auckland: Pearson Longman.

Yates-Smith, A. (1998). *Hine! E hine!: Rediscovering the feminine in Māori spirituality*. Unpublished doctoral dissertation, University of Waikato.

Chapter 15 Ka puta rā koe ki te whai ao ki te ao mārama: Where do babies come from?

Debbie Broughton

How are we connected to tūpuna that have passed on and to those yet to be born? Each generation has added layers to our understandings. About tūpuna. About whakapapa. But then the separation occurred. Not Papatūānuku and Ranginui. I mean the other separation. The myth that said we only lived once. The myth that said we were separate from our tūpuna, and they from us. I heard it was a deal done between the Pope and a doctor who wanted dead people to cut up. (Not sure if that just appeals because it's a morbid tale). The doctor got the dead people so the grave-robbing stopped. And the Pope claimed the souls.

Now that deal wouldn't have meant anything to us, but it was transplanted here. Where it grew. Where it was fertilised in churches and fed to us in schools. The schools that told us we didn't understand enough, we needed educating. The schools that allowed us to leave our shoes at the door as long as we left our understandings of the world there too. The schools where we were taught that our tūpuna were dead people.

But it wasn't us that made that deal. That separation myth is not ours. Because we have always understood that tūpuna are not dead people. The posts of our whare tūpuna speak of fibres entwined. Of beginnings that are endings, and endings that are more beginnings. Of whakapapa etched on faces before birth. Of ariki, of atua—representations of the beyond enacted. In a world of cycles and circles, death and birth are but layers of our journeys. That is imprinted upon our whakapapa. That is whakapapa.

And we have always understood how to tell stories. Stories with threads, humour, layers, whakapapa. Stories about everyday life. Because we have always known that coming to understand doesn't just happen in schools. The story I have to tell is not about dead people. Or about schools. Or about deals. It's a story about tūpuna. About where babies come from. It's a story about coming to understand, and challenging the deal. In everyday life. Outside the boxes.

Tūpuna and whakapapa

Ducking her head to avoid the top bunk, she gave Kora a kiss.

"Kei te pai bubba? Kia pai tō moe."

Kora stopped her before she pulled the bedroom door shut. "Mum, wait, I'm scared."

Mum sighed, used to Kora's stalling tactics at bedtime. Walking back into the room, she threw the toys down the end of the bed. Snuggling under the blanket she asked, "Why are you scared bubba?"

"Because what will happen to me when I die?"

Mum hesitated, tucking Kora's curls back in behind her right ear. "Well bubba, you're a tupuna, and when you die, you will still be a tupuna."

"What's a tupuna, Māmā?"

"Tūpuna are the old people. We all have tūpuna that look after us."

Kora raised her eyebrow in query, a whānau trait. "But what are they Mum? And what do they do?"

Taking a breath, she thought about how to reply. Talking about tūpuna sometimes sounded like she was talking about a religion, not her relations. She wondered whether that was because her parents sent her to Sunday school. They weren't really religious, but her aunty who taught the Sunday school was. Maybe they sent her there so they could sleep in on Sunday mornings. She didn't really know. Going there had left her with a muddled idea of what or who that God was. Tūpuna were different though. She didn't know it all, that was for sure. But

Nan had always talked to her about tūpuna. Over the past 6 months they had talked about them more than ever.

Six months ago. The first time I came back. Before I changed my mind.

"Tūpuna look after us," she said. "So we can look after our bubbas, so our bubbas know how to look after their bubbas."

Kora looked up at the ceiling. "Mum, are tūpuna with us all the time?"

"Āe."

"But Mum, what about when we are in the wharepaku, are they with us then?" Kora asked seriously.

"I think they wait outside," she replied, giving a reassuring smile and suppressing a giggle.

Jumping out from under the duvet she gave Kora another quick kiss on the forehead. She rearranged the toys on the bed and added, "You know you can mihi to your tūpuna bubba. You can ask them to look after you tonight, and then you don't need to be scared."

Kora's big blue eyes darted around the room. Then she said 'Tūpuna, ka taea e koutou te tiaki ahau? Ngā mihi."

Sitting down at her desk she opened her emails. She groaned as she spotted an email from the school. A week ago she had slipped into class, just before three. The kids were standing with hands clasped and heads bowed. Even a week on from that scene the memory still jolted here. She didn't think a kura of all places would be teaching Christian prayers. She'd called the principal to find out what was going on. Clicking open the email she scanned it quickly. It was a pānui for a whānau hui to talk about tikanga and karakia at the kura. It was a start.

Sinking back into her chair she gave a mihi to tūpuna for tonight's job. She had a letter to write for a hui the next day about her tūpuna land. Going to those hui with the suits wasn't really her thing. But Nan asked her to go. And she couldn't say no to Nan.

Writing letters for her whānau kept her up some nights. It also brought her tūpuna to life. Now they were more than just names written carefully in Koro's whakapapa book, tucked away at the top of her wardrobe. She pulled the photos of her tūpuna up on screen. The photos were grainy, mostly black-and-white scans, spanning generations.

Nan thought a cousin had the originals. She didn't know which cousin and whether they still had them. At least someone had scanned them and put them online. It did seem weird to have tūpuna jpegs rather than framed photos on the lounge wall. At some stage she'd see if the photos could be enlarged. She loved looking at their photos and imagining their lives.

Their clothing was a big clue to the generation each photo belonged to. The earliest photos were of tūpuna draped with kākāhu and hei tiki. As she moved through the generations she could see subtle changes in the clothes her tūpuna wore. These became big changes over time. The kākāhu were replaced by shirts, starched hard, and pants with razor-sharp creases. Hei tiki became pocket watches, neck ties and pearl chokers. Until, clothing-wise at least, her tūpuna didn't look any different from her Pākehā side. She wondered how they felt when those photos were taken. She wondered what, if anything, they accepted, along with the high-necked, white, buttoned-up dresses. She wondered, but she had no doubt that they were doing whatever they thought at the time was best. For her, for their mokopuna.

Lately she spent longer staring at one particular photo. A very dark photo, one of the earlier ones.

I remember that day. I remember that tāniko border that chased itself around my shoulders. I remember how the white collared shirt scratched.

Printing out a copy of her tupuna's photo she tucked it inside her notebook. Taking a printout instead of a photo to a hui was a bit different. She did it for herself, though, not for anyone else. Nan said to set her kawa. This was part of Mum's for important kaupapa.

Rain lashing the windscreen, she drove at snail's pace into town. Hitting Petone she saw dark clouds hunched over the city. She knew people would abandon the trains for the warmth of their cars. Finding a park would be a challenge. She felt her heart pumping faster. She would be cutting it fine.

But with perfect timing she found a park less than a block away. She could see Nan peering anxiously through the glass door of the office tower.

"You alright girl? All this waiting around, you tryna make me mimi my tarau? Let's go girl," Nan joked and was rewarded by a hint of a smile.

Mum took a deep breath to compose herself. Then she guided Nan through the lobby and up the lift to the fifth floor.

They were greeted promptly. They settled around the boardroom table for mihimihi. Her eyes flickered, remembering she hadn't said a mihi to tūpuna. She wondered whether it would matter. Running through scenarios in her head, she tried to figure out what to do. She couldn't leave the room now. She knew she shouldn't rely on someone else to mihi for her. She couldn't help but hope they would though.

Nan began their whakapapa to the people of the land. Very quickly she began flying through the generations, recalling their land, recalling their people. "Ka moe i a … Ka puta ki waho ko…".

Nearly 200 years have passed since we lived on that land. On our land. 200 years, seven generations. Then our pā was closed. We were moved. Onto other land. And now there is no-one. No-one.

Standing to sing Nan's waiata, she realised her chance to mihi to tūpuna was lost. Pushing the thought from her mind she grabbed some pineapple. The agenda moved on from mihimihi. She started writing.

That's when out of nowhere the coughing began. Damn, she thought, did that pineapple scratch my throat? She kept writing, the pen in one hand and the other one cupping her mouth. Her eyes scanned the room for a water jug, finding none. Cheeks flaming, she ducked out of the room. In a small staffroom to the right she spied a water jug. She quickly poured herself a glass. The water slid down her throat. She felt her heart return to its normal rhythm.

She took a quick look to make sure she was alone. "Nei rā te mihi ki a koutou e te kāhui tūpuna hei tautoko i te kaupapa o te rā. Nō reira tēnā koutou, tēnā koutou, tēnā koutou katoa."

Talking to tūpuna was something she was coming to understand more each day. She knew that if anyone wanted her to succeed, it was those who would eventually become her children or her mokopuna. She felt self-conscious about it sometimes though, especially talking out loud to her tūpuna. But Nan said speaking out loud had a different vibration to thought, so even though she didn't understand it yet, she did it.

When she first began talking with her tūpuna she thought it was her tupuna with the tāniko border on her kākāhu that was talking back to her. Lately, though, it seemed like that tupuna had moved on, and a different tupuna spoke to her now.

Remind them that they wanted us out. Our houses were moved so they wouldn't sully the white streets. We were moved so we wouldn't sully their white streets. Remind them, as they sit there in their suits.

She finished the water then walked back into the meeting, feeling calmer and hoping she hadn't missed much. Nan was sharing their connections with the pā. She was glad she hadn't missed this bit. She was always mesmerised hearing Nan talk about her tūpuna in such detail. It was as if she had been there. The stories they were there to tell were not the love stories that she had grown up with. They were the stories she had learnt as an adult. She wouldn't share those with Kora until she was old enough to bear their weight.

Hours later they walked out of the hui. She willed herself to slow down to keep pace with Nan. Her eyes were flashing with indignation and hurt from Nan's stories. But she felt lighter now. The board was rethinking its proposal for their land. Confrontation was hard on everyone, but she knew hui like that had to happen. Sometimes the board seemed to get dragged along by other people's agendas. As if they were there for the money as well. And they needed to be reminded of who they were.

Dropping Nan back home, she gave her a quick kiss on the cheek. Back in the car she said a mihi to her tūpuna for their support. Then she leant her head against the steering wheel and closed her eyes for a few seconds. A text jerked her back to reality. She put the car into drive and headed back to pick up Kora from school.

She put Kora to bed early that night.

"Mum!" Kora called out as she moved towards the door, "Wait Mum, I have another question."

Fighting back the urge to brush Kora off, she perched on the side of the bed.

"Mum, what happens after you are a tupuna?" Kora asked.

"After you're a tupuna, you come back again as a baby."

Kora squirmed beneath the blankets in excitement, "Will I come back as your baby Mum?"

"Maybe not as my baby, but I think you'll come back into our whānau."

"So whose baby will I come back as?" Kora persisted.

"I don't know, bubba. Maybe you will come back as Cole's mokopuna."

"Not Cole!" Kora squealed with delight and disgust. "Cole's got the bogey touch. He picks his nose and doesn't wash his hands!"

"Well let's hope by the time Cole is a koro, he would have stopped picking his nose. Or at least he will have learnt to wash his hands." Mum laughed. It felt good to laugh after a long day.

She snuck into the bathroom the next morning and confirmed her suspicions with a double-pack of tests from the pharmacy.

"Babe!" she began, burrowing under the blankets. "Babe, we're having another bubba."

Dad was startled, then threw his arms around her, holding on tight.

"I wonder which tupuna it is this time," she said, glancing over at the computer desk to the tupuna on her screensaver.

"Might be one of mine," he said.

"As long as it doesn't have your toe-jams," she laughed.

It was good to hear them so happy together again. It was tough on them when I changed my mind and didn't come back in again six months ago. But this time will be different, this time I will be different. Maybe I'll see a photo of the tupuna with the tāniko border and recognise myself. Or maybe I will have to relearn who I am, and how I am a tupuna too.

Te pae haumako—recreating our stories

It's been 200 years since the deal was brought to our whenua. Two hundred years of generation after generation being told in schools and in churches that tūpuna were dead people. But 200 years doesn't mean that our stories are lost, or that our understandings are irretrievable.

This book itself is a recollection, a collective remembering of our understandings. A spring for us to draw from. It can feed our stories, grow our perceptions, and help us heal the separation myth. If we let it, it can reawaken our memories of what is accurate, and what is ours.

Whether schools have a role to play in this, I'm not really sure. Most have not been set up to do this. But I do know that we don't need schools to shift our perceptions—about who we are, about who tūpuna are. Learning is not just something that happens once you walk through a school gate.

I'm not going to pretend it's an easy thing. Re-examining our understandings of where we come from before we are born. Rethinking where we go when we die. It's become a religion thing. It's become a belief thing. But at its core, it is about whakapapa. About challenging, recreating, and allowing each other to forget the boxes ever existed. It's about being brave about who we are.

Being brave can be as simple as just paying attention, being alert to what's happening in our everyday lives. The spare carpark that appears out of nowhere, the meat pack that you win the day before unexpected guests arrive. The signs that tūpuna give us every day of their support. The signs that tūpuna are not just dead people.

Tēnei te mōkai ki te kaupapa e mihi ana ki te kāhui tūpuna,
ki te pae haumako, ki te pae tapu.

Ngā mihi nui ki a Tungia Kaihau-Symonds rātou ko Watene Kaihau,
ko Sarah-Keita, ko Hariata mō ō koutou atawhai.

Tēnā koutou, tēnā koutou, tēnā koutou katoa.

Glossary

Aotearoa: New Zealand

atua: deity

atua wāhine: female energetic deities

atuatanga: divinity

awa atua: river carrying a deity/supernatural power

haka: Māori performing arts

hapū: a collection of related whānau

Hine-ahu-one: a deity

Hine-hau-one: a deity

Hinetitama: a deity

ikura: the monthly flow

ipu whenua: container for placenta

ira tangata: the life principle that held the key to creating a new species of mortal beings

iwi: tribe

ka'ao: the meshing of the cosmos, the netting of the universe

kai: food

kaiāwhina: voluntary teacher

kainga: home

kaitiaki: environmental caretaker and guardian

kapa haka: Māori performing arts

karakia: incantations; songs

kaumātua: elders

kaupapa Māori: Māori philosophy and principles

kawa o te marae: marae protocol

kei wareware i a tātou te ūkaipō: lest we forget the mother who nurtured us at her breast

kōhanga reo: preschool Māori-language nest

kōrero: talk

kuia: nannies and aunties

kura: school

kura kaupapa Māori: Māori-medium schooling

kura-ā-iwi: iwi-based schooling

mana: authority

mana motuhake:

mana wāhine: female authority

manaaki: support

Māoritanga: Māori way of life

marae: meeting house

marae-a-kura: meeting houses on school grounds

mātauranga mana wahine: Māori women's knowledges

mātauranga Māori: Māori knowledge

Matike Mai: visionary and communicator with the divine realms

Māui: a Polynesian deity and cultural hero

moko kauae: traditional Māori women's tattoo on the chin and lips

mokos (mokopuna): grandchildren

mōteatea: traditional chant

muka: flax fibre

Ngāti Kahungunu: a tribe

noa: common

Papatūānuku: Earth Mother

Pāremata Māori: Māori Parliament

pito: end; navel

pōwhiri: ritual of encounter

pūrākau: kaupapa Māori storytelling

rāhui: a form of sacredness

rangatahi Māori: Māori youth

rangatiratanga: self-determination

Ranginui: sky father

raranga: weaving

reo rumaki: language immersion

rerenga atua: flowing deity; supernatural power

taha Māori: Māori dimension

taiao: the web of life

tamariki: children

Tāne: a deity

tangata whenua: people of the land

tangatatanga: humanity

taonga: treasures

tapu: sacredness

tāpuhi: nurse in one's arms

Te Aho Matua: kaupapa Māori curriculum framework

te ao: the world of light

te ao hurihuri: the changing world

te ao Māori: the Māori world

te ira tangata: the human essence of a child, with physical, spiritual and emotional needs

te pā harakeke: a metaphor for Māori communities

Te Pō: The Darkness

Te Puni Kōkiri: Ministry of Māori Development

te reo Māori: the Māori language

teina: younger sibling

tika: correct

tikanga: practices/customs

tino rangatiratanga: self-determination

tīpuna: ancestors

tohu: qualification

tohunga: cultural expert

tuakana: older sibling

tukutuku: decorative fibre work

tūpuna: ancestors

Ūkaipō: beloved nurturer of humanity

waha kura: woven basket

waiata: songs and chants

wānanga: learning centre

whaea: mother

whaikōrero: oratory

whakairo: carving

whakapapa: genealogy

whānau: extended family

whanaungatanga: kinship

whare purokuroku: outreach centre

whare tangata: house of humanity; womb

whare wānanga: schools for teaching Māori genealogy of knowledge; schools of higher learning

wharekura: kaupapa Māori secondary schools

whenua: land

whenua Māori: Māori land

Author biographies

Linda Tuhiwai Smith
Ngāti Awa, Ngāti Porou

Linda has worked in the field of Māori education and health for many years, and is perhaps
best known for her work in spearheading the
development of kaupapa Māori research and having it recognised as a legitimate methodological
approach in its own right. Her book *Decolonising
Methodologies: Research and Indigenous Peoples* has been an international best seller in the indigenous world since its publication in 1998,
and she is widely sought after both here in Aotearoa and internationally
as a public speaker.

Starting out as a school teacher, Linda became a university lecturer
and researcher, and later Professor of Education at The University
of Auckland. Linda was a founding Joint Director of Ngā Pae o
te Māramatanga, New Zealand's first Māori Centre of Research
Excellence, from 2002 to 2007. She holds a host of research positions,
including as a member of the New Zealand Health Research Council,
where she is chair of the Māori Health Research Committee, and as
a member of the Marsden Fund Council, where she is convenor of
the Social Sciences Assessment Panel. Recent additional appointments
have included the Constitutional Advisory Panel Committee in New
Zealand and the High Panel—Science, Technology and Innovation for
Development in Paris.

Linda has a PhD in education and is currently Professor of Education
and Māori Development, Pro Vice-Chancellor Māori, at the University
of Waikato.

Jenny Lee-Morgan
Ngāti Mahuta

Jenny has extensive experience in teaching and kaupapa Māori research, and has been involved as a whānau member in kōhanga reo, kura kaupapa Māori, wharekura and mainstream secondary schools. In conjunction with other Māori education colleagues, and through Rautaki Ltd, an independent research and educational resource development company of which she was a director, Jenny co-conceptualised and co-developed the educational websites www.kaupapamaori.com and www.rangahau.co.nz on kaupapa Māori theory, research and action.

Jenny is also one of a number of leading Māori educators and researchers working to further develop and advance the field of kaupapa Māori research. Her innovations have focused on the revival and development of a pūrākau or story-telling method to share the real-life voices of research participants in a culturally consistent and thought-provoking manner.

Formerly a secondary school teacher of te reo Māori, Jenny has also worked in the community, business and tertiary education sectors, including as a lecturer in Māori education at The University of Auckland. Her publications include a book, *Jade Taniwha: Māori-Chinese Identity and Schooling*, published in 2007, which grew out of her MA thesis on identity and education. Jenny has a doctorate in education from The University of Auckland, and until recently was the Head of School at Te Puna Wānanga (School of Māori Education) in the Faculty of Education at The University of Auckland. She is currently on research and study leave to focus on writing about her research and experiences.

Jessica Hutchings
Ngāi Tahu

Jessica has been working at the cross-roads of indigenous knowledge, intellectual property rights, the politics of food and food sovereignty issues for the past two decades. An executive member of Te Waka Kai Ora (National Māori Organics Organisation) for many years, Jessica helped lead a project to develop a tikanga-based Māori food standard, Hua Parakore, and is herself a verified Hua Parakore food producer, growing kai for whānau on her small farm north of Wellington. She has published extensively in this area, including a recently released book *Hua Parakore Mara Kai: A Māori Food Sovereignty Handbook*, and up until recently she was a lecturer in environmental studies at Victoria University of Wellington.

An experienced kaupapa Māori researcher, Jessica has worked as an investment manager Māori for the Foundation for Research, Science & Technology, was the inaugural fellow at Te Mata o Te Tau, hosted by Massey University, and held a Health Research Council post-doctoral fellowship, also hosted by Massey University. She has a PhD in environmental studies from Victoria University of Wellington, and was the tumuaki of the kaupapa Māori research unit, Te Wāhanga, at the New Zealand Council for Educational Research until 2016.

Ranginui Walker
Whakatōhea

Over the last 40 years Ranginui Walker penned and published countless academic papers, magazine articles and books that told the history of colonial injustice in Aotearoa and the transformative developments that Māori have made in response, in particular in his ground-breaking book *Ka Whawhai Tonu Matou: Struggle Without End*, published in 1990. This considerable body of work has been hugely informative for both Māori and Pākehā, students, lecturers and laypeople alike, and his bold and authoritative voice was central in reshaping and redefining educational practices and politics in Aotearoa.

Ranginui was a primary school teacher, a community educator and a lecturer at Auckland Teachers College and The University of Auckland, where he gained a PhD in anthropology, and where he was appointed Associate Professor of Māori Studies in 1986 and Professor and Head of Department in 1993. He was a former secretary and chairman of the Auckland District Māori Council, a member of the New Zealand Māori Council, and a member of the Waitangi Tribunal. Ranginui was also a foundation member of and New Zealand delegate to the World Council of Indigenous Peoples, and received many honours in recognition of his work, including being appointed a Distinguished Companion of the New Zealand Order of Merit in 2001. He was a recipient of a Ngā Pae o te Māramatanga Te Tohu o te Māramatanga research excellence award in 2007, was awarded a Prime Minister's Literary Award in 2009, and received a Distinguished Alumni Award from The University of Auckland in 2012.

Moana Jackson
Ngāti Kahungunu, Ngāti Porou

Moana has worked with an extensive number of whānau, hapū, iwi and Māori organisations over the last four decades to assist them with a vast range of kaupapa—from drafting the original Wai 262 claim in the early 1980s, to leading the call for a separate Māori justice system in his 1988 research report *He Whaipaanga Hou*, through to taking a lead role in the campaign against the government's foreshore and seabed legislation in 2004. Moana is currently co-convenor of Matike Mai Aotearoa, an independent working group on constitutional transformation, whose brief is to develop a new constitution for Aotearoa that affirms rangatiratanga and tikanga Māori, and which he describes as his most exciting work to date.

Moana is very highly respected and trusted, both here in Aotearoa and overseas, where he has worked extensively on international indigenous issues, including the drafting of the United Nations Declaration on the Rights of Indigenous Peoples, and is regarded as an expert on indigenous constitutionalism. Moana was a judge on the International Tribunal of Indigenous Rights in Hawaii in 1993, and again in Canada in 1995. He was also counsel for the Bougainville Interim Government during the Bougainville peace process, and most recently was part of a United Nations delegation of human rights specialists to explore interventions into the Gaza situation.

Ani Mikaere
Ngāti Raukawa

Ani is one of the leading Māori commentators on the colonisation of tikanga Māori, which she names as the first law of Aotearoa. She has published and spoken extensively on this subject. Her publications include *The Balance Destroyed: The Consequences for Māori Women of the Colonisation of Tikanga Māori*, published in 2003, and *Colonising*

Myths—Māori Realities: He Rukuruku Whakaaro, a collection of articles and papers, published in 2011. In 2004 she was invited to deliver the Bruce Jesson Memorial lecture, where her address *Are We all New Zealanders Now?: A Māori Response to the Pākehā Quest for Indigeneity* explored the Pākehā search for legitimacy in Aotearoa.

Ani began her career as a legal academic at The University of Auckland from 1988 to 1990, followed by a term at the University of Waikato from 1991 to 2000. In 2001 she took up a position at Te Wānanga o Raukawa, heading the Ahunga Tikanga (Māori Laws and Philosophy) programme, which provided a much-welcomed shift in emphasis. Since 2010 Ani has been co-director of Te Kāhui Whakatupu Mātauranga at the Wānanga, promoting the expansion of the body of knowledge that has been bequeathed to contemporary Māori by earlier generations. She is co-organiser of a series of biannual symposia entitled *Kei Tua o Te Pae*, which explore the decolonisation and reclamation of tikanga and mātauranga. Ani has a Master of Jurisprudence from the University of Waikato and is currently working towards completing Te Kāurutanga, the most senior qualification awarded at Te Wānanga o Raukawa.

Sarah-Jane Tiakiwai
Waikato, Te Rarawa, Ngāti Awa, Ngāti Pikiao

Sarah-Jane Tiakiwai is the inaugural Academic Director for the Waikato-Tainui College for Research and Development, appointed in May 2010. The College is a Waikato-Tainui tribal institution which has a focus on developing leadership, engaging in innovative research and development initiatives, and working towards the preservation and maintenance of tribal culture and heritage.

Sarah-Jane previously worked in the wānanga and university sectors, holding a range of research, teaching and senior administrative and management positions, as well as running her own company. She has a strong background in and passion for iwi education and development.

Sarah-Jane was the first recipient of the post-settlement Waikato Raupatu doctoral scholarship offered by Waikato-Tainui, and her PhD examined the factors that contributed to the success of Māori in higher education. Sarah-Jane is from Waikato-Tainui and Te Rarawa, and also has whāngai connections to Ngāti Awa and Ngāti Pikiao.

Takawai Murphy
Ngāti Manawa, Ngāti Ruapani ki Waikaremoana, Tūhoe, Ngāti Rangitihi and Ngāti Kahungunu

Takawai is an inspiring and accomplished decolonisation educator who elicits high praise from both Māori and Pākehā participants alike for challenging them to develop greater understandings of Te Tiriti o Waitangi and insights into cross-cultural relationships without being confrontational. Starting out as a teacher, Takawai taught in schools for 20 years, many of them in senior positions, including as a principal. Frustrations with the school system, and particularly the limited educational response to the needs of Māori students (and staff members) in terms of recognising and valuing Māori language, identity and culture, led him to advocate for change for a number of years. In 1991, when change was not forthcoming and the only response was to silence or alienate him, Takawai left the school system and instead designed the Te Pūmaomao Nationhood Building course as a way of portraying his story and that of many Māori, and to empower participants to make a positive difference in their lives and the work they do.

He has now been presenting and evolving this programme for over 20 years to a wide range of participants, including Māori organisations, non-government organisations, local and regional councils, district health boards, and government departments. Ironically, in recent times the education sector has been one of the most responsive to the programme, which has been amended to focus on raising Māori educational achievement. Recently Takawai has also begun presenting an adapted version of this programme in Alaska to support the native Alaskans' resiliency project.

Veronica M. H. Tawhai
Ngāti Porou, Ngāti Uepohatu

Although self-described as an emerging kaupapa Māori educator and researcher, Veronica's
work in Māori and youth development, citizenship education, and Māori and youth political
participation and engagement has been widely
acclaimed and published in journals, conference
proceedings and books. She has co-edited two books, *Weeping Waters:
The Treaty of Waitangi and Constitutional Change*, published in 2010,
and *Always Speaking: The Treaty of Waitangi and Public Policy*, published in 2011. Veronica recently concluded her role as the national
co-ordinator of Matike Mai Aotearoa Rangatahi, the youth project of
the Independent Working Group on Constitutional Transformation,
and has presented widely on this kaupapa with and to rangatahi and
others throughout Aotearoa.

The significance of her work has attracted wide recognition, and
she has been appointed an associate scholar for the Centre for World
Indigenous Studies, served as a subcommissioner for UNESCO New
Zealand (Education Subcommission), and was awarded a research
fellowship at the National Centre for Indigenous Studies at the
Australian National University in 2013. She was also a recipient of the
Fulbright–Ngā Pae o te Māramatanga Indigenous Scholar Award in
the same year.

Veronica is a passionate advocate for an education system that
supports Māori student success, and is an academic mentor in her
community, an active kōhanga and kura kaupapa Māori parent, and
a life member and advisor for Te Mana Ākonga, the national Māori
tertiary students' association. She is currently completing a PhD on
citizenship education at Massey University and works there as a lecturer at Te Pūtahi-a-Toi, the School of Māori Art, Knowledge and
Education.

Leonie Pihama

Te Ātiawa, Ngā Māhanga ā Tairi,
Ngāti Māhanga

Leonie is a leading kaupapa Māori educator and researcher, and a strong advocate for the rangatiratanga of whānau, hapū and iwi. She has been working in the intersecting fields of education, health and whānau wellbeing for a number of decades, and has been involved in kōhanga reo, Māori-language immersion units and kura kaupapa Māori. She is widely published and sought after as a conference speaker, both here and overseas, and has contributed significantly to the development of the field of kaupapa Māori theory and research, including through her doctoral studies on mana wāhine as a theoretical framework.

In recognition of her academic work, Leonie has been a recipient of the Vice-Chancellor's University Development Fund (The University of Auckland) and a holder of the Hohua Tūtengaehe Post-Doctoral Research Fellowship (Health Research Council), and was awarded the inaugural Fulbright–Ngā Pae o te Māramatanga Indigenous Scholar Award in 2011, which enabled her to be hosted at the Indigenous Wellness Research Institute at the University of Washington and further expand kaupapa Māori theory. She has been a board member of Māori Television and was appointed to the Constitutional Advisory Panel Committee.

Previously a senior lecturer in Māori education at The University of Auckland, Leonie is also a former Director of the International Research Institute of Māori and Indigenous Education and Director of Māori and Indigenous Analysis Ltd. She has a PhD in education from The University of Auckland and is currently an Associate Professor and Director of the Te Kotahi Research Institute at the University of Waikato.

Mera Penehira

Ngāti Raukawa, Rangitāne, Ngāi Te Rangi

Mera is one of a number of Māori educators and researchers whose work is
contributing to the development of kaupapa Māori theory, research and action in
exciting new ways. Through her doctoral
research, which centred on traditional
knowledge and healing practices, she
examined the process of moko (traditional
Māori skin carving) and notions of mouri
as legitimate components of Māori well-
being, and developed a wider Māori framework of wellbeing (Mana
Kaitiakitanga) that brings together identity and spiritual, emotional,
and physical wellbeing. Her research drew on her own experiences
of receiving moko, and particularly moko kauae, and Mera has also
worked alongside tohunga ta moko, Christine Harvey, in an appren-
tice role.

The significance of her doctoral studies was recognised by the
Health Research Council and was funded within their International
Collaborative Indigenous Health Research Partnership programme,
and in 2010 she was awarded their Hohua Tūtengaehe Post-Doctoral
Research Fellowship in Māori health. In her post-doctoral research,
Mera explored Māori views on sexual and reproductive health and
developed a kaupapa Māori model of resistance and wellbeing for this
context. Prior to her current focus on health and wellbeing, she worked
in Māori and special education. Mera has a PhD from the University of
Waikato and is currently a lecturer in Māori education and Director of
Postgraduate Studies at Te Puna Wānanga (School of Māori Education)
in the Faculty of Education at The University of Auckland. She is also
co-academic director of the MAI ki Tamaki Māori doctoral student
mentoring programme.

Āneta Rāwiri

Whanganui Iwi me Ngāpuhi

Āneta started as a researcher in a number of Whanganui Iwi projects seeking to protect and regenerate ancestral heritage and decolonise research practice by placing the wellbeing of whānau, hapū, iwi, wai and whenua centre-stage. These included environmental and adult literacy projects that affirm whakapapa and rangatiratanga. Holding the pen and assuming authorship of project reports, the integrity and wisdom of her elders was woven by Āneta into stand-out reports that exemplify kaupapa Māori research in action.

She has recently been involved in a number of projects at Te Wānanga o Raukawa, including a case study to investigate the close relationship between mātauranga restoration and ecosystems restoration; and as a member of a number of national advisory groups established to advance the field of Māori adult literacy within kaupapa Māori frameworks. Āneta lives with her son in Raetihi among her whānau, hapū and wider iwi of Whanganui Iwi. She considers cherished and cherishing kin relationships to be essential to maintaining ancestral heritage and community wellbeing. She recently completed Tāhuhu Te Reo Māori (Master of Te Reo Māori), and is currently completing Tāhuhu Ahunga Tikanga (Master of Māori Laws and Philosophy) at Te Wānanga o Raukawa. Āneta currently holds the position of pūkenga within Te Whare Whakatupu Mātauranga at Te Wānanga o Raukawa.

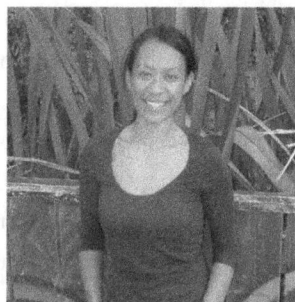

Naomi Simmonds

Ngāti Raukawa, Ngāti Huri

Naomi is a kaupapa Māori educator and researcher whose work has focused on decolonising maternity practices in Aotearoa through the reclamation of Māori birthing knowledges. Over the last 5 years she has developed this interest into a significant body

of published work that traverses the fields of education, gender studies, and geography. She has presented her work at conferences both here in Aotearoa and overseas, and is a board member of the Indigenous Peoples Specialty Group of the Association of American Geographers.

Naomi has also sought to contribute to the field of kaupapa Māori research, presenting on mana wahine methodologies, the value of wānanga as a research method, and the importance of community and researcher connectedness in the research process. Indeed, looking for and understanding connections underpins her work—between people, land, politics, place and history, and across disciplines, boundaries and borders—drawing together the experiences, tools and frameworks that decolonise the spaces in which we live.

Naomi has recently completed a PhD in geography at the University of Waikato and was awarded both a Tainui Education Trust doctoral scholarship and a Top Achievers doctoral scholarship in recognition of the significance of her work. Previously, Naomi was a resource management planner and is a certified independent environment hearings commissioner. She is also the environmental co-ordinator for her hapū of Ngāti Huri and Pikitū marae. Naomi has held a number of teaching and research roles at the University of Waikato and is currently a lecturer there in geography and environmental planning.

Kirsten Gabel
Ngāti Kahu, Te Paatu

Much of Kirsten's research work is grounded in mana wahine, and it explores a number of themes including traditional philosophies of Māori motherhood and maternal wellbeing, and reclaiming a role for atua wahine in our contemporary daily lives. She has published her work in a number of legal and other journals and has presented at conferences both here and in Australia. In 2014 she was a recipient of the He Kokonga Whare Writing Fellowship and used this opportunity to further her work by exploring Māori maternal knowledges and their relationship with and role in healing the intergenerational trauma of colonisation.

A second key focus area for Kirsten's research work is Māori tertiary student engagement and success, and she has completed a number of research projects for the University of Waikato in this field, including one on Māori students' experience of Māori student support initiatives and another on Māori student retention in the School of Law. Kirsten graduated with law degrees from the University of Waikato in 2002 and 2004, and subsequently worked as a national communications co-ordinator for the Māori Land Court. Returning to the University of Waikato in 2010, Kirsten was academic co-ordinator in the Office of the Pro Vice-Chancellor Māori, a research assistant on the Indigenous Wellbeing project, and the MAI ki Waikato co-ordinator from 2010 to 2011. She completed a PhD in 2013, and is currently employed as a research fellow in the School of Māori and Pacific Development at the University of Waikato.

Jo Smith
Kai Tahu, Kāti Mamoe, Waitaha

Jo is an experienced media educator and researcher with a focus on the ways in which colonial histories and the power they wield have an impact on and inform contemporary media practices. Importantly, her work has also sought to ask new questions about the ways in which media technologies and institutions can help shape new notions of identity, nationhood and community. To this end, she is currently working on a book-length study on the first 10 years of Māori Television.

Jo has published and presented extensively on her research in indigenous and postcolonial media, in conferences, journals and books, both here in Aotearoa and internationally, including chapters in the anthologies *The Fourth Eye: Māori Media in Aotearoa New Zealand*, published in 2013; and *Huihui: Navigating Art and Literature in the Pacific*, published in 2014; and as co-editor of a special issue of the *New Zealand Journal of Media Studies* on Taika Waititi's film *Boy* in 2012.

Jo's research work has been supported by a number of research grants and awards, including a Royal Society Fast Start Marsden Grant in 2008/09 for her project *Unsettled States: Settler-Native-Migrant Media*, and a 2012–2014 Standard Marsden Grant for *Onscreen Indigeneity: The Case of Māori Television*. Jo has a PhD from the University of Otago and was previously a lecturer at the Universities of Otago and Auckland. She is currently a senior lecturer in the media studies programme at Victoria University of Wellington.

Ngahuia Murphy
Ngāti Manawa, Ngāti Ruapani ki Waikaremoana, Tūhoe, Ngāti Kahungunu

Ngahuia grew up on the decolonisation kōrero of her parents, Takawai and Chris Murphy, which is also centre-stage in her work as an author, researcher, educator and performance artist. She has recently published two books as a result of her ground-breaking study of Māori pre-colonial stories, ceremonies and practices regarding menstruation, *Te Awa Atua: Menstruation in the Pre-colonial Māori World* and *Wai-whero: He Whakahirahira o te Ira Wahine: A Celebration of Womanhood*, which reclaim ancient teachings to empower contemporary Māori women and whānau.

Raised in Taranaki among the movement for the reclamation of te reo and tikanga Māori, Ngahuia acknowledges those people and that kaupapa for contributing to the strong foundations that underpin her work. The study earned her a first class master's degree from the University of Waikato, a Masters Research Award, and widespread interest and acclaim. Since completing the study in 2011, Ngahuia has presented her work around the country and internationally, including at the World Indigenous Peoples Conference on Education in 2014. Important to her is finding innovative and creative ways to share research findings, and to this end she has developed a bilingual sexual health resource for use in kura kaupapa Māori and schools, and set up the website www.waiwhero.com. Ngahuia is also an award-winning performance artist, winning the Arts Waikato Scholarship Award in 2009 for contemporary Māori dance and poetry. She is currently collaborating on an opera in te reo Māori celebrating atua wāhine and is working towards a PhD.

Debbie Broughton
Te Aitanga a Hauiti, Ngāpuhi, Taranaki, Ngāti Porou

Debbie is a kaupapa Māori researcher with an interest in exploring Māori knowledge systems and rediscovering the role of tūpuna in the inter-generational transmission of knowledge, and she has a passion for the revitalisation of their dialects. Knowledge and mātauranga feature in Debbie's work, including her recent paper on mātauranga, rangatiratanga and the future of New Zealand science, published in the *Journal of the Royal Society of New Zealand*, and in her bold and thought-provoking poetry, which centres on the knowledge-imparting presence of tūpuna in our everyday lives.

She has previously worked as a project manager for Te Rōpū Whāriki research centre at Massey University, as a research assistant on the Legal Māori Project which compiled the *Legal Māori Dictionary*, and as a policy analyst for the Human Rights Commission. More recently, Debbie was a pūkenga and kaiāwhina in the Ahunga Tikanga (Māori Laws and Philosophy) programme at Te Wānanga o Raukawa. Debbie has a law degree from Victoria University of Wellington, and after being admitted to the bar in 2010 she completed a Poutahu Ahunga Tikanga (postgraduate diploma in Māori Laws and Philosophy) the following year, and later a Tāhuhu Ahunga Tikanga (master's degree)— both at Te Wānanga o Raukawa. She is currently a kairangahau at Te Wāhanga, the kaupapa Māori research unit at the New Zealand Council for Educational Research, where she has mainly been engaged in a project investigating the preparedness of tertiary institutions to support learners and speakers of te reo Māori.

Index

www.ingramcontent.com/pod-product-compliance
Lightning Source LLC
Chambersburg PA
CBHW081738270326
41932CB00020B/3314